Number Works!

Graham Newman

STANLEY THORNES

Stanley Thornes (Publishers) Ltd

First published in 2000 by:

Stanley Thornes (Publishers) Ltd
Delta Place
27 Bath Road
Cheltenham
GL53 7TH

00 01 02 03 04 / 10 9 8 7 6 5 4 3 2 1

A catalogue record of this book is available from the British Library.

ISBN 0 7487 5448 2

Typeset by Florence Production Limited
Printed and bound in China by Dah Hua Printing Press Co. Ltd.

Introduction

This book has been written to help you with numeracy within the National Curriculum framework for Mathematics. The book is divided into different aspects of numeracy, and you can tell from the contents list which aspect you may wish to focus on.

Each chapter has been written to give you a variety of practice in a specific area of numeracy. The chapter starts with a short exercise (Exercise 1:1a) to test your skills in the work covered in that chapter. In the answer section you will see that each question in this exercise is related to one section in the chapter. If you cannot do a question, then you should look up the section that can help you. You may wish to work through the chapter anyway, in order to practise or consolidate your skills. A second exercise (Exercise 1:1b) is provided for you to test your skills again, once you have worked through the chapter, and to see how you have improved.

At the end of each chapter there are a number of activities, which give you an opportunity to apply the mathematics and your numeracy skills in a variety of ways. Some are to tackle alone, while others are for pairs or groups. In some cases these activities link in with the work in that specific chapter. Many of the activities can be attempted at any time.

At the end of the book (pages 222−223) there is a list of all the key words used in this book.

Contents

1 Number

You will use these words in this chapter.

KEY WORDS

units • tens • hundreds • thousands • ten thousand •
hundred thousand • million • digit • place value •
equal to • more than • ordering • ascending • descending •
greater than • less than • halfway • greatest • largest •
smallest • maximum • minimum • estimates •
consecutive • pattern • add • subtract • rounding •
to the nearest ten • to the nearest hundred

1 Diagnostic exercises

Exercise 1:1a

Write down the value of the red digit in these numbers.

1 5224   **2** 3354   **3** 2547   **4** 3042

Write these numbers in words.

5 907   **6** 1032   **7** 12 058

Write these numbers in figures.

8 Three thousand, four hundred and seven.

9 One hundred and four thousand, three hundred.

Write these numbers in order, starting with the smallest.

10 5012, 5100, 4900, 4907

11 868, 987, 799, 878, 796

12 Round these numbers to the nearest ten.

    a 423   **b** 778   **c** 1707   **d** 935

13 Round these numbers to the nearest hundred.

    a 1492   **b** 858   **c** 6044   **d** 729

Exercise 1:1b

Write down the value of the red digit in these numbers.

1 3746   **2** 8231   **3** 7062   **4** 3412

Write these numbers in words.

5 310   **6** 5507   **7** 11 301

Write these numbers in figures.

8 Five thousand and nineteen.

9 Three hundred and fifty thousand, three hundred and five.

Write these numbers in order, starting with the smallest.

10 2640, 1996, 3686, 2644

11 706, 732, 760, 687, 745

12 Round these numbers to the nearest ten.

    a 439   **b** 264   **c** 3806   **d** 545

13 Round these numbers to the nearest hundred.

    a 3424   **b** 756   **c** 5770   **d** 449

2 Place value

The value of each digit in a number is different.

You take 3427 pesetas on holiday.

    3   4   2   7

You could write this: $3 \times 1000 \ + \ 4 \times 100 \ + \ 2 \times 10 \ + \ 7 \times 1$

Every number can be written this way to show the value of every digit.

$734 = 7 \times 100 \ + \ 3 \times 10 \ + \ 4 \times 1$

$9086 = 9 \times 1000 \ + \ 0 \times 100 \ + \ 8 \times 10 \ + \ 6 \times 1$

Exercise 1:2

Write these numbers to show the value of each digit.

1	634	**2**	927	**3**	136	**4**	451
5	8369	**6**	7102	**7**	4516	**8**	8303
9	9412	**10**	3056	**11**	7503	**12**	2004

In the number 5742 the value of the digit 7 is $7 \times 100 = 700$

Exercise 1:3

Write down the value of the red digit in these numbers.

1	893	**2**	283	**3**	2721	**4**	2576
5	3417	**6**	7845	**7**	2857	**8**	9427
9	7982	**10**	2159	**11**	4712	**12**	6035

3 Numbers to words

How do you read numbers out loud?

Use number values.

237   Two hundred and thirty-seven

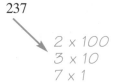

2×100
3×10
7×1 37

Write this number in words

1406   One thousand, four hundred and six.

1×1000
4×100
6×1

Exercise 1:4

Write these numbers in words.

1	285	**2**	405	**3**	270	**4**	658
5	5016	**6**	4607	**7**	4050	**8**	1850
9	1407	**10**	3089	**11**	2007	**12**	9800
13	7407	**14**	5044	**15**	2930	**16**	8361

4 Larger numbers to words

In larger numbers the digits can be grouped together.
Split them into threes, starting at the right-hand end.

1 2 3	4 5 6	7 8 9
millions	**thousands**	**hundreds, tens, units**

Write 205 427 in words.

205 427: *205* *thousands* *427* *hundreds, tens, units*

Put this together:

Two hundred and five **thousand**, four hundred and twenty-seven.

Write 2 400 040 in words.

2 400 040 *2* *millions* *400* *thousands* *040* *hundreds, tens, units*

Two **million**, four hundred **thousand** and forty.

Exercise 1:5

Write these numbers in words.

1	5647	**2**	4135	**3**	89 314	**4**	72 380
5	64 338	**6**	50 600	**7**	190 280	**8**	256 035
9	1 120 700	**10**	2 340 870	**11**	7 600 840	**12**	75 020 400

5 Words to numbers

We can write numbers in figures, or numerals.

Remember to write the digits in groups:

456   789

thousands   hundreds, tens, units

Three thousand, four hundred and twenty

3   420

thousands   hundreds, tens, units

Four hundred and four

404

thousands   hundreds, tens, units
There are none!

EXAMPLES

Exercise 1:6

Write these numbers in figures.

You could get someone to read them to you for you to write down.

1   Seven hundred and forty-four.
2   Four thousand two hundred and eighty-two.
3   Seven thousand four hundred and twenty-six.
4   Five hundred and two.
5   Three thousand nine hundred and seventy.
6   One thousand four hundred and ninety.
7   Eight thousand nine hundred and nine.
8   Eight hundred and seventy-six.
9   Two thousand three hundred and forty-two.
10 Seven thousand and twenty-seven.
11 Two thousand and two.
12 Six thousand four hundred and six.

6 Words to larger numbers

Remember how we group the digits in
large numbers:

123   456   789

millions   *thousands*   *hundreds, tens, units*

One million, four hundred thousand and seventeen.

1   400   017

millions   *thousands*   *hundreds, tens, units*

There are no hundreds, so be sure to put in a zero.

Answer: 1 400 017

Twelve million, twelve thousand and twelve.   *Zeros needed*

12   012   012

millions   *thousands*   *hundreds, tens, units*

Answer: 12 012 012

EXAMPLES

Exercise 1:7

Write these numbers in figures.

You could get someone to read them to you for you to write down.

1   Three million, five hundred thousand, four hundred.

2   Twelve thousand and forty.

3   One hundred and twenty-seven thousand, four hundred and three.

4   Eighty-one thousand, six hundred and twenty-seven.

5   Three hundred and three thousand, two hundred and seventy-one.

6   Ten thousand, nine hundred and ten.

7   Thirty thousand, seven hundred.

8   Thirteen thousand and four.

9   Twenty thousand, five hundred and fifty.

10   Ten thousand, six hundred.

11   One million, one hundred thousand and one.

12   Eight hundred and twenty-one thousand, four hundred.

7   Comparing number sizes

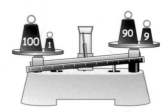

Numbers are ordered according to the value of each digit.

The greater the value, the more important a digit is.

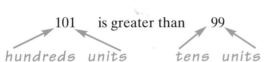

101   is greater than   99

hundreds units   *tens units*

The number 101 has **hundreds**. The number 99 does not have any hundreds, so 101 is larger than 99.

To write numbers in **ascending** order start with the **smallest**.
To write numbers in **descending** order start with the **largest**.

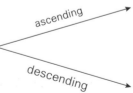
ascending
descending

Write these numbers in ascending order.

   7284, 7332, 7223, 8214, 7731

The largest value in these numbers is **thousands**.

Order by thousands: 7284, 7332, 7223, 7731 ← *smaller*

                      8214 ← *larger*

Next order by hundreds: 7284, 7223 ← *smaller*

                      7332

                      7731 ← *larger*

                      8214

EXAMPLE

Then order by tens:

7223 ⟵ *smaller*

7284 ⟵ *larger*

7332

7731

8214

Finally order by units. We don't need to do this in this example, but might need to for some groups of numbers.

In **ascending** order:

7223, 7284, 7332, 7731, 8214

Note: for **descending** order write the numbers in reverse:

8214, 7731, 7332, 7284, 7223

Exercise 1:8

Write these numbers in ascending order.

1 568, 587, 562, 495   **2** 201, 713, 431, 843

3 500, 498, 501, 489   **4** 630, 599, 723, 764

5 713, 533, 412, 711, 655   **6** 690, 621, 678, 673

7 281, 373, 186, 198, 93   **8** 6663, 6661, 6883, 6225

Write these numbers in descending order.

9 3645, 4587, 2996, 3640

10 6011, 6100, 5900, 5907

11 3003, 2890, 2752, 3100

12 7656, 8565, 8656, 8555

13 87 800, 88 722, 68 560, 78 600

14 48 560, 47 500, 78 600, 8850

15 98 800, 78 640, 100 000, 99 400

We use signs to compare the sizes of numbers.

> means greater than, or more than   e.g. 5 > 4

< means less than   e.g. 2 < 3

≥ means greater than or equal to

≤ means less than or equal to

= means equal to, or the same as

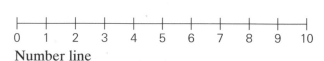

Number line

≥ 5 means greater than or equal to five.

On this number line, ≥ 5 means the numbers 5, 6, 7, 8, 9

Exercise 1:9

Replace ? with the correct sign.

1	2 ? 6	**2**	7 ? 3	**3**	9 ? 9	**4**	3 ? 5
5	6 ? 2	**6**	4 ? 4	**7**	14 ? 15	**8**	5 ? 9
9	12 ? 10	**10**	8 ? 3				

Write down the numbers on this number line that are described by the statement.

11	≥ 2	**12**	≤ 4	**13**	> 6	**14**	≥ 7
15	< 3	**16**	< 8	**17**	≤ 5	**18**	≥ 9
19	> 4	**20**	≤ 6				

8 Estimating numbers

How good are you at estimation?

To estimate you make a sensible guess.

Exercise 1:10

For each card, **do not count** the dots shown, but quickly try to guess how many there are.

Write down your estimates.

Then go back and count the exact number of dots on each card.

Compare your counted numbers with your estimates.

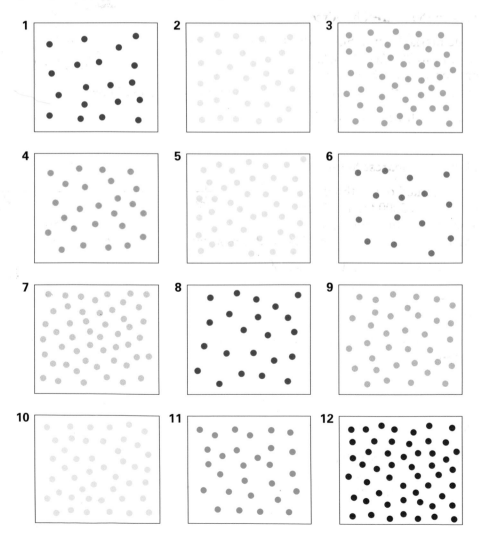

9 Rounding numbers

We round numbers when we want to find an approximate value, or when we want to make them simpler.

Rounding to the nearest ten

237 has 3 tens.

On a scale marked out in tens,
237 is nearer to 240 than to 230.
The number after the tens (the 7 units) is more than halfway to the next ten, so we **round up**.

237 rounded to the nearest 10 is 240.

Rounding to the nearest hundred

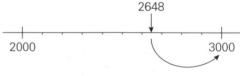

On a scale marked out in hundreds,
237 is nearer to 200 than to 300.
The number after the hundreds
(the 3 tens) is less than halfway to the next hundred, so we **round down**.

237 rounded to the nearest 100 is 200.

Rounding to the nearest thousand

On a scale marked out in thousands,
2648 is nearer to 3000 than to 2000.
The number after the thousands
(the 6 hundreds) is more than halfway to the next thousand, so we **round up**.

2648 rounded to the nearest 1000 is 3000.

Halfway

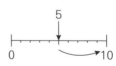

When a number is exactly halfway between two values,
we **round up**.

EXAMPLES

425 to the nearest 10 is 430.

550 to the nearest 100 is 600.

7490 to the nearest 1000 is 7000.

Exercise 1:11

Round to the nearest ten:

1	89	**2**	55	**3**	64	**4**	79
5	62	**6**	34	**7**	15	**8**	28
9	71	**10**	86	**11**	65	**12**	33

Round to the nearest hundred:

13	761	**14**	654	**15**	815	**16**	642
17	509	**18**	451	**19**	737	**20**	349
21	419	**22**	250	**23**	849	**24**	309

Round to the nearest thousand:

25	4278	**26**	3804	**27**	55 550	**28**	13 427
29	18 409	**30**	65 487	**31**	56 045	**32**	125 387
33	39 995	**34**	89 099	**35**	550 550		

ACTIVITIES

1   Reverse numbers

Write down any three-digit number.   *123*

There must be a difference of at least 2 between the hundreds and units digits.

Reverse the digits of the number you have chosen, and write this number down. This is the reverse number.   *321*

Subtract these two numbers.

Remember you must write the larger number on top.

$$\begin{array}{r} 321 \\ -\ 123 \\ \hline \\ \hline \end{array}$$

Write down the answer. Underneath write down the reverse of the answer.

Add the reverse answer to the answer.

$$\begin{array}{r} 198 \\ +\ 891 \\ \hline \end{array}$$

Try this with several numbers.

What do you notice?

2   Two-digit sums

Write down a three-digit number.   *123*

Using the three digits, write down 6 different two-digit numbers.

21   23   31   32   12   13

Add the 6 numbers you have made.

21 + 23 + 31 + 32 + 12 + 13 = 132

Divide this answer by the number you get when you add the three digits of your original number.

1 + 2 + 3 = 6
132 ÷ 6 = 22

Try this with several numbers.

What do you notice?

3 Max–min

Pick four different numbers from 0 to 9 inclusive.

a Write down the maximum number possible using your four digits.

b Write down the minimum number possible using your four digits.

c Subtract the minimum from the maximum.

d Write down the maximum and minimum numbers using the digits from your answer to **c**.

e Subtract the minimum from the maximum.

Write down your answer.

Repeat this with several other numbers of your choice.

What do you notice about the answer?

4 Consecutive numbers

Some numbers can be written as sums of **consecutive** numbers.

Consecutive numbers are numbers that follow each other.

3 = 1 + 2

4   cannot be done!

5 = 2 + 3

6 = 1 + 2 + 3

7 = 3 + 4

List all the numbers you can write as a series of sums of consecutive numbers.

5 The 100 race

A game for two players.

a Player A picks a number.

b Player B adds a number from 1 to 9 (inclusive).

c The players then take turns to add another number from 1 to 9.

Note: you can add the same number more than once.

The first player to reach 100 exactly wins the game.

6 Crossing the river

Two adults and two children want to cross a river.

None of them can swim, and they only have one small canoe, which they can all use.

The canoe holds either one adult, or two children.

How can they all get across?

7 Colours

Red and blue tiles are arranged to make these patterns:

$$1 + 2 + 3 \qquad 1 + 2 + 3$$

These patterns can then be put together to make a rectangle:

This shows that

$$1 + 2 + 3 + 1 + 2 + 3 = 4 + 4 + 4$$

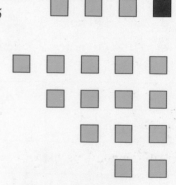

a Draw some more red and blue tiles to show:

$$1 + 2 + 3 + 4 + 1 + 2 + 3 + 4 = 5 + 5 + 5 + 5$$

b Draw the rectangle you get when this pattern is used twice.

Write down the sum of numbers it represents.

c If you use $1 + 2 + 3 + \ldots + 17 + 18 + 19$ twice to make a rectangle, how many columns and how many rows will it have?

8 Change

How many ways can you make 7p change?

$$7p = 5p + 2p$$

$$7p = 1p + 2p + 2p + 2p$$

a Show all possible ways of making 7p.

b Show all possible ways of making 8p.

c Show all possible ways of making 9p.

d Show all possible ways of making 10p.

9 Cash deposits

Whenever you pay money into a bank, you have to fill in a cash deposit slip, or credit slip.

This one has been filled in.

Date _____	**bank giro credit**	Notes £50		
		£20		
		£10	20	00
Paid in by _____		£5	15	00
BANK Plc		Coins £2 & £1		
		Other Coins		40
		Total Cash *	35	40
	J. BLOGGS			
Fee Box	Cheques		Cheques, etc		
Branch Sort Code	Account Number	Transaction Code		
11–11–11	1234567	84	£	35	40
Bank Plc	Please do not fold this counterfoil or write or mark below this line		

2 x £10 notes is £20.00

3 x £5 notes is £15.00

4 x 10p coins is £0.40

List these amounts in the table, as if you were filling in a credit slip.

a 3 × £10 notes, 4 × £5 notes, 9 × 10p coins and, loose change of 7p.

b 2 × £10 notes, 7 × £5 notes, 3 × 50p coins, 2 × 10p coins and loose change of 45p.

c 2 × £20 notes, 4 × £10 notes, 3 × £5 notes, 7 × 50p coins, 6 × 10p coins and loose change of 78p.

d 6 × £10 notes, 3 × £5 notes, 4 × 10p coins and loose change of 67p.

e 9 × £10 notes, 9 × £5 notes, 8 × 50p coins and 3 × 10p coins.

	a	b	c	d	e
Notes £50					
£20					
£10					
Coins £2 and £1					
Other coins					
Total cash					

Fill in all the totals.

2 Addition

□□

You will use these words in this chapter.

KEY WORDS

units • tens • hundreds • thousands • digit • amount • carry • add • sum • addition • total • maximum • minimum • largest • smallest • mental calculation • operation • combination

1 Diagnostic exercises

Exercise 2:1a

1
```
   23
 + 34
 ----
```

2
```
   46
 + 27
 ----
```

3
```
   83
 + 38
 ----
```

4
```
   563
 + 158
 -----
```

5
```
   5908
 + 2457
 ------
```

6 1207 + 135

7 6 + 4 + 2 + 8 + 7   **8** 12 + 35 + 46

9 What is the total cost of a 27p stamp and a 19p stamp?

10 Neil scores 83 on one test and 68 on another.

What is his total mark in the two tests?

11 A cable is 3420 mm long. A second cable 780 mm long.

What is the total length of the two cables?

12 408 people saw the school play on Thursday and 394 people on Friday.
What was the total attendance for the two days?

Exercise 2:1b

1
```
   42
 + 53
 ----
```

2
```
   35
 + 48
 ----
```

3
```
   87
 + 64
 ----
```

4
```
   475
 + 345
 -----
```

5
```
   2076
 + 4355
 ------
```

6 2456 + 627

7   5 + 8 + 3 + 2 + 7   **8**   23 + 33 + 104

9   One packet weighs 38 g and another weighs 46 g.
What is their total weight?

10   Ben has £29 and Alison has £37.
What is the total amount they have together?

11   One car has done 4260 miles and another 7084 miles.
What is the total mileage of the two cars?

12   On a farm there are two sheds. In the first shed there are 178 chickens.
In the second shed there are 205 chickens.
How many chickens are there altogether?

2 Addition without carrying

Always set out a sum in columns.
Add the units, then the tens.

35 is 3 tens and 5 units
41 is 4 tens and 1 unit

	T	U
+	3	5
	4	1
=	7	6

23 + 54 →

```
   2   3
 + 5   4
 ───────
   7   7     Answer: 77
 ───────
```

Exercise 2:2

1 52 + 46	**2** 36 + 13	**3** 13 + 46	**4** 31 + 63
5 12 + 55	**6** 45 + 24	**7** 63 + 21	**8** 46 + 32
9 27 + 32	**10** 84 + 13	**11** 25 + 72	**12** 78 + 21

13   Melissa had £67. She saved another £23.
How much does she have now?

14   Ravi had 71 stamps. His friend David had 25 stamps.
How many stamps did they have altogether?

15   A piece of wood is of 54 cm long. A second piece of wood is 43 cm
long. The two pieces are laid end to end.
What is the total length?

16   Martin has two apple trees. He picks 63 apples from one tree, and
34 apples from the other tree.
How many apples does he pick altogether?

3 Addition with carrying

Give yourself room for
your working:

The 1 (tens) as a carry goes here

```
  T   U
  3   6
  2   7
  ─────
      3
  1
```

```
      6   ......
  +   7   .......
  ─────
     13
```

The 3 (units) goes here

```
•••   3
••    2
•   + 1
  ─────
      6
```

```
  T   U
  3   6
  2   7
  ─────
  6   3
  1
```

Answer: 63

$18 + 25 \rightarrow$

```
    1   8
  + 2   5
  ───────
    4   3
    1
```

$39 + 27 \rightarrow$

```
    3   9
  + 2   7
  ───────
    6   6
    1
```

Exercise 2:3

1	12 + 39	**2**	55 + 37	**3**	47 + 19	**4**	38 + 53
5	13 + 78	**6**	66 + 26	**7**	24 + 57	**8**	26 + 67
9	14 + 68	**10**	37 + 48	**11**	62 + 29	**12**	18 + 35

13 There are 35 blue flowers and 47 yellow flowers in a garden. How many flowers are there altogether?

14 What is the total of 24p and 68p?

15 In a book there are 47 pages of writing and 15 pages of pictures. How many pages are there in the book altogether?

16 In a competition 37 fish were caught in the morning, and 25 in the afternoon. How many fish were caught altogether?

4 Far more carrying

Write the numbers
clearly in columns:

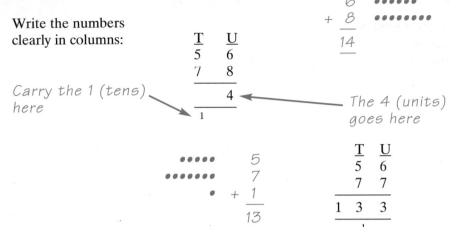

	T	U
	5	6
	7	8

Carry the 1 (tens) here

The 4 (units) goes here

```
      5
      7
  +   1
  ────
   13
```

	T	U
	5	6
	7	7
1	3	3
	1	

Answer: 133

EXAMPLE

$$36 + 77 \rightarrow$$

```
      3  6
  +   7  7
  ────────
   1  1  3
      1
```

$$87 + 45 \rightarrow$$

```
      8  7
  +   4  5
  ────────
   1  3  2
      1
```

Exercise 2:4

1	38 + 73	**2**	97 + 48	**3**	49 + 82	**4**	47 + 76
5	68 + 55	**6**	55 + 66	**7**	45 + 67	**8**	89 + 74
9	59 + 66	**10**	38 + 84	**11**	75 + 58	**12**	67 + 49

13 A set of scales has a 96 g weight and a 35 g weight.
What is the total weight on the scales?

14 Melanie has 86 stamps, and Shreena has 68 stamps.
How many stamps do they have altogether?

15 Barry takes 59 minutes to complete one test, and 53
minutes to do a second test.
What is the total time Barry spent completing the
tests?

16 A tank contains 97 litres of water. A further 58 litres of water is added.
How much docs the tank contain now?

5 Adding with hundreds

Work from the right (units) column.
Show all your carrying
in the correct column.

7 + 8 = 15

```
  H   T   U
  2   7   5
+ 3   8   4
──────────
  6   5   9
  1
```

2 + 3 + 1 = 6

5 + 4 = 9

*15 gives 5 down
and carry 1.*

Answer: 659

EXAMPLES

```
382 + 519  →    3   8   2
              + 5   1   9
              ───────────
                9   0   1
                1   1
```

```
668 + 156  →    6   6   8
              + 1   5   6
              ───────────
                8   2   4
                1   1
```

Exercise 2:5

1	465 + 207	**2**	166 + 379	**3**	264 + 144
4	628 + 182	**5**	775 + 155	**6**	263 + 127
7	458 + 186	**8**	278 + 367	**9**	305 + 176
10	278 + 155	**11**	326 + 157	**12**	343 + 178

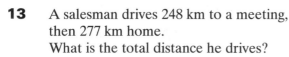

13 A salesman drives 248 km to a meeting,
then 277 km home.
What is the total distance he drives?

14 A kite is flying at a height of 618 metres.
It rises a further 287 metres.
How high is the kite flying now?

15 A piece of elastic 518 mm long is
stretched by another 203 mm.
What is its new length?

16 Over a season 409 pets were treated
at a vet's surgery. Over the next season
349 pets were treated.
What was the total number of pets treated?

6 Adding with thousands

Write your numbers in
very clear columns.
Separate the columns
with a space.

Th	H	T	U
2	7	4	8
+ 1	9	0	5
4	6	5	3
	1		1

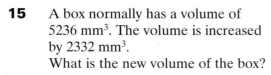

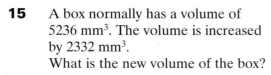

EXAMPLES

$1465 + 4207 \rightarrow$

	1	4	6	5
+	4	2	0	7
	5	6	7	2
			1	

$3564 + 5265 \rightarrow$

	3	5	6	4
+	5	2	6	5
	8	8	2	9
			1	

Exercise 2:6

1 1368 + 2554   **2** 2173 + 1346   **3** 1418 + 1289

4 4265 + 7409   **5** 3837 + 9116   **6** 5217 + 8254

7 4427 + 3573   **8** 8307 + 6485   **9** 9453 + 6234

10 5442 + 7361   **11** 3512 + 3375   **12** 9432 + 4153

13 A pool contains 7274 litres of water.
Another 2597 litres is added.
How much water is in the pool now?

14 In a factory 4580 chocolates
were packed in the morning,
and 5360 chocolates in the
afternoon.
What was the total number of
chocolates packed during the day?

15 A box normally has a volume of
5236 mm^3. The volume is increased
by 2332 mm^3.
What is the new volume of the box?

16 Worsley Wanderers FC had 8331 spectators at their first game, and
6522 at their second game.
What was the total attendance over the two games?

7 Finding totals

When writing numbers in a sum, always make sure they line up at the right-hand side.

Start by writing the "2" here

Th	H	T	U
	7	0	2
1	5	4	6
2	2	4	8
	1		

EXAMPLES

$1009 + 888 \rightarrow$

```
    1 0 0 9
  +   8 8 8
    -------
    1 8 9 7
        1
```

$27 + 999 \rightarrow$

```
        2 7
  +   9 9 9
    -------
    1 0 2 6
      1 1
```

Exercise 2:7

1	2155 + 508	**2**	213 + 3629	**3**	3176 + 807
4	69 + 5086	**5**	647 + 4308	**6**	5855 + 49
7	3867 + 813	**8**	828 + 1732	**9**	7106 + 88
10	1862 + 509	**11**	996 + 5016	**12**	47 + 5792

13 The mileage counter in a car showed 1417 miles.
The car is driven a journey of 98 miles.
What does the counter show now?

14 There are 1088 students in a hall. Another class of 35 students arrives.
What is the total number of students in the hall?

15 Liam has £1852 in his bank account.
He pays in another £397.
How much does he have now?

16 There are 6004 bricks in a builder's yard. Another 418 bricks are delivered.
What is the total number of bricks in the yard?

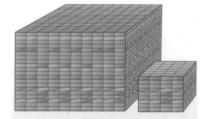

8 Mental calculation – single digits

To add up single
digit numbers mentally,
gather numbers into
pairs that are
easier to add.

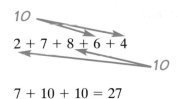

$2 + 7 + 8 + 6 + 4$

$7 + 10 + 10 = 27$

EXAMPLES

$2 + 7 + 6 + 7 + 5$

$2 + 14 + 6 + 5$

$2 + 20 + 5 = 27$

$3 + 4 + 6 + 2 + 3$

$10 + 5 + 3 = 18$

Exercise 2:8

Work out the answers mentally.

1 $8 + 9 + 6 + 3 + 4$ **2** $1 + 9 + 8 + 6 + 2$

3 $3 + 5 + 2 + 8 + 7$ **4** $3 + 4 + 6 + 3 + 8$

5 $7 + 8 + 6 + 3 + 4$ **6** $2 + 3 + 5 + 2 + 8$

7 $4 + 5 + 4 + 6 + 3$ **8** $2 + 3 + 4 + 5 + 8$

9 $8 + 5 + 9 + 3 + 2$ **10** $5 + 8 + 2 + 3 + 4$

11 $2 + 9 + 5 + 8 + 7$ **12** $4 + 8 + 5 + 9 + 6$

13 The scores thrown on an octagonal dice are:
6, 2, 3, 8, 7, 6, 5.
What is the total score?

14 The number of eggs found each day in a
chicken coop are 7, 8, 6, 5, 9, 4, 7.
What is the total number of eggs found in the week?

15 The number of books sold each hour from a market
stall is 7, 8, 3, 5, 4, 7.
What is the total number of books sold?

16 The number of fish in each tank in an aquarium are:
4, 8, 5, 7, 9, 8, 6. What is the total number of fish in the
aquarium?

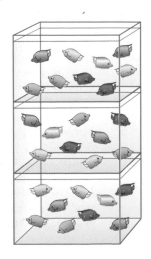

9 Mental calculation – two-digit numbers

To add two-digit numbers mentally group together units and tens that make easier numbers to add.

Units: 10

$$84 + 42 + 27 + 36$$

Tens: 100

Units: *10 + 2 + 7*   *=   19*
Tens: *100 + 40 + 30*   *=   170*

                                   189

EXAMPLE

10
11
$$12 + 36 + 35 + 88$$
60
90

Units: *10 + 11*   *=   21*
Tens: *60 + 90*   *=   150*

                               171

Exercise 2:9

Work out the answers mentally.

1	76 + 13 + 49	**2**	55 + 48 + 14	**3**	64 + 127 + 10
4	79 + 12 + 67	**5**	59 + 15 + 44	**6**	45 + 7 + 105
7	84 + 19 + 52 + 31	**8**	26 + 7 + 78	**9**	32 + 56 + 61
10	9 + 69 + 107	**11**	66 + 68 + 21 + 41	**12**	17 + 24 + 28 + 77

13   The numbers of CDs sold on a market stall on each of four days are 37, 44, 27 and 14.
What is the total number of CDs sold over the four days?

14   The amount of money collected by each charity worker is £53, £28, £29 and £59.
What is the total amount of money collected?

15   The number of burgers sold during lunchtime at three fast-food shops is 64, 39 and 53.
What is the total number of burgers sold?

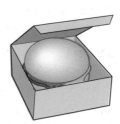

16   The weight of four boxes is 104 kg, 66 kg, 8 kg and 35 kg.
What is the total weight of the four boxes?

ACTIVITIES

1   Darts

In a game of darts, 3 darts are thrown,
and the score is added up.
Darts in this ring score double.
Darts in this ring score treble.

The score on this dartboard will be	
$13 + 10 + 10 + 2 + 2 + 2 = 39$	
A B C	

Write down the scores on these dartboards.

You could play your own game of darts and add up the scores.

2   Combinations

All numbers can be written as a sum or combination of other numbers.

How can you make the number 5 with other numbers?

Two numbers	Three numbers	Four numbers
$5 = 5 + 0$	$5 = 5 + 0 + 0$	$5 = 5 + 0 + 0 + 0$
$5 = 4 + 1$	$5 = 4 + 1 + 0$	$5 = 4 + 1 + 0 + 0$
$5 = 3 + 2$	$5 = 3 + 2 + 0$	$5 = 3 + 1 + 1 + 0$
	$5 = 3 + 1 + 1$	$5 = 3 + 2 + 0 + 0$
	$5 = 2 + 2 + 1$	$5 = 2 + 2 + 1 + 0$
		$5 = 2 + 1 + 1 + 1$

Pick at least one other number, and show how it can be made from other
numbers.

3 Coins

12p can be made with:

10p + 1p + 1p

or

5p + 5p + 1p + 1p

Use these coins: 1p, 2p, 5p, 10p

a Write down one combination of these coins for each amount from 1p to 30p.

b For each amount state the *minimum* number of coins needed.

c For each amount find *all* the possible combinations of the coins you could use.

4 Maximum and minimum

Using the digits 1, 2, 3 and 4 you can write down some two-digit numbers:

12, 13, 24, 43

What is the largest number you can write down?
What is the smallest number you can write down?

If you take away the smallest number from the largest number, you have the largest difference.

The largest difference is   43 − 12 = 31
The smallest difference is   23 − 14 = 9

The largest sum is   41 + 32 = 73
The smallest sum is   14 + 23 = 37

Now choose your own four digits.

a Write down all the numbers you can make from the four digits.

b Find the largest difference.

c Find the smallest difference.

d Find the largest sum.

e Find the smallest sum.

5   Operation grid

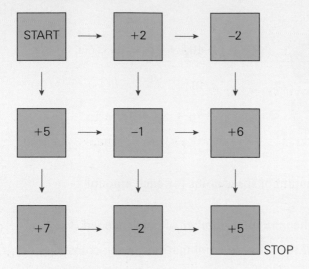

This is an operation grid.

You can start with any number, and you then follow the arrows along a route of your choice, to end up at the STOP point.

You must carry out all the operations on your chosen route.

a   Choose any number.
         Follow a route and work out the end result.

b   Which route will give you the lowest score?

c   Which route will give you the highest score?

d   Design your own operation grid.

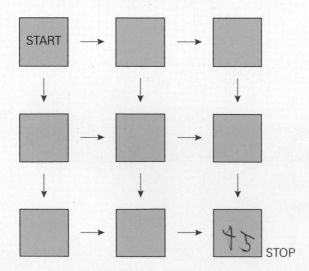

6   Estimates

Try this on your own, or with a partner.

> Write down a list of two-digit numbers. Start with between 4 and 6 numbers.
>
> Quickly estimate the total of the numbers.
>
> Then calculate the actual total.

a   Change one of the numbers, and estimate how this will change your answer.

b   Write down some more numbers to use.

c   Write down some three-digit numbers to use.

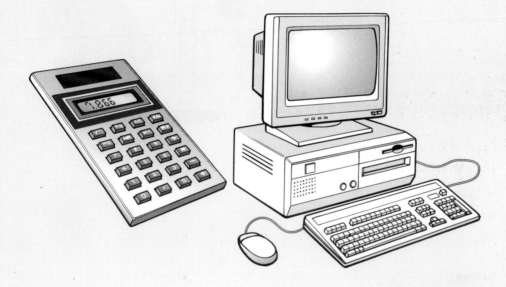

Computer
You could enter the numbers into a simple spreadsheet column, with a total. Enter different numbers into your list, and see how the total changes.

Calculator
You could use a calculator instead of a computer to work out the totals.

3 Subtraction

You will use these words in this chapter.

KEY WORDS

units • tens • hundreds • thousands • add • subtract •
take away • differences • borrowing • reduction •
counting down • counting up

1 Diagnostic exercises

Exercise 3:1a

1
$$\begin{array}{r} 76 \\ -\ 55 \\ \hline \end{array}$$

2
$$\begin{array}{r} 83 \\ -\ 27 \\ \hline \end{array}$$

3
$$\begin{array}{r} 527 \\ -154 \\ \hline \end{array}$$

4
$$\begin{array}{r} 4475 \\ -\ 738 \\ \hline \end{array}$$

5
$$\begin{array}{r} 607 \\ -\ 35 \\ \hline \end{array}$$

6
$$\begin{array}{r} 5600 \\ -\ 263 \\ \hline \end{array}$$

7 $2143 - 17$

8 $5408 - 777$

9 Ali buys 89 stamps and uses 45 of them.
How many does he have left?

10 The arrival times of 2467 trains were recorded. 274 trains were late.
How many arrived on time?

11 A car cost £7473 to buy.
It was sold for £519 less.
At what price was the car sold?

12 There are 5010 seats in a stadium. Season ticket holders have booked 704 seats.
How many seats are still available?

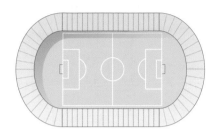

Exercise 3:1b

1   37
        − 24
        ⎯⎯

2   74
        − 36
        ⎯⎯

3   1254
        − 172
        ⎯⎯

4   2453
        − 187
        ⎯⎯

5   240
        − 16
        ⎯⎯

6   7050
        − 317
        ⎯⎯

7 3495 − 88

8 2034 − 407

9 Simon has 85 slabs to make a patio. He has laid 33.
How many does he have left to lay?

10 Hayley takes 4759 pesetas to spend on holiday. She returns with 483 pesetas.
How much did she spend?

11 A motorcycle costs £5222. Its price is reduced by £606.
What is the new price?

12 In the year 2000 a shipwreck is found. The boat sank 403 years before.
In which year did the ship sink?

2 Subtraction without borrowing

To do a subtraction you can either take away or add!
You need to work out the **differences** between numbers.

Count down:
8 7 6 5 4 3 (down 5)

or count up:
3 4 5 6 7 8 (up 5)

T	U
8	7
3	4

Count down:
7 6 5 4 (down 3)

or count up:
4 5 6 7 (up 3)

$$\begin{array}{cc} 8 & 7 \\ -\ 3 & 4 \\ \hline 5 & 3 \end{array}$$

EXAMPLE

Work out   93 − 21

$$\begin{array}{cc} 9 & 3 \\ -\ 2 & 1 \\ \hline 7 & 2 \end{array}$$

Exercise 3:2

1	38 − 21	**2**	57 − 45	**3**	73 − 31	**4**	66 − 32
5	56 − 23	**6**	49 − 27	**7**	84 − 54	**8**	48 − 23
9	85 − 41	**10**	65 − 32	**11**	98 − 54	**12**	75 − 54

13 Two coaches have been booked for a group of 89 pupils.
55 get on the first coach.
How many will there be on the second coach?

14 A builder has 94 days to build a garage.
After 63 days, how long has he left to
complete the job?

15 There are 46 lights in a hall. 32 are turned on.
How many are not turned on?

16 There are 77 children in a club. 44 are girls.
How many are boys?

3 Borrowing tens

If the number of units you are taking away from is not big enough, you have to borrow a ten.

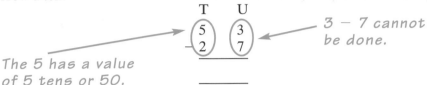

The 5 has a value of 5 tens or 50.

T U
5 3
− 2 7
_____

3 − 7 cannot be done.

We can move 10 to the next column to help us: $50 \rightarrow 40 + 10$

We write this:

50 − 10 = 40

T   U
$\cancel{5}^{4}$ $^{1}3$
− 2   7
_____
2   6

3 + 10 = 13

Work out: (a) 23 − 19   (b) 81 − 47

(a)
T U
2 3
− 1 9
_____

becomes:
$\cancel{2}^{1}$ $^{1}3$
− 1   9
_____
$\mathbf{?}$ 4

(b)
T U
8 1
− 4 7
_____

becomes:
$\cancel{8}^{7}$ $^{1}1$
4   7
_____
3   4

Exercise 3:3

1	46 − 27	**2**	84 − 48	**3**	45 − 29	**4**	73 − 35
5	65 − 37	**6**	93 − 56	**7**	85 − 48	**8**	46 − 19
9	58 − 19	**10**	83 − 45	**11**	94 − 36	**12**	73 − 37

13 There are 67 chocolates in a box. Someone eats 39 of them. How many are left?

14 Julie has £54. She spends £16 on a new skirt. How much money does she have left?

15 On a farm there are 96 chickens. 68 of the chickens are sold. How many chickens are left?

4 Borrowing hundreds

If the number of tens you are taking away from is not big enough, you have to borrow a hundred.

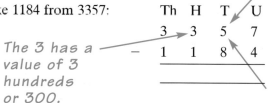

To take 1184 from 3357:

5 – 8 cannot be done.

Th	H	T	U
3	3	5	7
– 1	1	8	4

The 3 has a value of 3 hundreds or 300.

The 5 has a value of 5 tens or 50.

We can move 100 to the next column to help us: $300 \rightarrow 200 + 100$

We write this:

Th	H	T	U
3	$\cancel{3}^2$	$^1 5$	7
– 1	1	8	4
2	1	7	3

100 + 50 = 150

15 – 8 = 7

EXAMPLES

Work out (a) $342 - 19$ (b) $1574 - 383$

(a)
3	$\cancel{4}^2$	$^1 2$	0
–		1	9	0
3	2	3	0

(b)
1	$\cancel{5}^4$	$^1 7$	4
–		3	8	3
1	1	9	1

Exercise 3:4

1	$1277 - 209$	**2**	$546 - 448$	**3**	$449 - 176$
4	$4253 - 3172$	**5**	$2458 - 555$	**6**	$624 - 281$
7	$5443 - 2461$	**8**	$557 - 429$	**9**	$1342 - 522$
10	$643 - 361$	**11**	$2235 - 1333$	**12**	$1337 - 239$

13 Of a batch of 412 apples, 131 are too small to sell. How many apples can be sold?

14 A new boiler normally costs £4726. A discount of £385 reduces the price. What is the reduced price?

15 There are 357 pupils in a year group. 148 are girls. How many are boys?

16 A swimming pool can hold 4130 litres of water when full. There are 3330 litres of water already in the pool.
How many more litres are needed to fill it?

5 Borrowing more than once

You may have to borrow more than one time in a subtraction.

Th	H	T	U
− 2	6	⁴4³	⁽¹2⁾
	1	8	⑦

First borrow
12 − 7

Th	H	T	U
− 2	6	⁽⁴4³⁾	¹2
	1	⑧	7
			5

3 − 8
cannot be done.

Th	H	T	U
− 2	⁶6⁵	¹⁴4³	¹2
	1	8	7
2	4	5	5

Second borrow
13 − 8

EXAMPLES

Work out (a) 814 − 36   (b) 4574 − 608

(a)
	⁸8⁷	¹¹1⁰	¹4
−		3	6
	7	7	8

(b)
⁴4³	¹5	⁷7⁶	¹4
−		6	0	8
3	9	6	6

Exercise 3:5

1	3564 − 736	**2**	2958 − 479	**3**	2346 − 555
4	860 − 678	**5**	7863 − 981	**6**	160 − 88
7	5423 − 705	**8**	8785 − 2894	**9**	235 − 59
10	5464 − 3636	**11**	565 − 297	**12**	3370 − 1403

13 There are 475 sheep for sale at a market. 299 are sold.
How many sheep remain?

14 A new car cost £8670. Three years later its value had fallen to £5880.
What was the reduction in its value after three years?

15 Rajesh has £975. He buys a television for £487.
How much money does he have left?

£487

16 A tank contains 6597 litres of oil. 3809 litres are drained off.
How many litres of oil are left in the tank?

6 Borrowing from zero

You cannot borrow from a zero!
In this case you need to borrow from somewhere else.

To take 37 from 405:

$$\begin{array}{ccc} 4 & 0 & 5 \\ - & 3 & 7 \\ \hline \end{array}$$

You want to borrow from here, but can't.

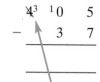

$$\begin{array}{ccc} \cancel{4}^3 & {}^10 & 5 \\ - & 3 & 7 \\ \hline \end{array}$$

Borrow from here first, so you can ...

$$\begin{array}{ccc} \cancel{4}^3 & {}^1\cancel{0}^9 & {}^15 \\ - & 3 & 7 \\ \hline 3 & 6 & 8 \end{array}$$

borrow from here!

Work out (a) 2017 − 555   (b) 703 − 48

(a)
$$\begin{array}{cccc} \cancel{2}^1 & {}^1\cancel{0}^9 & {}^11 & 7 \\ - & 5 & 5 & 5 \\ \hline 1 & 4 & 6 & 2 \end{array}$$

(b)
$$\begin{array}{ccc} \cancel{7}^6 & {}^1\cancel{0}^9 & {}^13 \\ - & 4 & 8 \\ \hline 6 & 5 & 5 \end{array}$$

Exercise 3:6

1	306 − 38	**2**	1069 − 74	**3**	503 − 45
4	3037 − 155	**5**	6018 − 4444	**6**	608 − 36
7	404 − 53	**8**	5024 − 367	**9**	5402 − 1035
10	204 − 47	**11**	6027 − 888	**12**	509 − 163

13 A piece of cheese weighs 505 g. A piece weighing 149 g is cut off.
What weight is the remaining piece?

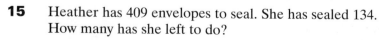

14 Alan took 4038 lire on holiday to Italy.
He returned with 482 lire.
How many lire had he spent on holiday?

15 Heather has 409 envelopes to seal. She has sealed 134.
How many has she left to do?

16 There are 2804 runners in a marathon race. After 3 hours, 1335 have finished. How many runners will take longer than 3 hours?

7 Borrowing from several zeros

You may have to borrow from several zeros.
If this is the case, keep borrowing until you get a number where you can use it.

To take 1009 from 3000:

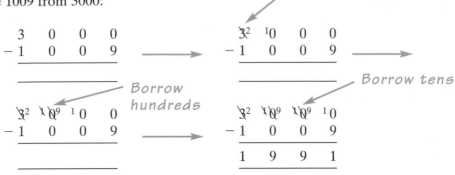

Work out: (a)   6030 − 444   (b)   5000 − 412

(a)   6030
      − 444
      _____

      $\cancel{6}^5$ $\cancel{0}^9$ $\cancel{3}^{12}$ $^1 0$
      −   4   4   4
      _____
              5   5   8   6

(b) $\cancel{5}^4$ $\cancel{0}^9$ $\cancel{0}^9$ $^1 0$
      −   4   1   2
      _____
              4   6   8   8

Exercise 3:7

1	4070 − 505	**2**	2000 − 182	**3**	6070 − 1458
4	5006 − 186	**5**	7003 − 2621	**6**	4020 − 178
7	3001 − 443	**8**	6050 − 3407	**9**	4040 − 1176
10	3030 − 263	**11**	5004 − 1205	**12**	8070 − 375

13 In the year 2000 a book was found that was written 325 years before. In which year was the book written?

14 Darren wins £6050 on the lottery. He spends £507 on a television. How much money does he have left?

15 A farmer has 7030 daffodil bulbs to sell. He sells 343 on the first day of his sale.
How many does he have left?

16 There are 9000 people in a stadium. 4178 are men.
How many are women?

ACTIVITIES

1 Tower of Hanoi

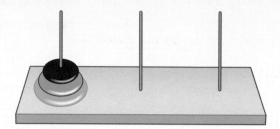

You have three discs of different sizes, and a board with three poles.
The discs fit on to the poles.

The object of the game is to move all the discs to the last pole.

The rules for moving the discs are:
   a) only one disc can be moved at a time.
   b) a move is when you take the top disc from one pole, and place it on another pole (perhaps on top of an existing disc).
   c) a larger disc may never be placed on top of a smaller disc.

How many moves do you need to move all three discs to the pole at the opposite end?

How many moves do you need for four discs? Five discs?

2 Taking counters

A game for two players.

20 counters are laid out in a row as shown.

The first player may take either one counter, or two counters.
The players then take turns to take either one counter, or two counters that must touch each other.

The player who takes the last counter is the winner.

3 Making 100

You have these digits to use **once** only:

1 2 3 4 5 6 7 8 9

You have the signs **+** and **−** which you may use many times.

Make the number 100 using the digits and the signs.

$$1 + 2 + 3 - 4 + 5 + 6 + 78 + 9 = 100$$

How many other ways can you make 100?

4 Hockey tournament

In a hockey tournament there are 12 teams.

You may call these teams A, B, C, etc., or give them different names.

In the tournament every team has to play all the other teams just once.
How many matches have to be played?
Make a list of all the matches.

How many matches have to be played if there are 13 teams?

How many matches have to be played if there are 14 teams?

Investigate the number of matches for a larger number of teams.

4 Times tables

You will use these words in this chapter.

KEY WORDS

times • altogether •
share • division •
divided by •
divide

1 Diagnostic exercises

Exercise 4:1a

For these questions write down the answer only.

1	6×2	**2**	3×5	**3**	4×10	**4**	7×4
5	8×3	**6**	7×6	**7**	4×8	**8**	6×9
9	$27 \div 3$	**10**	$45 \div 5$	**11**	$48 \div 6$	**12**	$63 \div 9$

13   Four pupils can sit around each table in a classroom.
How many pupils can sit around six tables?

14   There are eight chocolates in a packet.
How many chocolates are there altogether in 7 packets?

15   Four friends share 32 marbles equally between them.
How many marbles does each friend receive?

16   Derek can wash eight cars in an hour.
How many hours will he need to wash 64 cars at a garage?

Exercise 4:1b

For these questions write down the answer only.

1	8×2	**2**	6×5	**3**	7×10	**4**	4×4
5	9×3	**6**	6×8	**7**	8×7	**8**	4×9
9	$32 \div 4$	**10**	$50 \div 5$	**11**	$28 \div 7$	**12**	$72 \div 8$

13   Alan, Shamran and Louise each have eight stamps.
How many stamps do they have altogether?

2,4,6...

14 There are six eggs in a box.
What is the total number of eggs in six boxes?

15 There are 35 counters in a bag.
They are shared equally between 5 pupils.
How many counters does each pupil receive?

16 Bina has 45 tulip bulbs and some pots to plant them in.
She wants to plant 9 bulbs in each pot.
How many pots does she need?

2 Multiplying by 2, 5 and 10

You need to know these multiplication tables by heart, or be able to work out the facts quickly. These questions will help you practise.

Exercise 4:2a

For these questions write down the answer only.

1	3×2	**2**	7×5	**3**	4×10	**4**	5×2	**5**	2×5
6	8×5	**7**	3×10	**8**	6×2	**9**	6×10	**10**	3×5

11 What is the total value of two 5p coins?

12 Jeremy makes three journeys of 5 miles each.
What is his total mileage?

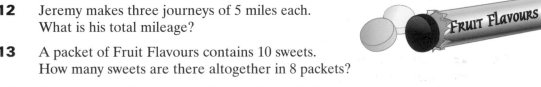

13 A packet of Fruit Flavours contains 10 sweets.
How many sweets are there altogether in 8 packets?

14 How many single socks are there in four pairs?

15 There are six 5-year-old children at a party.
What is their total age?

Exercise 4:2b

For these questions write down the answer only.

1	3×5	**2**	7×10	**3**	7×2	**4**	5×5	**5**	5×2
6	6×10	**7**	9×2	**8**	4×5	**9**	4×10	**10**	9×5

11 It takes a machine 7 seconds to stamp out a metal part.
How long does it take to stamp out 10 metal parts?

12 Lauren buys eight 2-litre packs of milk.
How much milk does she buy altogether?

13 What is the total weight of
nine 5 kg bags of potatoes?

14 What is the total value of
four 10p coins?

15 There are eight tennis
balls in a box.
How many tennis balls are
there altogether in 5 boxes?

3 Multiplying by 2, 3, 4, 5 and 10

You need to know these multiplication tables by heart, or be able to work out
the facts quickly. These questions will help you practise.

Exercise 4:3a

For these questions write down the answer only.

1	4×3	**2**	7×2	**3**	8×4	**4**	6×5	**5**	7×3
6	6×10	**7**	8×3	**8**	9×5	**9**	5×4	**10**	9×10

11 A car has four wheels.
How many wheels are there altogether on four cars?

12 What is the total value of five 5p coins?

13 A camera tripod has three legs.
How many legs are needed to make 9 tripods?

14 A box contains 10 pens.
How many pens are there altogether in 8 boxes?

15 A ladybird has 6 legs.
What is the total number of legs on 4 ladybirds?

Exercise 4:3b

For these questions write down the answer only.

1	8×2	**2**	5×3	**3**	6×10	**4**	9×4	**5**	7×5
6	6×3	**7**	8×5	**8**	7×4	**9**	7×3	**10**	5×10

11 What is the total weight of four 5 kg sacks of potatoes?

12 An octopus has 8 legs.
What is the total number of legs on 4 octopuses?

13 A farmer arranges his bee hives in rows of 8. There are 3 rows.
How many bee hives does he have?

14 What is the total value of seven 10p coins?

15 A table is sold with six chairs.
How many chairs do you get with four tables?

4 Multiplying by numbers up to 10

You need to know these multiplication tables by heart, or be able to work out the facts quickly.
These questions will help you practise.

Exercise 4:4a

For these questions write down the answer only.

1 9×6	**2** 8×8	**3** 6×6	**4** 6×4	**5** 9×7
6 7×8	**7** 8×9	**8** 9×3	**9** 7×7	**10** 6×9

11 A table has four legs.
How many legs are there altogether on eight tables?

12 Hitesh works 8 hours each day.
How many hours does he work in 7 days?

13 A box contains 6 golf balls.
What is the total number of golf balls in 8 boxes?

14 What is the total value of six 5p coins?

15 A wooden board game needs 9 pegs.
How many pegs are needed for 9 board games?

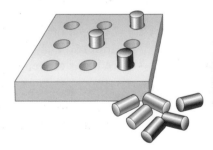

Exercise 4:4b

For these questions write down the answer only.

1 4×8	**2** 8×6	**3** 5×9	**4** 8×7	**5** 7×4
6 7×6	**7** 5×7	**8** 9×8	**9** 8×3	**10** 6×9

11 A boxed set contains 4 CDs.
What is the total number of CDs in 9 boxed sets?

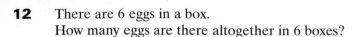

12   There are 6 eggs in a box.
How many eggs are there altogether in 6 boxes?

13   There are 7 days in a week.
How many days are there in 9 weeks?

14   What is the total value of eight 5p coins?

15   Tables are laid out in rows of 7 each.
How many tables are there in 7 rows?

5 Dividing by numbers up to 5

You can use multiplication facts to solve division problems.

EXAMPLES

36 ÷ 4   36 is in the 4 times table: 9 × 4 = 36, so 36 ÷ 4 = 9

24 ÷ 3   24 is in the 3 times table: 8 × 3 = 24, so 24 ÷ 3 = 8

Exercise 4:5a

For these questions write down the answer only.

| **1** | 16 ÷ 2 | **2** | 15 ÷ 3 | **3** | 40 ÷ 5 | **4** | 28 ÷ 4 | **5** | 40 ÷ 5 |
| **6** | 35 ÷ 5 | **7** | 8 ÷ 2 | **8** | 20 ÷ 4 | **9** | 27 ÷ 3 | **10** | 25 ÷ 5 |

11   A piece of wood 10 metres long is cut
into two equal pieces.
What is the length of each piece of wood?

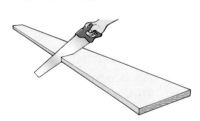

12   How many times does 3 divide into 24?

13   A bingo prize of £32 is shared equally
by 4 people.
How much does each receive?

14   20 counters are put into five equal piles.
How many counters are there in each pile?

15   Daniel has a 15-hour project to do over 5 days.
He plans to spend an equal time each day
on the project.
How many hours is this for each day?

Exercise 4:5b

For these questions write down the answer only.

| **1** | $16 \div 4$ | **2** | $6 \div 2$ | **3** | $12 \div 3$ | **4** | $50 \div 5$ | **5** | $30 \div 5$ |
| **6** | $12 \div 2$ | **7** | $18 \div 3$ | **8** | $45 \div 5$ | **9** | $40 \div 5$ | **10** | $24 \div 4$ |

11 A piece of cheese weighs 36 kg.
It is cut into four pieces of equal weight.
What weight is each piece?

12 How many times can you take 5 from 25?

13 A cartoon is 14 minutes long. It is divided into two equal parts.
How long is each part?

14 A pile of 5p coins has a total value of 60p.
How many coins are there?

15 21 pens are divided equally between three people.
How many pens does each person receive?

6 Dividing by numbers up to 10

You can use multiplication facts to solve division problems.

EXAMPLES

$42 \div 7$ 42 is in the 7 times table: $6 \times 7 = 42$, so $42 \div 7 = 6$

$63 \div 9$ 63 is in the 9 times table: $7 \times 9 = 63$, so $63 \div 9 = 7$

Exercise 4:6a

For these questions write down the answer only.

| **1** | $36 \div 6$ | **2** | $49 \div 7$ | **3** | $54 \div 9$ | **4** | $40 \div 8$ | **5** | $48 \div 6$ |
| **6** | $56 \div 8$ | **7** | $36 \div 9$ | **8** | $30 \div 6$ | **9** | $63 \div 7$ | **10** | $70 \div 10$ |

11 A prize of £64 is shared equally between eight people.
How much does each receive?

12 54 eggs are packed in boxes.
Each box contains 6 eggs.
How many boxes are used?

13 How many times can you take 7 from 42?

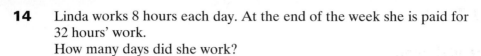

14 Linda works 8 hours each day. At the end of the week she is paid for 32 hours' work.
How many days did she work?

15 In a hall the chairs are arranged in rows of 9.
How many rows can be made using 72 chairs?

Exercise 4:6b

For these questions write down the answer only.

1 $27 \div 9$ **2** $42 \div 6$ **3** $56 \div 7$ **4** $54 \div 6$ **5** $48 \div 8$

6 $45 \div 9$ **7** $64 \div 8$ **8** $24 \div 6$ **9** $81 \div 9$ **10** $35 \div 7$

11 There are seven days in a week.
How many weeks is 28 days?

12 What is 72 divided by 8?

13 A tube of sweets contains 9 chocolates.
There are 63 chocolates to be packed.
How many tubes is this?

14 36 counters are divided equally between 9 pupils.
How many counters does each pupil receive?

15 48 children are divided into 6 equal groups.
How many children are there in each group?

ACTIVITIES

1 Handshakes

You are in a room with two other people
(three of you altogether).
You all want to shake hands with each other.
You can shake hands with each other person
once only.
How many handshakes take place?

How many handshakes would take place
with four people? Five people?

Continue this investigation.
How would you work it out for 50 people?

2 Lines

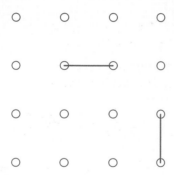

A game for two players.

Take turns to link any two dots that are next to each other with a straight
line.
You may NOT join two dots diagonally.
The straight line must only join any two dots, and must not go through a third
dot.

If you cannot find two dots next to each other to join, then you lose the
game.

Try the game with a larger playing board.

3 Magic squares

This is a magic square.

Add the numbers in each row — you get 15.
Add the numbers in each column — you get 15!
Add the numbers in each diagonal — you get 15!!

4	9	2
3	5	7
8	1	6

This is why it is called a magic square.
Whether you add the numbers in a row, a column, or a diagonal, you will always get the same total.

Copy and complete these magic squares:

	1	
		7
4	9	2

	9	
7	5	
	1	8

		7
	6	8
5		3

3		5
8		
7	2	

5	12	7
10		
		11

	3	
5	7	9
6		

		7
4		
9	10	5

	12	7
	10	
13	8	

4		8
	7	3
		10

Design your own magic square.

4   The wall

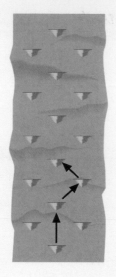

A game for two players.

The diagram represents the hand holds on a climbing wall.
A climber can move up the wall from one hand hold to another.

The first player tells the climber which hand hold to move to from the bottom
of the wall.
The other player then gives the next direction.

The player who gives the instruction to the climber to move to the very top
hand hold is the winner.

Play the game several times, and try to work out how you can always win the
game.

5   The restaurant

Starters
Soup	£1.10
Prawn cocktail	£1.80
Fruit juice	80p

Multiplication

Main Meal
(with fries, side order)
Hamburger	£5.60
Cheeseburger	£5.90
Grilled Steak	£7.10
Omelette	£2.20
Fried plaice	£4.50
Chicken curry	£3.90

Sandwiches
Cheese	£1.30
Cheese and tomato	£1.60
Chicken	£1.70
Prawn	£1.90
Tuna	£1.90

Desserts
Chocolate cake	£1.30
Apple pie	£1.30
Cheesecake	£1.80
Ice cream	£1.10

Drinks
Coffee	£1.10
Tea	90p
Cola	£1.00

Find the total cost for each of these orders:

1   Cheeseburger and cola.

2   Tuna sandwich and coffee.

3   Chicken sandwich and ice cream.

4   Chicken curry and tea.

5   Soup, grilled steak and cheesecake.

6   Prawn cocktail, omelette and apple pie.

7   Fruit juice, fried plaice, apple pie and coffee.

8   Soup, cheese & tomato sandwich, ice cream and cola.

9   Prawn cocktail, grilled steak, apple pie and tea.

10   Fruit juice, chicken curry, chocolate cake and coffee.

Now write your own orders for the restaurant.
For each one find out the total cost.

Make up your own menu and work out the cost of some orders.

5 Multiplication

You will use these words in this chapter.

KEY WORDS
times • product • multiply
• multiple of digits •
total • operation •
double • largest product •
smallest product

1 Diagnostic exercises

Exercise 5:1a

1   32
    × 5
    ——

2   20
    × 6
    ——

3   402
    × 6
    ——

4   824
    × 4
    ——

5 Every day a ferry sails across a lake.
The ferry has been running for 465 weeks.
How many sailings has it made?

6   2417
    ×   6
    ——

7 342 × 10

8 In an experiment a dice is thrown 100 times. 502 people do the experiment. How many times is the dice thrown?

9 124 × 80

10 A box contains 300 screws. A shop has a stock of 230 boxes. What is the total number of screws stored by the shop?

11   32
    ×13
    ——

12   142
    × 24
    ——

Exercise 5:1b

1	27	2	40	3	216	4	782
	× 5		× 8		× 6		× 4
	———		———		———		———

5 A game needs 9 wooden counters. 542 games are made. How many wooden counters are needed?

6	4624	7	604 × 1000
	× 7		
	———		

8 There are 132 foreign stamps in a packet. What is the total number of stamps in 10 packets?

9	213 × 30	10	410 × 400	11	26	12	243
					×14		× 35
					———		———

2 Multiplying by single digits

It helps if you know your times tables by heart, or can work out the facts quickly.

To work out 24 multiplied by 6:

$$\begin{array}{r} 24 \\ \times\ 6 \\ \hline \end{array}$$

This is 20 x 6 = 120
and 4 x 6 =

$$\begin{array}{r} 120 \\ 24 \\ \hline 144 \end{array}$$

Another way:

4 x 6 = 24

$$\begin{array}{r} 24 \\ \times\ 6 \\ \hline 4 \\ {\scriptstyle 2} \end{array}$$

Write the tens here

Write the units here

$$\begin{array}{r} 24 \\ \times\ 6 \\ \hline 144 \\ {\scriptstyle 2} \end{array}$$

2 x 6 = 12
+2 carried
14

$$\begin{array}{r} 45 \\ \times\ 7 \\ \hline 315 \\ {\scriptstyle 3} \end{array}$$

$$\begin{array}{r} 60 \\ \times\ 4 \\ \hline 240 \end{array}$$

Exercise 5:2

1	36×3	**2**	47×6	**3**	18×4	**4**	23×7
5	65×4	**6**	72×5	**7**	59×3	**8**	96×7
9	35×8	**10**	89×5	**11**	44×8	**12**	67×6

13 A coach can carry up to 63 people.
How many people can four full coaches carry?

14 What is the product of 39 and 6?

15 The school bought forty-five books.
Each book cost £9.
What was the total cost of the books?

16 There are 7 days in one week.
How many days are there in 28 weeks?

3 Multiplying with one carry

$$\begin{array}{r} 1\,0\,8 \\ \times \quad 4 \\ \hline \\ \hline \end{array}$$

This is 100 x 4 = 400
and 8 x 4 = 32
432

Another way:

$$\begin{array}{r} 1\,0\,8 \\ \times \quad 4 \\ \hline 2 \\ {\scriptstyle 3} \end{array}$$

8 x 4 = 32

$$\begin{array}{r} 1\,0\,8 \\ \times \quad 4 \\ \hline 3\,2 \\ {\scriptstyle 3} \end{array}$$

0 x 4 = 0
+3 carried
3

$$\begin{array}{r} 1\,0\,8 \\ \times \quad 4 \\ \hline 4\,3\,2 \\ {\scriptstyle 3} \end{array}$$

1 x 4 = 4

EXAMPLES

$$\begin{array}{r} 1\,1\,3 \\ \times \quad 7 \\ \hline 7\,9\,1 \\ {\scriptstyle 2} \end{array}$$

$$\begin{array}{r} 5\,6\,0 \\ \times \quad 5 \\ \hline 2\,8\,0\,0 \\ {\scriptstyle 3} \end{array}$$

Exercise 5:3

1	123×4	**2**	402×9	**3**	212×8	**4**	202×7
5	430×6	**6**	412×5	**7**	504×8	**8**	313×7
9	142×4	**10**	605×9	**11**	524×3	**12**	303×7

13 There are 318 cars in a car park.
Each car has 4 wheels.
What is the total number of wheels for
all of these cars?

14 Martin collects 5p coins. He has 413 of them.
What is the total value of all his coins,
in pence?

15 There are 704 pupils at a school. Each pupil has to carry 9 books.
What is the total number of books carried at the school?

16 What is the product of 512 and 7?

4 Multiplication with more carries

$$\begin{array}{r} 2\,8\,4 \\ \times \quad 7 \\ \hline \\ \hline \end{array}$$

This is $200 \times 7 = 1400$
$80 \times 7 = 560$
$4 \times 7 = 28$
$\overline{1988}$

Another way:

$$\begin{array}{r} 2\,8\,4 \\ \times \quad 7 \\ \hline 8 \\ \hline \end{array}$$
$$_2$$
$\longrightarrow$
$$\begin{array}{r} 2\,8\,4 \\ \times \quad 7 \\ \hline 8\,8 \\ \hline \end{array}$$
$$_{5\ 2}$$
$\longrightarrow$
$$\begin{array}{r} 2\,8\,4 \\ \times \quad 7 \\ \hline 1\,9\,8\,8 \\ \hline \end{array}$$
$$_{5\ 2}$$

$4 \times 7 = 28$

$8 \times 7 = 56$
$+ 2$
$\overline{58}$

$2 \times 7 = 14$
$+ 5$
$\overline{19}$

$$\begin{array}{r} 5\,4\,2 \\ \times \quad 6 \\ \hline 3\,2\,5\,2 \\ \hline {\scriptstyle 2\ 1} \end{array}$$

$$\begin{array}{r} 4\,1\,7 \\ \times \quad 9 \\ \hline 3\,7\,5\,3 \\ \hline {\scriptstyle 1\ 6} \end{array}$$

Exercise 5:4

1	189×8	**2**	217×7	**3**	257×8	**4**	118×9
5	387×6	**6**	524×7	**7**	287×5	**8**	618×8
9	184×6	**10**	332×9	**11**	358×7	**12**	568×4

13 In a stadium there are 465 rows of seats, with 8 seats to each row.
What is the total number of seats?

14 There are 9 skittles in a game.
How many skittles are needed for 156 games?

15 Four workers have each picked 588 strawberries.
What is the total number of strawberries picked?

16 In a leap year there are 366 days.
How many days are there in 6 leap years?

5 Multiplying by 10, 100, 1000

We can use what we know about place value to work out these multiplications.

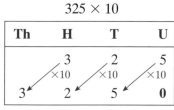

$325 \times 10 = 3250$

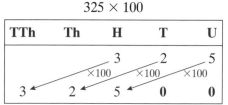

$325 \times 100 = 32\,5000$

$$325 \times 1000$$

HTh	TTh	Th	H	T	Th
			3	2	5
		$\times 1000$	$\times 1000$	$\times 1000$	
3	2	5	0	0	0

$325 \times 1000 = 325\,000$

When we multiply by **10** the digits change by **one** column.
When we multiply by **100** the digits change by **two** columns.
When we multiply by **1000** the digits change by **three** columns.

EXAMPLES

$56 \times 10 = 560$ $351 \times 100 = 35\,100$ $67 \times 1000 = 67\,000$

Exercise 5:5

1	86 × 100	**2**	680 × 1000	**3**	85 × 10
4	67 × 100	**5**	431 × 10	**6**	101 × 100
7	82 × 1000	**8**	282 × 10	**9**	596 × 1000
10	87 × 10	**11**	30 × 100	**12**	672 × 1000
13	140 × 100	**14**	15 × 1000	**15**	270 × 10

16 How many pence are there in £70?

17 There are 1000 counters in a bag. What is the total number of counters in 487 bags?

18 What is the product of 100 and 200?

6 Multiplying by multiples of 10

Break the multiple of 10 into a single digit and a multiple of tens.

$$24 \times 30$$
$$= 24 \times 3 \times 10$$

$$
\begin{array}{r}
24 \\
\times\ 3 \\
\hline
72 \\
\end{array} \times 10
$$

$$= 720$$

$$41 \times 600$$
$$= 41 \times 6 \times 100$$

$$
\begin{array}{r}
41 \\
\times\ 6 \\
\hline
246 \\
\end{array} \times 100
$$

$$= 24\,600$$

EXAMPLES

$$36 \times 70 = 36 \times 7 \times 10 = 252 \times 10 = 2520$$

$$67 \times 4000 = 67 \times 4 \times 1000 = 268 \times 1000 = 268\,000$$

Exercise 5:6

1	26 × 40	**2**	44 × 3000	**3**	37 × 400
4	141 × 60	**5**	37 × 500	**6**	124 × 60
7	61 × 5000	**8**	81 × 300	**9**	61 × 4000
10	137 × 800	**11**	26 × 30	**12**	122 × 70
13	12 × 300	**14**	321 × 7000	**15**	54 × 50

16 There are 365 days in a year. How many days are there in 800 years? Ignore leap years.

17 A box contains 30 matches.
How many matches are there in 42 boxes?

Contents 30 matches

18 Each of 44 workers received a £6000 share of a lottery prize.
What was the total prize money won by the group?

7 Multiplying two 2-digit numbers

68×42

$$This \ is \ 68 \times 40 = 68 \times 4 \times 10 \ = 2720$$
$$and \ 68 \times 2 \ = \ \ \ 136$$
$$2856$$

You can also set this out as a long multiplication:

```
    68           68           68           68
  × 42         × 42         × 42         × 42
  ─────        ─────        ─────        ─────
      0         2720         2720         2720
                              136          136
                                          ────
                                          2856
```

Multiply by the 4 first, but as the value of the 4 is 40, put the 0 down first.

68 x 40

68 x 2 on the next line

You should always check your answer using approximation.

68×42 can be written as approximate numbers:

$70 \times 40 = 2800.$

Note: 2800 is *not* the answer to 68×42!
Comparison: 2800 is *near to* 2856
This shows that 2856 is the expected size for the answer.

Answer: $68 \times 42 = 2856$

EXAMPLES

```
41 × 38        4 1              84 × 57         8 4
             ×   3 8                          ×   5 7
             ───────                          ───────
             1 2 3 0                          4 2 0 0
               3 2 8                          5 8 8
             ───────                          ───────
             1 5 4 8                          4 7 8 8
```

Check:
40 x 40
= 1600

Check:
80 x 60
= 4800

Exercise 5:7

1 38 × 44	**2** 78 × 19	**3** 41 × 53	**4** 58 × 81
5 52 × 78	**6** 67 × 82	**7** 32 × 67	**8** 29 × 73
9 88 × 21	**10** 49 × 74	**11** 89 × 61	**12** 42 × 66
13 74 × 32	**14** 36 × 85	**15** 52 × 69	**16** 94 × 47

17 There are 78 rows of seats in a stadium. Each row has 86 seats. What is the total number of seats in the stadium?

18 A coach can carry 59 people when full.
A trip for the whole school needs 22 coaches.
What is the maximum number of people
going on the trip?

19 There are about 48 books on each shelf
of a library, and 98 shelves.
About how many books are there in the library,
if all the shelves are full?

20 What is 73 times 57?

8 Multiplying by a 2-digit number

To multiply a number by a 2-digit number you have to break the problem
down into parts.

613 × 39

This is 613 x 30 = 613 x 3 x 10 = 18 390
and 619 x 9 =   5 517
                                   ─────
                                   23 907

You can also set this out as a long multiplication:

```
    6 1 3          6 1 3            6 1 3            6 1 3
  ×   3 9        ×   3 9          ×   3 9          ×   3 9
  ───────        ───────          ───────          ───────
        0        1 8 3 9 0        1 8 3 9 0        1 8 3 9 0
                                    5 5 1 7          5 5 1 7
                                                   ─────────
                                                   2 3 9 0 7
```

Multiply by the 3
first, but as the
value of the 3 is 30,   613 x 30
put the 0 down first.
                           613 x 9

You should always check your answers using approximation.

613×39 can be written as approximate numbers: $600 \times 40 = 24\,000$

Note: 24 000 is *not* the answer to 613×39!
Comparison: 23 907 is *near to* 24 000
This shows that 23 907 is about the expected size of the answer.

Answer: $613 \times 39 = 23\,907$

643×56

```
      6 4 3
    ×   5 6
  ─────────
    3 2 1 5 0
      3 8 5 8
  ─────────
    3 6 0 0 8
```
Check:
600 x 60
= 36 000

2369×86

```
      2 3 6 9
    ×     8 6
  ───────────
    1 8 9 5 2 0
      1 4 2 1 4
  ───────────
    2 0 3 7 3 4
```
Check:
2000 x 90
= 180 000

Exercise 5:8

1 497×98 **2** 763×48 **3** 1143×71 **4** 492×94

5 1812×39 **6** 246×84 **7** 421×28 **8** 1821×72

9 507×19 **10** 1945×88 **11** 631×82 **12** 532×39

13 There are 1204 ball bearings in a box. Each ball bearing weighs 21 g.
What is the combined weight of all the ball bearings?

14 A football supporter's club charges its 473 members
a fee of £15 for a trip to a match.
What is the total amount collected?

15 What is the product of 1119 and 68?

16 A machine can make 65 combs in one pressing.
The machine makes 845 pressings in a day.
How many combs can be made each day?

ACTIVITIES

1   The darts game

A game for 2 players.

Start with the number 101.
Player A takes away any number between 1 and 9
(inclusive), OR **double** one of these numbers.

Player B does the same.

Both players then take turns at taking away.

The winner is the first player to reach 0 exactly.

2   Multiplication routes

There are three different
routes you can follow in
the diagram:

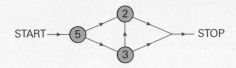

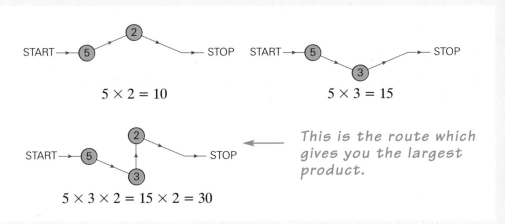

$5 \times 2 = 10$

$5 \times 3 = 15$

This is the route which
gives you the largest
product.

$5 \times 3 \times 2 = 15 \times 2 = 30$

Find out which route gives you the biggest answer in each of these diagrams.

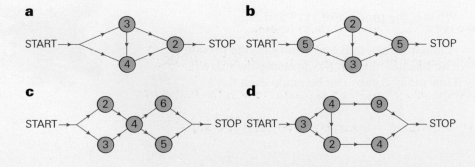

a

b

c

d

3 That number again!

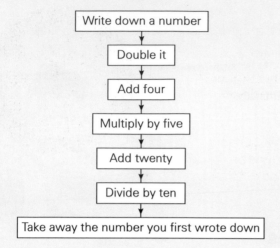

Write down a number
↓
Double it
↓
Add four
↓
Multiply by five
↓
Add twenty
↓
Divide by ten
↓
Take away the number you first wrote down

Try this with several numbers.
What do you notice about the answer?

Will you always get this answer, whatever number you try?

4 Number times

You can use the four digits 1, 2, 3 and 4 to make some multiplication problems.

$$213 \times 4 = 852$$
$$12 \times 34 = 408$$

The largest product you can make is $42 \times 31 = 1302$
The smallest product you can make is $13 \times 24 = 312$

Now choose your own four digits to use.

Find the largest product you can make with the four digits.

Find the smallest product you can make with the four digits.

You could extend the problem to consider five digits.

6 Division

□□□

You will use these words in this chapter.

KEY WORDS

- share • divide • remainder
- divided by • fraction
- decimal • halve • third
- quarter • quotient • divisor

1 Diagnostic exercises

Exercise 6:1a

Work these out. Show any remainder with your answer.

1 4)804   **2** 6)1806   **3** 2)3427   **4** 5)7463

Give your answer as a decimal:

5 2)3579   **6** 8)6159

Work out:

7 70 000 ÷ 100   **8** 85 000 ÷ 1000   **9** 18 280 ÷ 40

10 28 000 ÷ 700   **11** 4158 ÷ 27

12 Carrots are packed in 3 kg bags. There are 25 kg of carrots. How many full bags is this?

Exercise 6:1b

Work these out. Show any remainder with your answer.

1 3)963   **2** 5)3550   **3** 4)5237   **4** 7)9354

Give your answer as a decimal:

5 5)3534   **6** 4)6457

Work out:

7　9000 ÷ 10　　　**8**　45 000 ÷ 100　　　**9**　522 000 ÷ 6000

10　64 000 ÷ 80　　**11**　7439 ÷ 43

12　Eggs are sold in boxes of six. The hens have laid 52 eggs.
　　How many full boxes is this?

2　Single digit division (no remainders)

It helps to know your times tables.

$$1407 \div 7 \quad 7\overline{)1407}^{2} \longrightarrow 7\overline{)1407}^{20} \longrightarrow 7\overline{)1407}^{201}$$

$$14 \div 7 = 2 \quad 0 \div 7 = 0 \quad 7 \div 7 = 1$$

EXAMPLES

$$3\overline{)2796}^{932} \qquad 5\overline{)3005}^{601}$$

The expression "halve" or fraction "half" means "divide by 2".
To find a third, divide by 3.
To find a quarter, divide by 4.

Exercise 6:2

1　$2\overline{)846}$　　**2**　$4\overline{)1684}$　　**3**　$5\overline{)4555}$　　**4**　$3\overline{)1839}$

5　$6\overline{)1860}$　　**6**　$2\overline{)1248}$　　**7**　$4\overline{)3208}$　　**8**　$6\overline{)4806}$

9　2406 ÷ 3　**10**　3066 ÷ 6　**11**　1262 ÷ 2　**12**　3690 ÷ 9

13　5050 ÷ 5　**14**　2169 ÷ 3　**15**　3577 ÷ 7　**16**　2404 ÷ 4

17　What is 1536 divided by 3?

18　A driver makes 4 journeys of equal distance in his car.
　　His total mileage is 3684 km.
　　What is the distance of each single journey?

19　Prize money of £2408 is divided equally
　　between 8 people.
　　How much will each person receive?

20　2005 nails are to be shared equally into 5 boxes.
　　How many nails will there be in each box?

3 Single digit division (with remainders)

It helps to know your times tables.

Sometimes numbers do not divide exactly, and we are left with a remainder.

5572 ÷ 6

$$\begin{array}{r} 9 \\ 6\overline{)\,5\,5^1 7\,2} \end{array}$$

9 x 6 = 54
55 − 54 = r 1

$$\begin{array}{r} 9\,2 \\ 6\overline{)\,5\,5^1 7^5 2} \end{array}$$

2 x 6 = 12
17 − 12 = r 5

$$\begin{array}{r} 9\,2\,8 \ \text{r4} \\ 6\overline{)\,5\,5^1 7^5 2} \end{array}$$

8 x 6 = 48
52 − 48 = r 4

So   5572 ÷ 6 = 928 remainder 4

Called the quotient   *Called the divisor*   *Called the remainder*

EXAMPLES

$$\begin{array}{r} 1\,3\,8\,5\ \text{r2} \\ 3\overline{)\,4\,1\,5\,7} \end{array}$$

$$\begin{array}{r} 5\,9\,9\ \text{r4} \\ 7\overline{)\,4\,1\,9\,7} \end{array}$$

Exercise 6:3

1	2)6215	**2**	5)4292	**3**	3)2437	**4**	5)3761
5	4)1463	**6**	2)1631	**7**	6)5071	**8**	3)3872
9	4979 ÷ 7	**10**	7634 ÷ 4	**11**	4276 ÷ 6	**12**	3767 ÷ 9
13	4213 ÷ 8	**14**	7387 ÷ 9	**15**	89 794 ÷ 8	**16**	24 784 ÷ 7

17   What is the remainder when 3975 is divided by 4?

18   There are 1330 counters in a box.
These are shared between 6 people so each
person has the same number of counters.
How many counters does each person have?

19   What is the remainder when 7129 is
divided by 5?

20   How many days are left over when 64 018
days is divided into weeks?

JULY 2000					
Monday		3	10	17	24	31
Tuesday		4	11	18	25	
Wednesday		5	12	19	26	
Thursday		6	13	20	27	
Friday		7	14	21	28	
Saturday	1	8	15	22	29	
Sunday	2	9	16	23	30	

4 Single digit division (as a decimal)

Instead of writing a remainder, you can write the remainder as a decimal part of the answer.

$1745 \div 4$

$$4 \overline{) 1\,7^1 4\,5} \qquad\longrightarrow\qquad 4 \overline{) 1\,7\,^14^25} \qquad\longrightarrow\qquad 4 \overline{) 1\,7^14^25}$$

with remainder **1**

$4 \times 4 = 16$ $3 \times 4 = 12$ $6 \times 4 = 24$
$17 - 6 = r1$ $14 - 2 = r2$ $25 - 24 = r1$

Now add a decimal point and a zero 0 on to the end of the number, so you can continue dividing:

$$4 \overline{)1\,7^14^25\,.^10^2} \qquad\qquad 4 \overline{)1\,7^14^25\,.^10^20}$$

$2 \times 4 = 8$ $\longrightarrow$ $5 \times 4 = 20$
$10 - 8 = r2$ no remainder

So $1745 \div 4 = 436.25$

EXAMPLES

$$5 \overline{)3\,2^21^18\,.^30}\qquad 6\,4\,3\,.\,6$$

$$8 \overline{)4\,2^21^53\,.^70^60^40}\qquad 5\,2\,6\,.\,8\,7\,5$$

Exercise 6:4

1 $3817 \div 2$	**2** $3927 \div 4$	**3** $4524 \div 5$	**4** $5337 \div 8$
5 $3913 \div 4$	**6** $4637 \div 8$	**7** $92617 \div 2$	**8** $3837 \div 5$
9 $3462 \div 8$	**10** $8784 \div 5$	**11** $15387 \div 2$	**12** $2958 \div 4$

13 A cable is 56 427 mm long.
It is cut into two pieces of equal length.
What is the length of each piece?

14 What is the exact answer when
4 is divided into 6597?

15 A total weight of 9756 g of salt is
shared equally into five containers.
What weight of salt will be in each container?

16 Divide 8 into 8675.
What is the exact answer?

5 Dividing by 10, 100, 1000

We can use what we know about place value to work out these divisions.

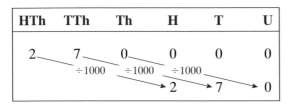

$$420 \div 10$$

Th	H	T	U
	4	2	0
	$\div 10 \to 4$	$\div 10 \to 2$	

$$420 \div 10 = 42$$

$$5300 \div 100$$

Th	H	T	U
5	3	0	0
	$\div 100$	$\div 100 \to 5$	$\to 3$

$$5300 \div 100 = 53$$

$$270\,000 \div 1000$$

HTh	TTh	Th	H	T	U
2	7	0	0	0	0
	$\div 1000$	$\div 1000$	$\div 1000$		
			2	7	0

$$270\,000 \div 1000 = 270$$

EXAMPLES

$$1400 \times 10 = 140 \quad 303\,000 \times 10 = 30\,300 \quad 15\,000 \times 1000 = 15$$

Exercise 6:5

Write down the answers.

1	$70\,900 \div 100$	**2**	$9000 \div 1000$	**3**	$6500 \div 10$
4	$400 \div 100$	**5**	$700 \div 10$	**6**	$5000 \div 100$
7	$800\,000 \div 1000$	**8**	$2000 \div 10$	**9**	$59\,000 \div 1000$
10	$1500 \div 10$	**11**	$8200 \div 100$	**12**	$40\,000 \div 1000$
13	$140\,000 \div 100$	**14**	$17\,000 \div 1000$	**15**	$43\,000 \div 10$
16	$25\,000 \div 100$				

17 There are 1000 g in one kilogram.
How many kilograms are the same as 250 000 g?

18 A bonus of £4000 is shared equally by 100 workers.
How much does each receive?

19 How many £10 notes make £9000?

20 There are 100 cm in one metre.
How many metres are the same as 72 000 cm?

6 Dividing by multiples of 10

Break the multiple of 10 into a single digit and a multiple of tens.
For example, $30 = 3 \times 10$

$3900 \div 30$

$= 3900 \div (3 \times 10)$
$= 3900 \div 3$ then $\div 10$

$$\begin{array}{r} 1300 \\ 3\,)\overline{3900} \end{array}$$

then $1300 \div 10 = 130$

$252\,000 \div 700$

$= 252\,000 \div (7 \times 100)$
$= 252\,000 \div 7$ then $\div 100$

$$\begin{array}{r} 36\,000 \\ 7\,)\overline{252\,000} \end{array}$$

then $3600 \div 100 = 360$

$46\,000 \div 400 = 46\,000 \div 4$ then $\div 100 = 11\,500 \div 100 = 115$

$56\,000 \div 80 = 56\,000 \div 8$ then $\div 10 = 700 \div 10 = 70$

Exercise 6:6

1	$880 \div 40$	**2**	$78\,000 \div 30$	**3**	$96\,000 \div 600$
4	$36\,000 \div 6000$	**5**	$84\,000 \div 300$	**6**	$4800 \div 20$
7	$7440 \div 80$	**8**	$5200 \div 40$	**9**	$72\,000 \div 6000$
10	$68\,600 \div 70$	**11**	$47\,700 \div 90$	**12**	$74\,000 \div 200$
13	$8720 \div 80$	**14**	$7500 \div 300$	**15**	$171\,000 \div 90$

16 $85\,400 \div 700$

17 One box contains 400 transistors.
How many boxes are needed for 84 000 transistors?

18 How many times does 600 divide into 88 200?

19 There are 30 seats in each row in a concert hall.
Altogether there are 36 000 seats.
How many rows of seats are there?

20 What should 900 be multiplied by to give an answer of 73 800?

7 Dividing by a two-digit number

Work out: 2996 × 14

By a short division method:

$$\begin{array}{r} 2 \\ 14\,\overline{)\,2\,9^{1}9\,6} \end{array}$$
2 r1

⟶

$$\begin{array}{r} 2\,1 \\ 14\,\overline{)\,2\,9^{1}9^{5}6} \end{array}$$
1 r5

⟶

$$\begin{array}{r} 2\,1\,4 \\ 14\,\overline{)\,2\,9^{1}9^{5}6} \end{array}$$
4 r0

By a long division method:

To divide by a 2-digit number you have to break the problem down into stages.

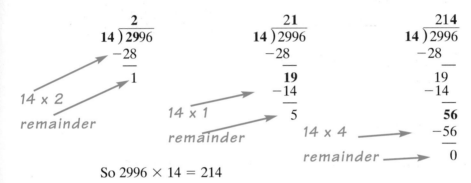

14 x 2
remainder

14 x 1
remainder

14 x 4
remainder

$$\begin{array}{r} 2 \\ 14\,\overline{)\,2996} \\ -28 \\ \hline 1 \end{array}$$

$$\begin{array}{r} 21 \\ 14\,\overline{)\,2996} \\ -28 \\ \hline 19 \\ -14 \\ \hline 5 \end{array}$$

$$\begin{array}{r} 214 \\ 14\,\overline{)\,2996} \\ -28 \\ \hline 19 \\ -14 \\ \hline 56 \\ -56 \\ \hline 0 \end{array}$$

So 2996 × 14 = 214

You can check your answer using multiplication and approximation.

Does 214 × 14 = 2996?

Approximation: 200 × 14 = 2800

Comparison: 2800 is near to 2996

This shows that 214 is the expected size for the answer.

Answer: 2996 ÷ 14 = 214

EXAMPLES

$$\begin{array}{r} 444 \\ 13\,\overline{)\,5772} \\ -52 \\ \hline 57 \\ -52 \\ \hline 52 \\ -52 \\ \hline 0 \end{array}$$

$$\begin{array}{r} 233 \\ 31\,\overline{)\,7223} \\ -62 \\ \hline 102 \\ -93 \\ \hline 93 \\ -93 \\ \hline 0 \end{array}$$

Exercise 6:7

1 544 ÷ 17	**2** 627 ÷ 19	**3** 770 ÷ 14	**4** 432 ÷ 12
5 627 ÷ 19	**6** 4012 ÷ 59	**7** 8140 ÷ 22	**8** 3648 ÷ 57
9 6764 ÷ 76	**10** 2820 ÷ 47	**11** 1152 ÷ 18	**12** 6435 ÷ 65
13 3773 ÷ 49	**14** 8162 ÷ 22	**15** 5160 ÷ 15	**16** 13041 ÷ 21

17 Boyband's "best hits" CD costs £16.
They have sold their stock for £5680.
How many CDs have they sold?

18 A lottery prize of £16 492 is shared equally
between 31 colleagues.
How much does each receive?

19 What should 17 be multiplied by to give
an answer of 5899?

20 A shop sells 23 televisions for a total of £4899.
How much does each cost?

8 Rounding remainders

Sometimes when we are dividing in real situations we need a whole number
for the answer.
Sometimes we need to round the remainder up, and sometimes we need to
round it down.

a Julie needs 11 litres of paint.
It is sold in 5-litre tins.
How many tins of paint should she buy?

2 tins would give her $2 \times 5 = 10$ litres,
which is not enough.

She would need to buy 3 tins (15 litres)

b 380 stamps are to be put into packets
of 50 for sale.
How many packets can be sold?

$380 \div 50 = 7$ packets with 30 stamps
remaining.
The remainder cannot make another full
packet, so cannot be sold.

The number of full packets for sale is 7.

EXAMPLES

Exercise 6:8

1 Video tapes are sold in packs of 5.
How many packs can be made from a box of 38 video tapes?

2 Pencils are sold in boxes of 15. A teacher needs 100 pencils.
How many boxes should she buy?

3 In a game there are 4 players in a team.
How many teams can be made from a group of 35 people?

4 A coach can carry 55 passengers.
How many coaches are needed to take 250 pupils on a school outing?

5 An empty tank has a capacity of 75 litres.
How many 7-litre containers can you empty into the tank before it overflows?

6 How many whole weeks are there in 60 days?

7 Shreena has £1.58.
She wants to change this for 20p coins.
How many 20p coins can she get for her £1.58?

8 The number of people allowed in a hotel lift is 12.
How many trips of the lift are needed for a group of 50 people?

ACTIVITIES

1 Number chains

This is a number chain:

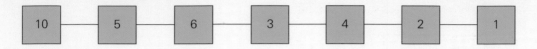

Make a number chain following these simple rules:

a Write down any number.

b For the next number:

    (i)   add 1 if the last number was **odd**

    (ii)   divide by 2 if the last number was **even**.

c Repeat step **b** until you get to 1.

Start with different numbers and write out their number chains.

Which numbers less than 100 make the longest chains?

What about numbers greater than 100?

2 Remainders

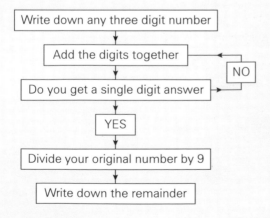

Try this with several numbers.
Write down what you notice from your answers.

3 Sliding counters

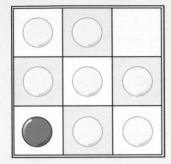

Eight counters are placed on a 3 × 3 board as shown.

By sliding one counter at a time, how many moves do you need to move the blue counter from the bottom left-hand corner to the top right-hand corner? Diagonal movements are **not** allowed.

What is the shortest route?
How many moves is it?

You could extend the game by using a larger board.
Your board could be a rectangle rather than a square.

4 Number maze

This is a number maze.

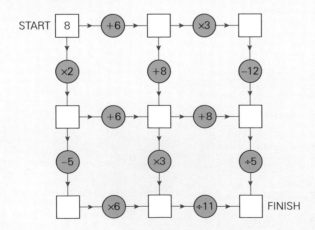

Each circle shows an operation.
A number needs to be written in each square.

a   Start with the number 8.
    Work through the number maze, filling in all the numbers.
    Find the missing FINISH number.

b   Start with some different numbers.
    Do you get the same results?

c   Try the number maze below.
    Start with the number 6, then try other numbers.

Design your own number maze.

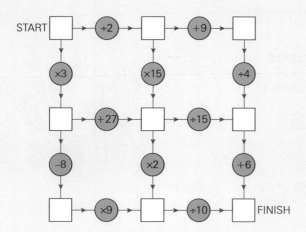

7 Decimals

You will use these words in this chapter.

KEY WORDS
- place value • decimal value • order • size • significant
- ascending • descending • decimal • fraction
- decimal point • decimal place • estimation • estimate
- tenth • hundredth • thousandth

1 Diagnostic exercises

Exercise 7:1a

Write these fractions as decimals.

1   **2**   **3**

Write these decimals as fractions.

4   0.7   **5**   0.42   **6**   8.03

Estimate the readings on these scales.

7 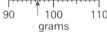   **8** 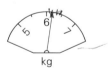   **9**

Write these decimals in ascending order.

10   0.04, 0.4, 0.004   **11**   6.10, 65.4, 6.52, 66.3

Work out:

12 $7.875 + 0.68 + 0.909$ **13** $2 + 20.7 + 670.5 + 1.085$

14   Bill has £5.43 He spends £2.49
How much does he have left?

15   A rope is 6 m long. A piece 2.07 m long is cut off.
What length is left?

16 7.225×8 **17** 0.007×6

18 0.4×1.3 **19** $0.5 \div 100$ **20**   Divide 9.12 by 6.

Exercise 7:1b

Write these fractions as decimals.

1   **2**   **3**

Write these decimals as fractions.

4   0.37   **5**   0.3   **6**   4.042

Estimate the readings on these scales.

7   **8**

(scale showing 60, 61, 62 grams)

9

Write these decimals in ascending order.

10   0.132, 0.232, 0.012   **11**   4.0, 0.04, 0.85, 5.8

Work out:

12   9.96 + 8.5 + 0.064 + 0.97   **13**   4 + 17.5 + 0.87 + 10.65

14   Kirsty has £6.56. She spends £3.49.
How much does she have left?

15   A silicon wafer is 0.55 mm thick.
Its thickness is reduced by 0.055 mm.
What is its new thickness?

16 4.037×5 **17** 0.08×9

18 2.4×0.6 **19** $1.42 \div 100$

20   Divide 4.552 by 8.

2 Decimal values

Each whole number can be divided into tenths.

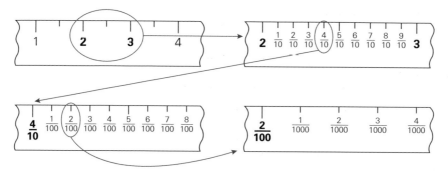

Each tenth can be divided into hundredths.

Each hundredth can be divided into thousandths.

These smaller numbers are called decimal values.

H	T	U	.	$\frac{1}{10}$	$\frac{1}{100}$	$\frac{1}{1000}$
		2	.	3		
		0	.	0	4	7

The value of the 3 in 2.3 is $\frac{3}{10}$

The value of the 4 in 0.041 is $\frac{4}{100}$

The value of the 7 in 0.047 is $\frac{7}{1000}$

Writing fractions as decimals

$\frac{33}{1000}$ is a fraction written in thousandths.

We write the numerator of the fraction with its right-hand digit in the thousandth column.

$\frac{33}{1000}$ can be written
0.033

U	.	$\frac{1}{10}$	$\frac{1}{100}$	$\frac{1}{1000}$
0	.	0	3	3

Up to thousandths column

$\frac{19}{100}$ can be written
0.19

U	.	$\frac{1}{10}$	$\frac{1}{100}$
0	.	1	9

Up to hundredths column

$\frac{8}{10}$ can be written
0.8

U	.	$\frac{1}{10}$
0	.	8

Up to tenths column

Writing decimals as fractions

0.09 can be written

$\frac{9}{100}$

U	.	$\frac{1}{10}$	$\frac{1}{100}$
0	.	0	9

0.008 can be written

$\frac{8}{1000}$

U	.	$\frac{1}{10}$	$\frac{1}{100}$	$\frac{1}{1000}$
0	.	0	0	8

0.17 can be written

$\frac{17}{100}$

U	.	$\frac{1}{10}$	$\frac{1}{1000}$
0	.	1	7

Write these decimals as fractions:

$0.8 = \frac{8}{10}$ $\qquad$ $0.017 = \frac{17}{1000}$ $\qquad$ $3.14 = 3\frac{14}{100}$

Write these fractions as decimals:

$\frac{4}{100} = 0.04$ $\qquad$ $\frac{24}{100} = 0.24$ $\qquad$ $2\frac{7}{1000} = 2.007$

Exercise 7:2

Write these decimals as fractions.

1	0.33	**2**	0.4	**3**	0.135	**5**	0.09
6	0.1	**7**	0.49	**8**	0.031	**9**	0.6
10	0.07	**11**	2.9	**12**	5.303	**13**	6.009

Write these fractions as decimals.

14	$\frac{3}{10}$	**15**	$\frac{16}{100}$	**16**	$\frac{17}{1000}$	**17**	$\frac{7}{10}$
18	$\frac{7}{100}$	**19**	$\frac{2}{10}$	**20**	$\frac{153}{1000}$	**21**	$\frac{37}{100}$
22	$\frac{321}{1000}$	**23**	$7\frac{56}{100}$	**24**	$3\frac{4}{10}$	**25**	$5\frac{57}{1000}$

3 Using decimals in estimation

Decimals divide a measurement into smaller parts.

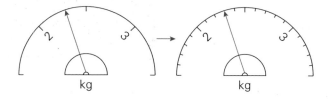

Imagine the decimal values are shown to help you give an estimate: about 2.3 kg.

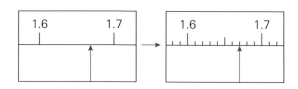

Estimate: about 1.67

Exercise 7:3

Estimate these readings.

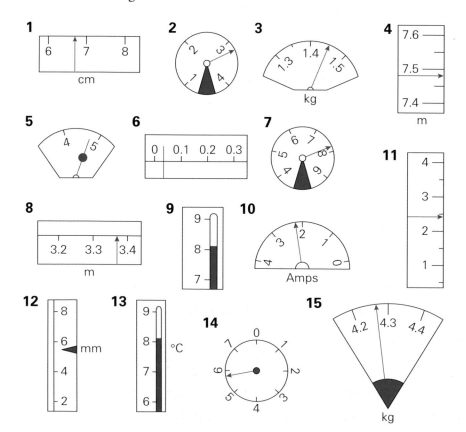

4 Ordering decimals

To order decimals you have to look at the value of each decimal place.

1/10   5/100   9/1000

0 . 1 5 9   0 . 1 5 9

To order decimal numbers, start with the digits at the front of the numbers (the most significant).

EXAMPLE

Write in ascending order (smallest first):

0.629, 0.509, 0.612, 0.55, 0.621

Order the first digits ( )	Order the second digits ( )	Order the third digits ( )
0.509	0.509	0.509
0.55	0.55	0.55
....	....	....
0.629	0.612	0.612
		....
0.612	0.629	0.621
0.621	0.621	0.629

Ascending order: 0.509, 0.55, 0.612, 0.621, 0.629

Note:

For descending order, reverse the list: 0.629, 0.621, 0.612, etc.

Exercise 7:4

Write in ascending order:

1 0.51, 0.59, 0.52

2 0.022, 0.049, 0.032

3 6.039, 6.009, 6.109

4 9.099, 9.909, 9.990

5 2.3, 0.23, 3.2, 0.32

6 10.9, 1.09, 9.09, 9.90

Write in descending order:

7 0.243, 0.343, 0.023

8 0.8, 0.008, 0.0888

9 5.0069, 5.009, 5.0079

10 0.44, 4.4, 0.04, 0.4

11 1.26, 0.526, 0.56, 0.126

12 0.110, 1.0, 1.01, 0.011

5 Adding decimals

To add decimals, write the digits with the same place value under each other. The decimal points should be line up under each other.

$$2 + 1.04 + 0.9 + 15.412 = 19.352$$

```
       2
    1 . 0 4
    0 . 9
 + 1 5 . 4 1 2
 ─────────────
  1 9 . 3 5 2
      1
```

The gaps have value zero.
2 is the same as 2.00

Add together: **a** $4 + 2.112 + 5.3$ **b** $5.48 + 9 + 1.073$

a
```
      4
    2 . 1 1 2
 +  5 . 3
 ───────────
  1 1 . 4 1 2
```

b
```
    5 . 4 8
    9
 +  1 . 0 7 3
 ───────────
  1 5 . 5 5 3
```

Exercise 7:5

Write out these addition sums and work out the answers.

1 $3.7 + 2.06 + 6.1$ **2** $4.8 + 7 + 2.5$

3 $2.52 + 0.81 + 3.73$ **4** $0.86 + 9.5 + 0.07$

5 $4.57 + 10.8 + 0.09 + 2$ **6** $2.38 + 0.9 + 0.075$

7 $0.086 + 0.7 + 0.915 + 0.3$ **8** $11.07 + 1.87 + 0.9 + 4$

9 $0.875 + 6.3 + 0.008 + 0.72$ **10** $2.7 + 18 + 3.1 + 0.985$

11 $43 + 7.6 + 0.58 + 2.35$ **12** $32 + 2.56 + 0.78 + 8.3$

13 The costs of some groceries are £1.72, £0.46, £1.08, and £0.83. Find the total cost.

14 Metal parts weighing 8.5 kg, 17 kg, 1.6 kg and 1.08 kg are to be delivered by air freight. What is the total weight of the parts?

15 Oil is kept in four containers. The quantities in each container are 1.085 litres, 2 litres, 2.07 litres and 6.75 litres. What is the total quantity of oil?

16 These times were recorded in a Science experiment: 10.65 s, 0.875 s, 3 s, 18.5 s. Find the total of these times.

6 Subtracting decimals

To subtract a decimal from another decimal, write the digits with the same place value under each other.

The decimal points should line up under each other.

Fill in any gaps in the numbers with zeros, particularly in the number you are taking away from (the number on the top line).

$$4.51 - 3.27$$

$$
\begin{array}{r}
4.\overset{4}{\cancel{5}}{}^{1}1 \\
-\ 3.2\,7 \\
\hline
1.2\,4 \\
\hline
\end{array}
$$

$$7.6 - 5.42$$

Fill in the gap with zero.

$$
\begin{array}{r}
7.6\,\mathbf{0} \\
-\ 5.4\,2 \\
\hline
 \\
\hline
\end{array}
$$

$$
\begin{array}{r}
7.\overset{5}{\cancel{6}}{}^{1}0 \\
-\ 5.4\,2 \\
\hline
2.1\,8 \\
\hline
\end{array}
$$

EXAMPLES

Subtract:

a $3.14 - 1.03$ **b** $5.4 - 2.22$

a
$$
\begin{array}{r}
3\overset{2}{\cancel{.}}{}^{1}1\,4 \\
-\ 1.9\,3 \\
\hline
1.2\,1 \\
\hline
\end{array}
$$

b
$$
\begin{array}{r}
5.\overset{3}{\cancel{4}}{}^{1}0 \\
-\ 2.2\,2 \\
\hline
3.1\,8 \\
\hline
\end{array}
$$

Exercise 7:6

Write out these sums and work out the answers.

1 $5.45 - 5.38$	**2** $5.14 - 4.07$	**3** $4.32 - 3.38$	
4 $4.06 - 1.26$	**5** $6.07 - 5.09$	**6** $7.27 - 4.2$	
7 $5.05 - 4.4$	**8** $5 - 1.4$	**9** $7.03 - 6.7$	
10 $8.2 - 5.06$	**11** $3.3 - 1.07$	**12** $4 - 0.38$	
13 $0.703 - 0.65$	**14** $0.13 - 0.012$	**15** $0.05 - 0.037$	
16 $0.44 - 0.044$	**17** $0.93 - 0.093$	**18** $4 - 3.07$	
19 $9 - 8.88$	**20** $10 - 1.01$		

21   There are 4.3 litres of water in a tank. 1.35 litres is poured out. How much water is left in the tank?

22 A metal pole is 8 m long. A piece 3.94 m long breaks off. What is the reduced length of the pole?

23 Martin has £9.84 He spend £4.99 on a new tie. How much money does he have left?

24 A calculator shows 0.44
What would you expect it to show
if you subtracted 0.08?

7 Multiplying decimals

When multiplying decimal numbers we set out the sum like this:

5.8×3 1.75×4 13.15×4

```
    5 . 8              1 . 7 5                1 3 . 1 5
×       3            ×       4              ×         4
─────────            ─────────              ───────────
  1 7 . 4              7 . 0 0                5 4 . 6 0
    2                  3   2                  1     2
```

The decimal point in the answer is lined up with the decimal point in the top number.

Note: Give the answer to the same accuracy as the number we started with.

5.8 is given to **one** decimal place.	1.75 is given to **two** decimal places.	13.15 is given to **two** decimal places.
The answer 17.4 is given to **one** decimal place.	The answer 7.00 is given to **two** decimal places.	The answer 54.60 is given to **two** decimal places.

EXAMPLE

2.41×23

```
        2 . 4 1
×         2 3
─────────────
    4 8 2 0          241 x 20
      7 2 3
─────────────
    5 5 . 4 3        241 x 3
        1
```

Check: 2.41 is given to two decimal places. 55.43 is given to two decimal places.

Answer 55.43

This type of problem is called long multiplication.
There is more about long multiplication on page 57.

Exercise 7:7a

Write out these multiplication problems and work out the answers.

1	5.51×6	**2**	5.05×7	**3**	7.75×8
4	3.026×5	**5**	6.125×8	**6**	3.085×4
7	2.06×3	**8**	3.24×16	**9**	0.213×8
10	8.842×4	**11**	4.69×9	**12**	1.051×5
13	2.403×37	**14**	0.008×5	**15**	0.036×26
16	3.12×14				

17 Find the total cost of 8 vases at £7.24 each.

18 A metal part is 2.403 m long. Eight of these parts are laid end to end. What is the total length?

19 Find the total cost of 15 books at £6.18 each.

20 The capacity of a glass is 0.44 litres. 28 glasses can be filled from a container.
What is the capacity of the container?

When multiplying two decimal numbers together, we need to make sure the size of the answer matches the sizes of the numbers we start with.

$$0.3 \times 0.2$$

Each number has **1** digit after the decimal point.
So the answer will have $1 + 1 = $ **2** digits
after the decimal point.

2 digits after the decimal point.

3 x 2 = 6 $0.3 \times 0.2 = 0.06$

0.1×0.4 0.6×2.1 26×0.3

1 + 1 = 2 digits after the point.   *1 + 1 = 2 digits after the point.*   *1 digit after the point.*

$0.1 \times 0.4 = \mathbf{0.04}$ $0.6 \times 2.1 = \mathbf{1.26}$ $26 \times 0.3 = \mathbf{7.8}$

1 × 4 = 4   *6 × 21 = 126*   *26 × 3 = 78*

Exercise 7:7b

1	32×0.4	**2**	54×0.9	**3**	2.06×0.4
4	146×0.7	**5**	4.6×0.7	**6**	5.6×0.8
7	2.18×0.05	**8**	3.24×0.06	**9**	0.67×0.9
10	3.4×0.6	**11**	1.2×0.8	**12**	0.95×0.7
13	0.102×0.8	**14**	0.508×0.04	**15**	0.0687×0.5

16 Find the product of 0.6 and 0.07.

17 Multiply 0.85 by 0.7.

18 A washer is 0.3 cm thick. 35 washers are stacked one on top of another. What is the height of the stack?

8 Multiplying and dividing by 10 and 100

Multiplying by 10, 100, or any other power of ten, the digits move to the left. You may need to insert zeros to fill the gaps.

7.24×10

T	U	.	$^1/_{10}$	$^1/_{100}$
$\times 10$	7	.	2	4
7	2	.	4	

$7.24 \times 10 = 72.4$

5.3×100

H	T	U	.	$^1/_{10}$	$^1/_{100}$
		5	.	3	
5	3	0			

$5.3 \times 100 = 530$

Add a zero to fill the gap.

$9.07 \times 10 \ = 90.7$

$73.2 \times 100 = 7320$

$42.1 \times 10 = 421 \quad \text{(or 421.0)}$

The zero is not needed.

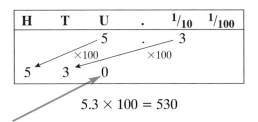

Exercise 7:8a

1	3.42 × 10	**2**	12.3 × 100	**3**	65.1 × 10
4	0.31 × 10	**5**	27.5 × 100	**6**	5.9 × 100
7	0.334 × 10	**8**	0.16 × 100	**9**	21.45 × 10
10	12.44 × 100	**11**	63.9 × 10	**12**	0.09 × 100
13	0.07 × 10	**14**	0.008 × 100	**15**	2.2 × 10

16 A bag of sweets costs £0.85
How much will 100 bags of sweets cost?

17 A box of fireworks costs £28.35.
How much do 10 boxes cost?

18 One rubber ring is 0.03 metres thick.
What is the height of a stack of 100 rings?

Dividing by 10, 100, or any other power of ten, the digits move to the right.
You may need to insert zeros to fill the gaps.

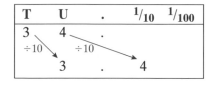

34 ÷ 10

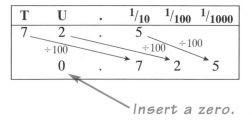

72.5 ÷ 100

Insert a zero.

EXAMPLES

804 × 10 = 80.4   12.4 × 10 = 1.24

237 × 100 = 2.37

Exercise 7:8b

1	89.7 ÷ 10	**2**	21.3 ÷ 100	**3**	2.21 ÷ 10
4	4.2 ÷ 10	**5**	27.5 ÷ 100	**6**	2.9 ÷ 100
7	7.9 ÷ 10	**8**	0.15 ÷ 100	**9**	21.31 ÷ 10
10	0.49 ÷ 100	**11**	0.41 ÷ 10	**12**	0.03 ÷ 100
13	0.04 ÷ 10	**14**	0.002 ÷ 100	**15**	1.03 ÷ 10

16 A piece of cheese weighs 15 kg.
It is cut into 100 equal pieces.
What is the weight of each piece, in
kilograms?

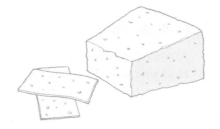

17 £32.80 is divided equally
between 10 people.
How much does each person receive?

18 A bottle contains 5 litres of oil. It is
divided into 100 equal measures.
How much oil is in each measure, in litres?

9 Division

When dividing into a decimal, keep the decimal points lined up.

$74.4 ÷ 6$

$$
\begin{array}{r}
1\,2.\,4 \\
6\,)\,\overline{7^{1}4.^{2}4}
\end{array}
$$
The decimal points are kept in line.

$63.77 ÷ 4$

Remainder of 1 here, so carry on:

$$
\begin{array}{r}
1\,5.\,9\,4 \\
4\,)\,\overline{6^{2}3.^{3}7^{1}7}
\end{array}
$$

Add zeros and continue dividing until there is no more remainder.

$$
\begin{array}{r}
1\,5.\,9\,4\,2\,5 \\
4\,)\,\overline{6^{2}3.^{3}7^{1}7^{1}0^{2}0}
\end{array}
$$

For more on division see page 64.

a $2.013 \div 3$ **b** $11.11 \div 8$

a

$$\begin{array}{r} 0.671 \\ 3\overline{)2.{}^{2}0\,1^{1}3} \end{array}$$

b

$$8\overline{)11.11} \longrightarrow \begin{array}{r} 1.38875 \\ 8\overline{)1^{1}1.{}^{3}1^{7}1^{7}0^{6}0^{4}0} \end{array}$$

Exercise 7:9

Write out these division sums and work out the answers.

1	$4.374 \div 3$	**2**	$9.5052 \div 6$	**3**	$3.572 \div 4$
4	$15.924 \div 6$	**5**	$6.4512 \div 4$	**6**	$9.5424 \div 7$
7	$17.354 \div 5$	**8**	$21.411 \div 3$	**9**	$35.542 \div 8$
10	$9.5047 \div 5$	**11**	$66.513 \div 6$	**12**	$8.0822 \div 8$
13	$103.471 \div 4$	**14**	$477.21 \div 5$	**15**	$710.74 \div 8$

16   A fruit cake weighing 9.55 kg is divided into quarters.
What is the weight of each quarter?

17   4.8 litres of fruit juice is divided equally between 5 jars.
How much is there in each jar, in litres?

18   A rope is 9.45 m long. It is cut into six pieces of equal length.
How long is each piece?

3.1

A game for two players.

The first player picks a number from: 0.1, 0.2, 0.3, 0.4 or 0.5.

The second player picks one of these number, and adds it to the first number.

The players then take turns to pick another number, adding it to the previous total.

The winner of the game is the one who can get first to the number **3.1**

2 Estimating a square root

To estimate the square root of 61:

    $8 \times 8 = 64$ so $\sqrt{64} = 8$

    $7 \times 7 = 49$ so $\sqrt{49} = 7$

So $\sqrt{61}$ is slightly less than 8.

    8.9? 8.8?

You choose.

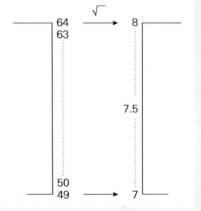

Write down 10 numbers between 1 and 100. Two players can take turns to choose a number and guess its square root.

Check with a calculator.

Score 1 point if the units digit is correct.

Score 2 points if the units and the tenths digit (the first figure after the decimal point) is correct.

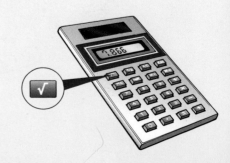

3   Fencing

A farmer wants to build a pen to hold a goat. The pen is to be built against a wall, so that only three sides of fencing are needed.

He starts with 12 metres of fencing.
He puts up the pen like this:

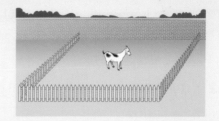

The area of this pen is $3 \times 6 = 18$ m^2.

Can the fencing be arranged a different way so that the farmer can have a greater area of grass for the goat to eat?

You could try using decimal measurements of a metre.

The farmer decides to investigate how we could get the greatest area of grass for different lengths of fencing.

Start with 10 metres, 11 metres, and so on.
In each case find the arrangements of fencing that would give the farmer the greatest area.
You may wish to use squared paper or graph paper to draw diagrams of the pen.

4   Post office

Weight up to	First class	Second class
60 g	26p	19p
100 g	39p	31p
150 g	52p	40p
200 g	66p	50p
250 g	77p	61p
300 g	88p	70p
350 g	£1.00	80p
400 g	£1.14	92p
450 g	£1.30	£1.05
500 g	£1.45	£1.20
600 g	£1.75	£1.40
700 g	£2.20	£1.60
750 g	£2.35	£1.70
800 g	£2.55	
900 g	£2.80	
1000 g	£3.05	

The table shows the postage rate for letters for within the UK (1999/2000).

EXAMPLES

1   Find the postage cost for a 455 g letter, second class.

455 g is more than 450 g, so £1.05 is not enough.

The next weight is 500 g (£1.20)

It will cost £1.20

2   Find the cost of posting a 850 g package.

From the table, packages over 750 g have to be posted first class.
The next weight after 850 g in the table is 900 g.
It will cost £2.80

Use the table to find the cost of posting:

a   a first class letter, weight 520 g

b   a second class letter, weight 290 g

c   a first class letter, weight 75 g

d   a second class letter, weight 305 g

e   a package, weight 775 g

Weigh some of the smaller objects in your room, and find out how much it would cost to post them.

Is the difference between the cost of first class and the cost of second class the same for all the weights?

How much would you save if you wrapped two 300 g packages together?
Give the difference for both first and second class postage rates.

How much does it cost to send a 1000 g package by Parcel Force?
Is it any cheaper than letter post?
You will need to get the Parcel Force rates from your local Post Office.

8 Number properties and sequences

□□□

You will use these words in this chapter.

KEY WORDS

> • odd • even • multiple • factor • prime • prime factor • smallest • largest • lowest • highest • term (of a sequence) • common multiple • common factor • differences • next • consecutive • sequence • series • predict • pattern • rule • square • square root • square number • triangle number • minus number • negative number

1 Diagnostic exercises

Exercise 8:1a

> 2   3   6   8   9   11

From this list of numbers write down:

1   the odd numbers   **2**   the even numbers

3   any multiples of 3   **4**   any factors of 12.

5   Write down all the factors of the number 10.

6   Write down the smallest number that is a common multiple of 2 and 7.

7   Write down the largest number that is a common factor of 10 and 12.

8   Find the square of 7.

9   Write the number 90 as the product of its prime factors.

10   **a**   Draw the next two diagrams in this sequence.

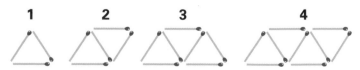

1   2   3   4

b Complete the table.

Diagram number	1	2	3	4	5	6
Number of lines	3	5	7	9		

Find the missing terms in these number sequences:

11 7, 9, 11, 13, __ , __   **12** 61, 59, __ , __ , 53, 51

13 1, 2, 4, 7, __ , __

14 Find the rule for the number sequence 6, 7, 8, 9, 10, ...

15 Find the rule for the number sequence 4, 6, 8, 10, ...

16 Find the rule for this number sequence, and use it to find the 20th term: 4, 7, 10, 13, ...

Exercise 8:1b

> 3   6   7   8   12   15

From this list of numbers write down:

1 the odd numbers   **2** the even numbers

3 any multiples of 4   **4** any factors of 15.

5 Write down all the factors of the number 16.

6 Write down the smallest number that is a common multiple of 6 and 12.

7 Write down the largest number that is a common factor of 16 and 20.

8 Find the square of 6.

9 Write the number 24 as the product of its prime factors.

10 **a** Draw the next two diagrams in this sequence.

b Complete the table.

Diagram number	1	2	3	4	5
Number of lines	5	8	11		

Find the missing terms in these number sequences:

11   6, 12, 18, 24, __ , __

12   17, 15, __ , __ , 9, 7

13   6, 11, 16, 21, __ , __

14   Find the rule for the number sequence 5, 6, 7, 8, ...

15   Find the rule for the number sequence 2, 5, 8, 11, ...

16   Find the rule for this number sequence, and use it to find the 20th term: 1, 3, 5, 7, ...

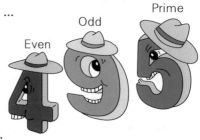

Even   Odd   Prime

2   Number names

Consecutive numbers are numbers that follow each other:
     1, 2, 3, 4, 5, …

A number is called an **even** number if it is in the 2 times table.

     2, 4, 6, 8, 10, ... are even numbers.

A number is called an **odd** number if it **is not** in the 2 times table.

     1, 3, 5, 7, 9, 11, ... are odd numbers.

A number is called a **multiple** if it is in the times table of another number.

     12 is a multiple of 3:   3, 6, 9, **12**, 15, 18, …

     15 is a multiple of 5:   5, 10, **15**, 20, 25, 30, ...

A number is called a **factor** if it can divide exactly (with no remainder) into another number.

     3 is a factor of **12** since 3 divides exactly into 12.

     All the factors of 6 are 1, 2, 3 and 6.

Write down the 9th odd number.

          1, 3, 5, 7, 9, 11, 13, 15, **17**, 19, 21, ...
                              9th

Write down the first five multiples of 9.

          9, 18, 27, 36, 45

Find all the factors of: **a** 7   **b** 9   **c** 20

a   The factors of 7 are 1 and 7.

b   The factors of 9 are 1, 3 and 9.

c   The factors of 20 are 1, 2, 4, 5, 10 and 20.

Exercise 8:2

1 Write down the 12th odd number.

2 Write down the 9th even number.

3 Write down the 15th even number.

4 Write down the 17th odd number.

5 From the list of numbers write down:

18   23   37   40   51   65   74

    a all the even numbers

    b all the odd numbers.

6 Write down the first five multiples of 8.

7 Write down the first six multiples of 5.

8 Write down the first seven multiples of 6.

9 From the list write down:

3   8   15   19   24   30   37   40

    a the multiples of 4

    b the multiples of 5

    c the multiples of 6.

10 Write down **two** factors of each number:

    a 18   **b** 30   **c** 20   **d** 52

11 Write down **all** the factors of each number:

    a 6   **b** 21   **c** 12   **d** 42

12 From the list of numbers write down those numbers that are:

2   6   8   10   12   15

    a factors of 8   **b** factors of 12   **c** factors of 30

3 Common multiples and factors

A number is called a **common multiple** if it is in the times table of two or more other numbers.

> 3 times table: 3, 6, 9, 12, **15**, 18, …
> 5 times table: 5, 10, **15**, 20, 25, …
> So **15** is a common multiple of 3 and 5.

A number is called a **common factor** if it can divide exactly into two or more other numbers.

A common factor of 6 and 15 is 3, since 3 is a factor of 6, and 3 is also a factor of 15.

Find two common multiples of 3 and 4.
4 times table: 4, 8, **12**, 16, 20, **24**, 28, …
3 times table: 3, 6, 9, **12**, 15, 18, 21, **24**, …
12 and 24 are common multiples of 3 and 4.

Find the **lowest** common multiple of 3 and 4.
Common multiples of 3 and 4 are 12 and 24.
The **lowest** common multiple is 12.

Find the common factors of 12 and 18.
The factors of 12 are **1**, **2**, **3**, 4, **6** and 12.
The factors of 18 are **1**, **2**, **3**, **6**, 9 and 18.
So the common factors are 1, 2, 3 and 6.

Find the **highest** common factor of 12 and 18.
The common factors are 1, 2, 3 and 6.
The **highest** common factor is 6.

Exercise 8:3

1 Write down a common multiple of each pair of numbers.

   a 3 and 4   **b** 6 and 24   **c** 8 and 12

   d 20 and 8   **e** 4 and 6   **f** 9 and 12

2 Write down the lowest common multiple of each pair of numbers.

   a 8 and 12   **b** 4 and 5   **c** 3 and 9

   d 12 and 16   **e** 6 and 15   **f** 8 and 18

3   Write down a common factor of each pair of numbers.

     a 6 and 9   **b** 7 and 21   **c** 45 and 48

     d 12 and 18   **e** 21 and 35   **f** 60 and 45

4   Write down the highest common factor of each pair of numbers.

     a 6 and 8   **b** 8 and 12   **c** 25 and 35

     d 40 and 48   **e** 16 and 24   **f** 42 and 63

4 Special numbers

A **prime** number has no factors other than 1 and itself.

The first five prime numbers are 2, 3, 5, 7 and 11.
Note that 1 is not a prime number.

A number is called a **prime factor** if it is a factor, and also a prime number.

The factors of 12 are 1, 2, 3, 4, 6, 12.
The prime factors of 12 are 2 and 3.

The **square numbers** are numbers that can be formed into a square:

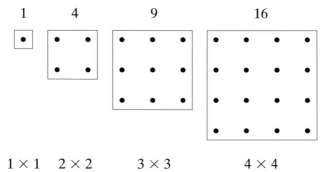

We say the square of a number is a number that is multiplied by itself.

    The square of 3 is $3 \times 3 = 9$, or $3^2 = 9$.

The **triangle numbers** are numbers that can be formed into a triangle:

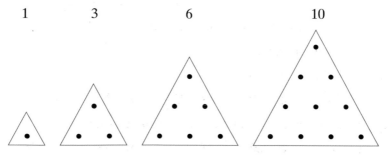

a Write down the prime numbers between 10 and 20.

    11, 13, 17, 19.

b Write down the prime factors of 15.

The factors of 15 are 1, 3, 5, 15.
The prime factors of 15 are 3 and 5.

c Write the number 24 as a product of its prime factors.

The prime factors of 24 are 2 and 3.
We can write 24 as a series of multiplications using the prime factors 2 and 3: $24 = 2 \times 2 \times 2 \times 3$

d Write down the square of 5. $5 \times 5 = 25$

e Work out 8^2. $8 \times 8 = 64$

Exercise 8:4

1 Write down the prime numbers between:

    a 40 and 50   **b** 70 and 80

2 Write down the 7th and 8th prime numbers.

3 Write down the prime number(s) from each list.

    a 2, 4, 5, 9, 10, 12, 13.   **b** 1, 3, 6, 7, 11, 15, 18.

    c 4, 9, 14, 17, 22, 23, 29, 30.   **d** 3, 8, 9, 11, 16, 17, 20, 21.

4 Write down the next three square numbers after 1, 4, 9, 16, ...

5 Write down the square numbers from each list.

    a 2, 4, 22, 31, 49, 60.   **b** 5, 9, 10, 16, 23, 30.

    c 2, 3, 9, 21, 29, 36, 42.   **d** 1, 4, 10, 25, 45, 64, 72.

6 Write down the next three triangle numbers after 1, 3, 6, 10, ...

7 Find the 10th triangle number.

8 Write down the prime factors of:

    a 12   **b** 21   **c** 40   **d** 25   **e** 18   **f** 28

9 Write these numbers as the product of their prime factors:

    a 18   **b** 60   **c** 20   **d** 45   **e** 36   **f** 70

10 Work out:

 a 4^2 **b** 7^2 **c** the square of 9.

11 The area of a square is 121 cm².
What is the length of one side of the square?

12 Find which number, when multiplied by itself, gives 169.

5 Sequences of diagrams

A sequence is a series or pattern of diagrams or numbers.

Sequences can be shown using a series of diagrams, which can be added to (extended) once you have seen the pattern that is being built up.

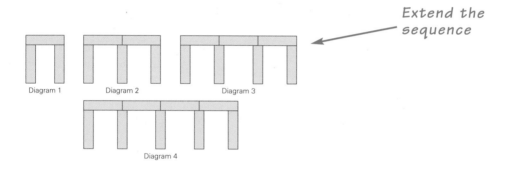

Show the sequence of numbers of blocks in a table.

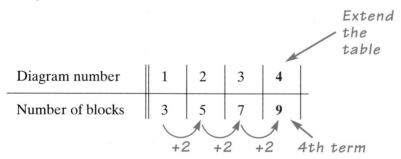

Diagram number	1	2	3	4
Number of blocks	3	5	7	9

+2   +2   +2   4th term

See the pattern?

The number of blocks gives us a number sequence.
Each number in the sequence is called a term.

If you can see the pattern you can predict the next term in the series.

Exercise 8:5

For each sequence of diagrams:

a   draw the next two diagrams in the sequence

b   draw a table to show the series of numbers up to the 5th term.

1

Number of dots

2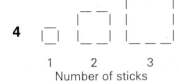

Number of lines

3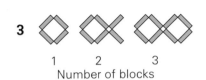

Number of blocks

4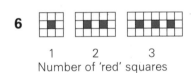

Number of sticks

5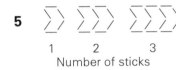

Number of sticks

6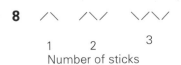

Number of 'red' squares

7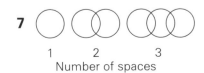

Number of spaces

8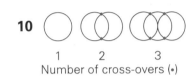

Number of sticks

9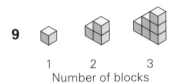

Number of blocks

10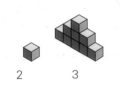

Number of cross-overs (•)

11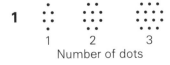

12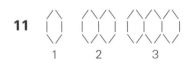

6 Number sequences

To complete a number sequence we need to know how the sequence is built up.

We can use number differences to help.

Number sequence: 19, 22, 25, 28, ...
Find the next two terms.

Find the differences between the numbers:

19   22   25   28
   +3   +3   +3

This sequence goes up 3 each time.

Continuing the sequence:

28   31   34
   +3   +3

The next two terms are 31 and 34.

EXAMPLE

Find the missing numbers in this number sequence:

33, 31, 29, ___ , ___ , 23, 21

Find the number differences first:

33   31   29   The numbers go
   −2   −2   down 2 each time.

The sequence is: 33, 31, 29, **27**, **25**, 23, 21

The missing numbers are 27 and 25.

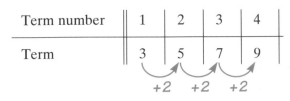

Exercise 8:6

Find the missing numbers in these number sequences.

1 9, 14, 19, 24, __, __   **2** 17, 20, 23, 26, __, __

3 5, 7, 9, __, __   **4** 2, 6, 10, 14, __, __

5 4, 9, 19, 34, __, __   **6** 9, 11, 14, __, __, 29

7 15, 23, 31, 39, __, __   **8** 2, 4, __, __, 22, 32

9 20, 17, 14, 11, __, __   **10** 8, 10, 14, __, __, 38

11 53, 46, 39, 32, __, __   **12** 4, 7, 12, 19, __, __

13 9, 13, 20, 30, __, __   **14** 4, 9, 16, 25, __, __

15 8, 13, 23, 38, __, __   **16** 10, 28, __, __, 70, 80

17 12, 22, __, __, 58, 72   **18** 8, 28, 45, 59, __, __

19 15, 27, 44, 65, __, __   **20** 11, 14, 19, __, __, 56

7 Finding rules

With all number sequences we need to know how the sequence is built up.

We can find a rule to describe the number sequence.

Number sequence 3, 5, 7, 9, ...

Write the sequence in a table:

Term number	1	2	3	4
Term	3	5	7	9

+2   +2   +2

The number difference is 2.

Each term has been changed as shown.

How has it been changed?

Each term has been multiplied by 2, and 1 added. The rule is × 2 + 1

$1 \rightarrow 3$
$2 \rightarrow 5$
$3 \rightarrow 7$
$4 \rightarrow 9$

× 2 + 1

The number difference gives you the number you multiply by in your rule. You may need to add another number too.

Find the rule for the sequence: 5, 8, 11, 14, ...

In a table:

Term number	1	2	3	4
Term	5	8	11	14

+3   +3   +3

The number difference is 3, so each term is multiplied by 3. What do we need to add each time?

1 → 5
2 → 8
3 → 11
4 → 14

Each term is multiplied by 3, then 2 is added.

The rule is × 3 + 2

Exercise 8:7

For these number sequences:

a find the next two terms

b find the rule for the sequence.

1 0, 1, 2, 3, 4   **2** 4, 5, 6, 7, 8

3 0, 2, 4, 6, 8   **4** 4, 7, 10, 13, 16

5 7, 11, 15, 19, 23   **6** 1, 4, 7, 10, 13

7 5, 7, 9, 11, 13   **8** 1, 5, 9, 13, 17

9 5, 8, 11, 14, 17   **10** 3, 8, 13, 18, 23

11 6, 8, 10, 12, 14   **12** 6, 9, 12, 15, 18

8 Using rules

Once we have found the rule for the number sequence we can use it to find other terms.

Number sequence: 3, 5, 7, 9, ...

Written as a table:

Term number	1	2	3	4
Term	3	5	7	9

The rule is: $\times 2 + 1$

To find the 10th term: **10** $\times 2 + 1 = 20 + 1 = 21$

To find the 20th term: **20** $\times 2 + 1 = 40 + 1 = 41$

a Find the rule for the sequence 1, 4, 7, 10, ...
b Find the 12th term for this sequence.

a Written as a table:

Term number	1	2	3	4
Term	1	4	7	10

The rule is: $\times 3 - 2$

b To find the 12th term: **12** $\times 3 - 2 = 36 - 2 = 34$

Exercise 8:8

For each number sequence:

a find the rule.

b use your rule to find the terms asked for.

1 2, 5, 8, 11,...   Find the 6th and 10th terms.

2 5, 9, 13, 17, ...   Find the 10th and 15th terms.

3 0, 2, 4, 6, ...   Find the 8th and 15th terms.

4 6, 10, 14, 18,...   Find the 7th and 10th terms.

5 6, 8, 10, 12, ...   Find the 12th and 20th terms.

6 3, 7, 11, 15, ...   Find the 10th and 15th terms.

7 7, 12, 17, 22, ...   Find the 8th and 10th terms.

8 0, 3, 6, 9, ...   Find the 12th and 15th terms.

9 8, 12, 16, 20,...   Find the 10th and 20th terms.

10 6, 11, 16, 21, ...   Find the 8th and 10th terms.

11 2, 6, 10, 14, ...   Find the 10th and 15th terms.

12 2, 7, 12, 17, ...   Find the 15th and 20th terms.

ACTIVITIES

1   Frogs

Two frogs always start on squares as far apart as possible.

A frog can either **hop** onto an adjacent square, or **jump** over one other frog to the vacant square immediately beyond it.

The red frog can only move from left to right.
The blue frog can only move from right to left.

What is the smallest number of moves needed to swap the two frogs over?

You can change the activity by having a longer row, but you must always have one blank square between frogs of different colours.

You do not need to have the same numbers of each colour of frog.

Here are some examples of different arrangements you could investigate:

    a   two frogs of each colour on a row of 5 squares

    b   three frogs of each colour on a row of 7 squares

    c   one red and two blue frogs on a row of 4 squares

    d   two red and three blue frogs on a row of 6 squares.

2   Number maze

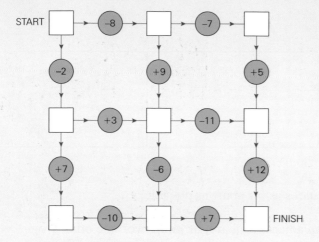

This number maze uses positive and negative numbers.

Each circle shows an operation.

a   Start with the number 4. Work through the number maze, filling in all the squares.

What is the FINISH number?

b   Try starting with different numbers.

Do you get the same results?

Try the number maze opposite. Start with the number 5, then try other numbers.

Design your own number maze.

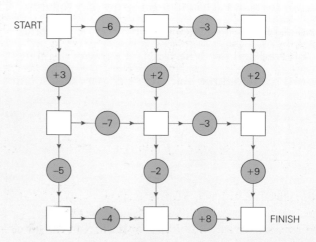

3   Spinner game

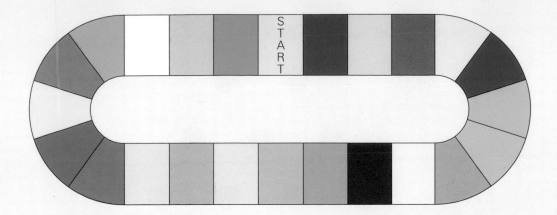

In this game you move around the board with a counter.

A score of **+3** means you move **forward 3 spaces**.
A score of **−2** means move **backward 2 spaces**.

The winner is the first one to go completely around the course.

You may pick one of these spinners to play the game:

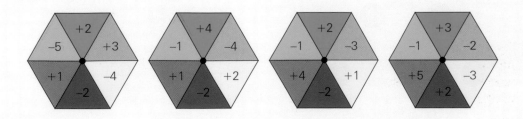

Make the spinners by copying them on to card and pushing a pencil through the middle.

Play the game to get a feel for the spinners and how they score.

Which spinner would you pick in order to win the game?

4   Number pyramids

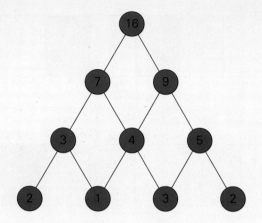

Can you spot the patterns in this number pyramid?

Add each pair of numbers from the bottom upwards to give the number above.

Using this rule, find the missing numbers in the pyramids below and opposite.

Then make up some number pyramids of your own.

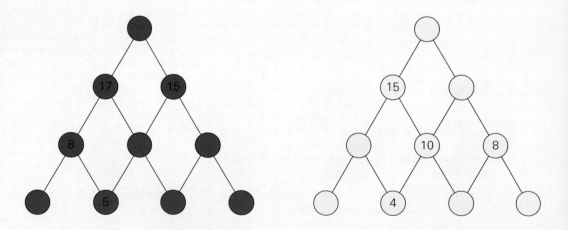

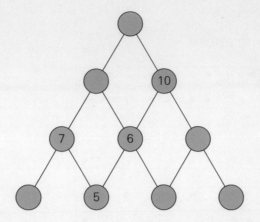

5   Cards

1 storey   2 storeys   3 storeys

The diagram shows how to build a house of cards.

For a one-storey house you need 2 cards.

For a two-storey house you need 7 cards.

For a three-storey house you need 15 cards.

a   Either by working with the numbers, or by drawing diagrams, find out
how many cards you need for a five-storey house.

b   How many cards do you need for a ten-storey house?

6 Patterns

Copy and complete each pattern.

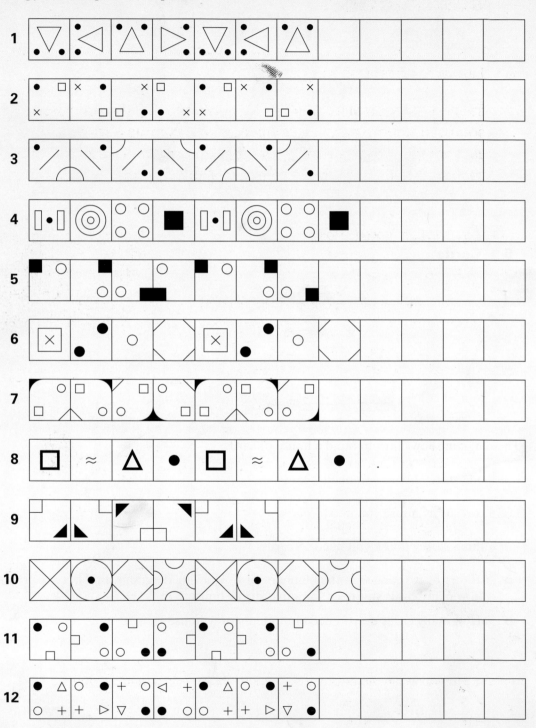

9 Fractions – addition and subtraction

□□□

You will use these words in this chapter.

1 Diagnostic exercises

Exercise 9:1a

Write down the fraction of the diagram that is shaded:

1

2

3 Copy and complete the diagram so that $\frac{3}{5}$ is shaded.

4 Complete this list of equivalent fractions.

$$\frac{1}{4} = \frac{2}{8} = \frac{3}{?} = \frac{?}{?} = \frac{?}{?}$$

Copy and complete:

5 $\dfrac{1}{3} = \dfrac{2}{?}$ **6** $\dfrac{2}{7} = \dfrac{?}{35}$

Find the common denominators and write these fractions in ascending order:

7 $\dfrac{2}{5}, \dfrac{3}{8}$ **8** $\dfrac{1}{4}, \dfrac{5}{6}$

Cancel these fractions to their lowest terms:

9 $\dfrac{9}{12}$ **10** $\dfrac{30}{36}$ **11** $\dfrac{56}{77}$

Work out:

12 $\dfrac{5}{8} + \dfrac{2}{8}$ **13** $\dfrac{3}{4} + \dfrac{1}{16}$ **14** $\dfrac{7}{10} - \dfrac{3}{10}$ **15** $\dfrac{2}{3} - \dfrac{1}{6}$

Exercise 9:1b

Write down the fraction that is shaded:

1   **2** 

3   Copy and complete the diagram so that $\frac{4}{7}$ is shaded.

4   Complete this list of equivalent fractions.

$$\frac{2}{5} = \frac{4}{10} = \frac{6}{?} = \frac{?}{?} = \frac{?}{?}$$

Copy and complete:

5 $\dfrac{1}{6} = \dfrac{?}{18}$ **6** $\dfrac{4}{5} = \dfrac{?}{20}$

Find the common denominators and write these fractions in ascending order:

7 $\dfrac{1}{4}, \dfrac{2}{5}$ **8** $\dfrac{3}{4}, \dfrac{3}{8}$

Cancel these fractions to their lowest terms:

9 $\dfrac{6}{10}$ **10** $\dfrac{35}{42}$ **11** $\dfrac{25}{55}$

Work out:

12 $\dfrac{2}{9} + \dfrac{5}{9}$ **13** $\dfrac{5}{8} + \dfrac{1}{32}$ **14** $\dfrac{5}{6} - \dfrac{3}{6}$ **15** $\dfrac{3}{4} - \dfrac{1}{8}$

2 Simple fractions

This pizza is divided into three pieces.

Each piece is $\frac{1}{3}$.

A fraction has a top number and a bottom number, which is like a code:

The top number is called the **numerator**, "how many pieces you have".

$$\dfrac{1}{3}$$

The bottom number is called the **denominator**, "the number of pieces the whole is divided into".

 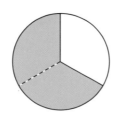 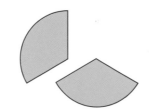 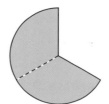

There are two pieces together here, so $\dfrac{1}{3} + \dfrac{1}{3} = \dfrac{2}{3}$

The more pieces the pizza is cut into, the smaller the pieces are.

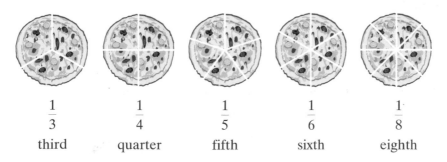

$\dfrac{1}{3}$	$\dfrac{1}{4}$	$\dfrac{1}{5}$	$\dfrac{1}{6}$	$\dfrac{1}{8}$
third	quarter	fifth	sixth	eighth

The larger the denominator, the smaller the fraction.

What fraction is shaded?

Answer: $\frac{3}{5}$

Shade $\frac{5}{6}$ of this shape:

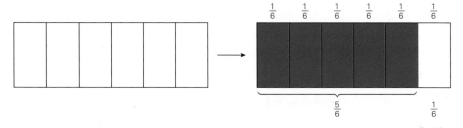

Copy and complete the diagram so that $\frac{3}{7}$ is shaded:

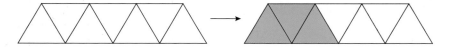

Exercise 9:2

Write down the fraction that is shaded:

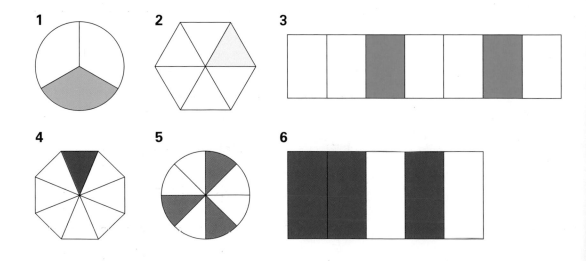

1

2

3

4

5

6

7 **8** **9**

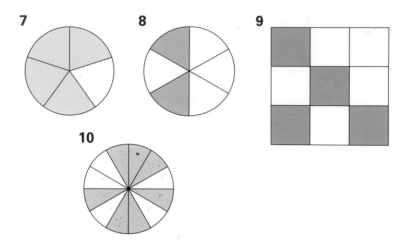

10

Copy and complete the diagrams so that the fraction asked for is shaded.

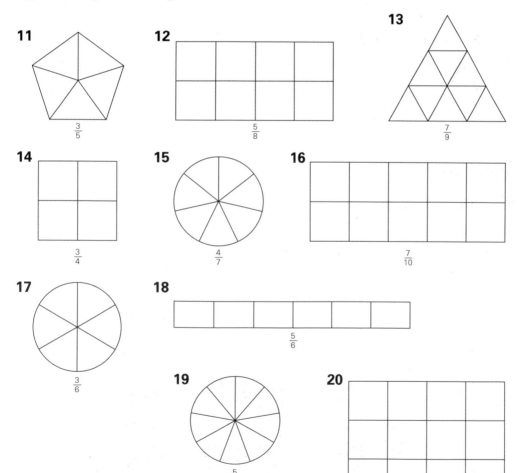

11

$\frac{3}{5}$

12

$\frac{5}{8}$

13

$\frac{7}{9}$

14

$\frac{3}{4}$

15

$\frac{4}{7}$

16

$\frac{7}{10}$

17

$\frac{3}{6}$

18

$\frac{5}{6}$

19

$\frac{5}{9}$

20

$\frac{7}{12}$

3 Comparing fractions

The fraction block shows many common fractions.
You can compare fractions by comparing the sizes of the blocks.

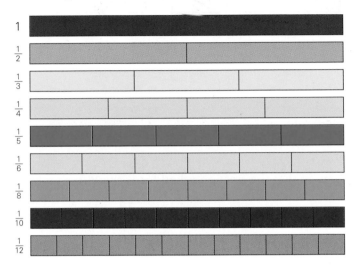

Exercise 9:3

Use the fraction block to fill in the fractions that are the same.

1 $\dfrac{1}{2} = \dfrac{2}{?} = \dfrac{?}{6} = \dfrac{?}{8} = \dfrac{?}{10} = \dfrac{6}{?}$

2 $\dfrac{2}{3} = \dfrac{?}{6} = \dfrac{8}{?}$ **3** $\dfrac{9}{12} = \dfrac{?}{4} = \dfrac{?}{8}$

4 $\dfrac{6}{10} = \dfrac{?}{5}$ **5** $\dfrac{10}{12} = \dfrac{?}{6}$ **6** $\dfrac{?}{6} = \dfrac{1}{3}$

7 $\dfrac{3}{4} = \dfrac{?}{8}$ **8** $\dfrac{?}{10} = \dfrac{2}{5}$

Write these fractions in ascending order (smallest first):

9 $\dfrac{3}{4}, \dfrac{2}{6}, \dfrac{2}{3}, \dfrac{1}{5}$ **10** $\dfrac{7}{12}, \dfrac{5}{6}, \dfrac{1}{4}, \dfrac{7}{10}, \dfrac{1}{2}$

11 $\dfrac{9}{12}, \dfrac{2}{3}, \dfrac{4}{5}, \dfrac{7}{8}$ **12** $\dfrac{2}{5}, \dfrac{3}{6}, \dfrac{4}{12}, \dfrac{3}{8}, \dfrac{1}{4}$

4 Equivalent fractions

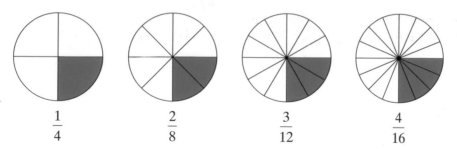

$$\frac{1}{4} \qquad \frac{2}{8} \qquad \frac{3}{12} \qquad \frac{4}{16}$$

These shaded sections are all the same size , even though the fraction appears to be different.
The fractions are *not* different!

The fractions are **equivalent** fractions. They have exactly the same value.

We can write a list of equivalent fractions.

To find equivalent fractions, multiply the
numerator and the denominator
by the same number.

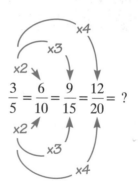

$$\frac{3}{5} = \frac{6}{10} = \frac{9}{15} = \frac{12}{20} = \ ?$$

Complete these equivalent fractions:

a $\dfrac{2}{4} = \dfrac{4}{?}$ **b** $\dfrac{3}{8} = \dfrac{?}{24}$ **c** $\dfrac{?}{3} = \dfrac{10}{15}$

a $\dfrac{2}{4} \overset{\times 2}{=} \dfrac{4}{?}$ **b** $\dfrac{3}{8} \underset{\times 3}{=} \dfrac{?}{24}$ **c** $\dfrac{?}{3} \underset{\times 5}{=} \dfrac{10}{15}$

$$\dfrac{2}{4} \underset{\times 2}{=} \dfrac{4}{8} \qquad \dfrac{3}{9} \overset{\times 3}{=} \dfrac{9}{24} \qquad \dfrac{2}{3} \overset{\times 5}{=} \dfrac{10}{15}$$

Exercise 9:4

Complete these equivalent fractions.

1 $\dfrac{1}{3} = \dfrac{2}{6} = \dfrac{?}{9} = \dfrac{?}{?}$

2 $\dfrac{1}{5} = \dfrac{?}{10} = \dfrac{?}{15} = \dfrac{?}{?}$

3 $\dfrac{3}{4} = \dfrac{?}{8} = \dfrac{?}{12} = \dfrac{?}{?}$

4 $\dfrac{5}{6} = \dfrac{?}{12} = \dfrac{?}{18} = \dfrac{?}{?}$

5 $\dfrac{2}{7} = \dfrac{?}{?} = \dfrac{?}{?} = \dfrac{?}{?}$

6 $\dfrac{2}{3} = \dfrac{4}{?} = \dfrac{?}{9} = \dfrac{?}{?}$

7 $\dfrac{4}{5} = \dfrac{?}{?} = \dfrac{?}{?} = \dfrac{?}{?}$

8 $\dfrac{4}{?} = \dfrac{?}{?} = \dfrac{?}{9} = \dfrac{?}{?}$

9 $\dfrac{2}{3} = \dfrac{?}{12}$

10 $\dfrac{5}{9} = \dfrac{15}{?}$

11 $\dfrac{3}{4} = \dfrac{?}{16}$

12 $\dfrac{5}{6} = \dfrac{?}{30}$

13 $\dfrac{?}{5} = \dfrac{14}{35}$

14 $\dfrac{2}{3} = \dfrac{?}{9}$

15 $\dfrac{3}{4} = \dfrac{?}{12}$

16 $\dfrac{?}{7} = \dfrac{12}{28}$

17 $\dfrac{7}{9} = \dfrac{?}{63}$

18 $\dfrac{?}{8} = \dfrac{16}{64}$

19 $\dfrac{6}{7} = \dfrac{24}{?}$

20 $\dfrac{3}{10} = \dfrac{?}{90}$

Draw diagrams to show that the fractions in each pair are equivalent.

21 $\dfrac{1}{2}$ and $\dfrac{3}{6}$

22 $\dfrac{1}{3}$ and $\dfrac{3}{9}$

23 $\dfrac{2}{3}$ and $\dfrac{8}{12}$

24 $\dfrac{6}{8}$ and $\dfrac{3}{4}$

25 $\dfrac{2}{5}$ and $\dfrac{4}{10}$

5 Ordering fractions

Another way of ordering fractions in to write them all as equivalent fractions with the same denominator, called the **common denominator**.

Write these fractions in ascending order: $\dfrac{1}{4}, \dfrac{2}{5}, \dfrac{3}{8}$

We need to find a common denominator for 4, 5 and 8.

That is, a single number which 4, 5 and 8 will divide into.
4, 5 and 8 are all factors of 40.
40 is the lowest common multiple of 4, 5 and 8.
(For more about lowest common multiples, see page 95.)

Writing all the fractions with 40 as the denominator:

$$\underset{\times 10}{\overset{\times 10}{\dfrac{1}{4}}} = \dfrac{10}{40} \qquad\qquad \underset{\times 8}{\overset{\times 8}{\dfrac{2}{5}}} = \dfrac{16}{40} \qquad\qquad \underset{\times 5}{\overset{\times 5}{\dfrac{3}{8}}} = \dfrac{15}{40}$$

smallest   *largest*

In order: $\dfrac{10}{40}, \dfrac{15}{40}, \dfrac{16}{40}$ *Look at the numerators and put them in order.*

The original fractions in ascending order: $\dfrac{1}{4}, \dfrac{3}{8}, \dfrac{2}{5}$

In descending order: $\dfrac{2}{5}, \dfrac{3}{8}, \dfrac{1}{4}$

Exercise 9:5

Find the common denominators and write these fractions in ascending order.

1 $\dfrac{2}{3}, \dfrac{3}{4}$ 　　　　**2** $\dfrac{1}{3}, \dfrac{2}{7}$ 　　　　**3** $\dfrac{3}{8}, \dfrac{4}{10}$

4 $\dfrac{4}{5}, \dfrac{5}{7}$ 　　　　**5** $\dfrac{7}{9}, \dfrac{9}{10}$ 　　　　**6** $\dfrac{5}{8}, \dfrac{3}{4}$

Find the common denominators and write these fractions in descending order.

7 $\dfrac{5}{7}, \dfrac{8}{12}$ 　　　　**8** $\dfrac{7}{8}, \dfrac{2}{3}$ 　　　　**9** $\dfrac{3}{10}, \dfrac{2}{6}$

10 $\dfrac{4}{5}, \dfrac{9}{12}$ 　　　　**11** $\dfrac{8}{9}, \dfrac{7}{10}$ 　　　　**12** $\dfrac{4}{7}, \dfrac{3}{5}$

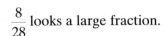

6 Cancelling fractions

$\frac{8}{28}$ looks a large fraction.

One of its equivalent fractions is $\frac{2}{7}$.

Fractions are easier to understand, compare and work with when numerators and denominators are smaller numbers.

To write a fraction as an equivalent fraction using smaller numbers we use **cancelling.**

After cancelling the fraction is written in its **simplest form**, or to its **lowest terms**.

Cancel these fractions to their lowest terms.

a $\frac{18}{24}$ Which number is a common factor of 18 and 24? (Which number goes into 18 and 24) **6**

So divide both numbers by 6:

$\frac{18}{24}\overset{\div 6}{\underset{\div 6}{=}}\frac{3}{4}$ Can you find any other numbers (other than 1) that are factors of 3 and 4? If not, these numbers are the lowest terms.

b $\frac{48}{120}$ A common factor of 48 and 120 is **6**.

So divide both numbers by 6.

$\frac{48}{120}\overset{\div 6}{\underset{\div 6}{=}}\frac{8}{20}$ Can you find any other numbers (other than 1) that are factors of 8 and 20? Yes: 4 is a factor.

Divide by 4:

$\frac{8}{20}\overset{\div 4}{\underset{\div 4}{=}}\frac{2}{5}$ There are no numbers (other than 1) that are factors of 2 and 5. So these are the lowest terms.

EXAMPLES

Exercise 9:6

Cancel these fractions to their lowest terms.

1 $\dfrac{6}{8}$ **2** $\dfrac{24}{32}$ **3** $\dfrac{80}{90}$ **4** $\dfrac{6}{9}$ **5** $\dfrac{16}{24}$

6 $\dfrac{7}{35}$ **7** $\dfrac{8}{10}$ **8** $\dfrac{48}{72}$ **9** $\dfrac{12}{24}$ **10** $\dfrac{21}{28}$

11 $\dfrac{3}{12}$ **12** $\dfrac{36}{64}$ **13** $\dfrac{24}{30}$ **14** $\dfrac{12}{15}$ **15** $\dfrac{28}{70}$

16 $\dfrac{48}{60}$ **17** $\dfrac{56}{80}$ **18** $\dfrac{33}{90}$ **19** $\dfrac{52}{64}$ **20** $\dfrac{42}{48}$

7   Adding simple fractions

You can add fractions that have the same denominator.

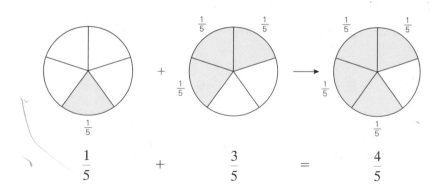

Add the numerators. Keep the denominators the same.

$$\frac{1}{5} \quad + \quad \frac{3}{5} \quad = \quad \frac{4}{5}$$

If the denominators are different, you need to find a common denominator. (See page 119).

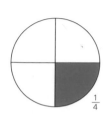

$$\frac{1}{4} \quad + \quad \frac{2}{8}$$

is the same as: $\dfrac{2}{8} + \dfrac{2}{8} = \dfrac{4}{8}$

With a common denominator.

Then cancel: $\dfrac{4}{8} = \dfrac{1}{2}$

a $\dfrac{1}{4} + \dfrac{3}{8}$ $\dfrac{1}{4} \overset{\times 2}{\underset{\times 2}{=}} \dfrac{2}{8}$

$\dfrac{2}{8} + \dfrac{3}{8} = \dfrac{5}{8}$

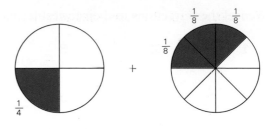

b $\dfrac{7}{10} + \dfrac{1}{5}$ $\dfrac{1}{5} \overset{\times 2}{\underset{\times 2}{=}} \dfrac{2}{10}$

$\dfrac{7}{10} + \dfrac{2}{10} = \dfrac{9}{10}$

Exercise 9:7

Work out the answer as a fraction in its lowest terms.

1 $\dfrac{1}{4} + \dfrac{1}{4}$ **2** $\dfrac{2}{5} + \dfrac{1}{5}$ **3** $\dfrac{3}{6} + \dfrac{2}{6}$

4 $\dfrac{2}{9} + \dfrac{5}{9}$ **5** $\dfrac{3}{8} + \dfrac{2}{8}$ **6** $\dfrac{4}{7} + \dfrac{3}{7}$

7 $\dfrac{2}{10} + \dfrac{5}{10}$ **8** $\dfrac{7}{12} + \dfrac{3}{12}$ **9** $\dfrac{1}{4} + \dfrac{1}{16}$

10 $\dfrac{1}{3} + \dfrac{7}{12}$ **11** $\dfrac{1}{2} + \dfrac{1}{8}$ **12** $\dfrac{1}{8} + \dfrac{3}{16}$

13 $\dfrac{3}{4} + \dfrac{1}{32}$ **14** $\dfrac{7}{16} + \dfrac{3}{32}$ **15** $\dfrac{1}{4} + \dfrac{11}{32}$

16 $\dfrac{1}{2} + \dfrac{13}{32}$

17 Ranjeet paints $\frac{1}{4}$ of a room on Monday, and $\frac{3}{8}$ of the room on Tuesday. Over these two days, what fraction of the room does he paint?

18 Annie is doing a long walk. She completes $\frac{5}{16}$ of the walk on Saturday, and $\frac{5}{32}$ of the walk on Sunday.
What fraction of the walk has she completed over the weekend?

8 Subtracting simple fractions

You can subtract fractions that have the same denominator.

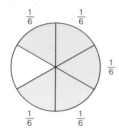 $-$ 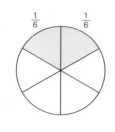 $=$

$$\frac{5}{6} \qquad - \qquad \frac{2}{6} \qquad = \qquad \frac{3}{6}$$

Subtract the numerators. Keep the denominators the same.

$$\frac{5}{8} - \frac{2}{8} = \frac{3}{8}$$ *Subtract the numerators.*
Keep the denominators the same.

When the denominators are different you need to find a common denominator. (See page 119.)

$$\frac{15}{16} - \frac{3}{4} \qquad\qquad \frac{3}{4} \overset{\times 4}{\underset{\times 4}{=}} \frac{12}{16}$$

$$\frac{15}{16} - \frac{12}{16} = \frac{3}{16}$$

EXAMPLES

a $\dfrac{5}{8} - \dfrac{2}{8} = \dfrac{3}{8}$ *Subtract the numerators.*
Keep the denominators the same.

b $\dfrac{5}{6} - \dfrac{7}{12}$ $\qquad \dfrac{5}{6} \overset{\times 2}{\underset{\times 2}{=}} \dfrac{10}{12}$

$$\frac{10}{12} - \frac{7}{12} = \frac{3}{12}$$

Cancelling: $\dfrac{3}{12} \overset{\div 3}{\underset{\div 3}{=}} \dfrac{1}{4}$

Exercise 9:8

Work out the answer as a fraction in its simplest terms.

1 $\dfrac{8}{9} - \dfrac{4}{9}$

2 $\dfrac{5}{7} - \dfrac{3}{7}$

3 $\dfrac{7}{10} - \dfrac{3}{10}$

4 $\dfrac{11}{12} - \dfrac{4}{12}$

5 $\dfrac{7}{8} - \dfrac{1}{2}$

6 $\dfrac{7}{9} - \dfrac{2}{3}$

7 $\dfrac{3}{4} - \dfrac{3}{8}$

8 $\dfrac{13}{16} - \dfrac{3}{4}$

9 $\dfrac{7}{8} - \dfrac{1}{4}$

10 $\dfrac{5}{8} - \dfrac{1}{2}$

11 $\dfrac{3}{4} - \dfrac{5}{32}$

12 $\dfrac{7}{8} - \dfrac{13}{16}$

13 $\dfrac{3}{4} - \dfrac{9}{16}$

14 $\dfrac{7}{12} - \dfrac{1}{3}$

15 $\dfrac{13}{16} - \dfrac{1}{2}$

16 $\dfrac{7}{8} - \dfrac{3}{4}$

17 There is $\frac{3}{8}$ of a wedding cake left, but $\frac{1}{4}$ of the cake has already been promised to someone. This piece is cut off.
What fraction of the original wedding cake is left?

18 $\frac{7}{16}$ of a garden needs digging. Mr Brown digs one quarter of the garden.
What fraction now needs diggin

ACTIVITIES

1 Calculator digits

You can use some or all of the digit keys on your calculator:

You must not use any twice.

You may also use any of the operation keys:

How many numbers can you make using these keys?

$1 = 1$
$2 = 1 \times 2$
$3 = 1 + 2$
$4 = 12 \div 3$
etc.

2 Uminoes

$\frac{1}{2}$	$\frac{2}{6}$

$\frac{2}{8}$	$\frac{3}{9}$

$\frac{1}{10}$	$\frac{3}{4}$

$\frac{6}{8}$	$\frac{3}{6}$

$\frac{3}{10}$	$\frac{3}{30}$

$\frac{1}{3}$	$\frac{2}{4}$

This is a game based on dominoes, for 2 to 6 players.
First you need to make the cards to play the game.

Cut out 60 cards (uminoes), 3 cm by 6 cm.

Draw a line down the centre of each card, dividing them into two squares (do *not* cut them into two pieces!).

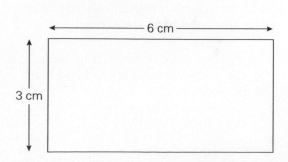

Next write out the fractions that you are going to use in the game.
Here is a list of common fractions:

$$\frac{1}{2}, \frac{1}{4}, \frac{3}{4}, \frac{1}{3}, \frac{2}{3}, \frac{1}{5}, \frac{2}{5}, \frac{3}{5}, \frac{4}{5}, \frac{1}{6}, \frac{5}{6}, \frac{1}{8}, \frac{3}{8}, \frac{5}{8}, \frac{7}{8}, \frac{1}{10}, \frac{3}{10}, \frac{5}{10}, \frac{7}{10}, \frac{9}{10}$$

For each fraction in your list, write out the first three equivalent fractions.

For example $\quad \frac{1}{2} \rightarrow \frac{2}{4}, \frac{3}{6}, \frac{4}{8}; \frac{1}{4} \rightarrow \frac{2}{8}, \frac{3}{12}, \frac{4}{16}.$

Now write two fractions from your lists on to each umino.
You may write the same fraction on several uminoes if you wish.

To play the game:

> Turn all the uminoes face down, shuffle, and share them out equally.
> One player starts by putting an umino down.
> The next player checks to see if they can match a fraction on either
> end of the umino (or the line of uminoes) with one of theirs.
> If so, put it down on the end.

Continue to take turns.
The winner is the first to
run out of uminoes.

3   Number trees

Which numbers have a family tree?

Take each digit in the number and find its
square.
Add the squares together, and start again.
You must stop when you get to 1.

Family trees come in all different sizes.
Choose your own numbers and find their
family trees.

Try the numbers 9, 17 and 25.

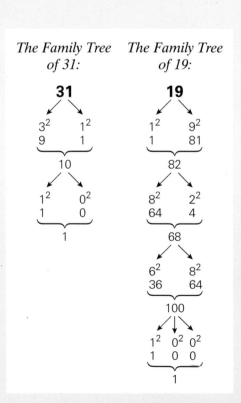

The Family Tree of 31:

31
$3^2 \quad 1^2$
$9 \quad 1$
10
$1^2 \quad 0^2$
$1 \quad 0$
1

The Family Tree of 19:

19
$1^2 \quad 9^2$
$1 \quad 81$
82
$8^2 \quad 2^2$
$64 \quad 4$
68
$6^2 \quad 8^2$
$36 \quad 64$
100
$1^2 \quad 0^2 \quad 0^2$
$1 \quad 0 \quad 0$
1

4   Missing numbers

In these diagrams the numbers in the squares are the sums of the numbers in the two circles either side.

a   Fill in the missing numbers in these triangular diagrams:

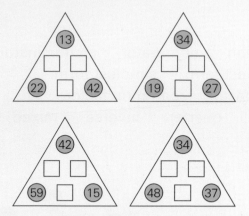

b   Fill in the missing numbers in these rectangular diagrams:

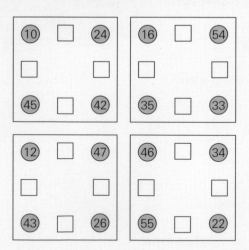

10 Fractions – multiplication and division

You will use these words in this chapter.

> • fraction • equivalent fraction • numerator • denominator •
> common denominator • lowest term • simplest form •
> ascending • descending • factor • common factor •
> cancelling • quantity • half • quarter • inverse • mixed
> number • improper fraction

1 Diagnostic exercises

Exercise 10:1a

Write these mixed numbers as top-heavy (improper) fractions.

1 $2\frac{1}{4}$ **2** $4\frac{1}{3}$ **3** $1\frac{3}{5}$

Write these top-heavy (improper) fractions as mixed numbers.

4 $\dfrac{8}{3}$ **5** $\dfrac{13}{5}$ **6** $\dfrac{23}{7}$

Write these fractions in ascending order.

7 $2\frac{5}{7}$, $2\frac{8}{9}$ **8** $3\frac{2}{5}$, $2\frac{3}{4}$, $3\frac{5}{6}$

For these questions give your answer in its simplest form.

9   A packet of stamps contains 5 first class and 15 second class stamps. What fraction of the stamps in the packets are first class stamps?

10   Jomo gains 28 marks out of 40 in a test. Write his result as a fraction.

11   Find $\frac{1}{5}$ of 30 mm.   **12**   Find $\frac{5}{6}$ of £9.

13 $\dfrac{3}{4} \times \dfrac{5}{9}$ **14** $4 \times \dfrac{5}{6}$ **15** $\dfrac{5}{6} \div \dfrac{2}{7}$ **16** $\dfrac{7}{8} \div 3$

Exercise 10:1b

Write these mixed numbers as top-heavy (improper) fractions.

1 $2\frac{1}{3}$ **2** $3\frac{1}{2}$ **3** $5\frac{3}{4}$

Write these top-heavy (improper) fractions as mixed numbers.

4 $\dfrac{7}{2}$ **5** $\dfrac{11}{4}$ **6** $\dfrac{29}{8}$

Write these fractions in ascending order.

7 $3\frac{2}{5}, 3\frac{1}{4}$ **8** $5\frac{3}{4}, 5\frac{2}{3}, 4\frac{4}{7}$

For these questions give your answer in its simplest form.

9 In a year group there are 48 boys and 52 girls.

Write down the fraction of the year group who are girls.

10 In a survey 100 out of 240 vehicles were cars.

What fraction of the vehicles surveyed were cars?

11 Find $\frac{1}{8}$ of £4.   **12** Find $\frac{3}{5}$ of 80 kg.

13 $\dfrac{3}{8} \times \dfrac{4}{11}$ **14** $\dfrac{2}{5} \times 6$ **15** $\dfrac{4}{9} \div \dfrac{5}{6}$ **16** $\dfrac{3}{7} \div 4$

2 Mixed numbers

Mixed numbers have a whole number part and a fraction part.

       $4\frac{2}{3}$ or "four and two thirds"
       Fraction part: $\frac{2}{3}$
       Whole number part: 4 whole ones

Improper fractions are fractions that are "top heavy".
The numerator is greater than the denominator:

       $\dfrac{14}{3}, \dfrac{5}{4}, \dfrac{10}{8}$

Whole numbers can be written as improper fractions.

4 written as thirds is:

$4 \times 3 = 12$ parts

$4 = \dfrac{12}{3}$ ⟵ *parts*

⟵ *fraction*

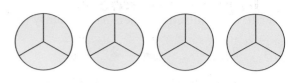

3 written as sixths is:

$3 \times 6 = 18$ parts

$3 = \dfrac{18}{6}$ ⟵ *parts*

⟵ *fraction*

Mixed numbers can be written as improper fractions.

$4\frac{2}{3}$ can be written as thirds:

$4\frac{2}{3}$

$\frac{2}{3}$ is a fraction already.

Total: $\dfrac{2}{3} + \dfrac{12}{3} = \dfrac{14}{3}$

$4 = \dfrac{12}{3}$ as an improper fraction.

a $2\frac{1}{4}$

$\dfrac{1}{4}$ is a fraction already.

$2 = \dfrac{8}{4}$ as an improper fraction.

Total: $\dfrac{1}{4} + \dfrac{8}{4} = \dfrac{9}{4}$

b $1\frac{2}{7} = \dfrac{7}{7} + \dfrac{2}{7} = \dfrac{9}{7}$ **c** $4\frac{3}{5} = \dfrac{20}{5} + \dfrac{3}{5} = \dfrac{23}{5}$

EXAMPLES

Exercise 10:2

Write these mixed numbers as improper fractions.

1 $4\frac{1}{2}$ **2** $3\frac{5}{6}$ **3** $7\frac{2}{5}$ **4** $4\frac{1}{4}$

5 $8\frac{2}{3}$ **6** $9\frac{2}{3}$ **7** $2\frac{2}{3}$ **8** $3\frac{1}{3}$

9 $2\frac{3}{7}$ **10** $5\frac{4}{5}$ **11** $5\frac{7}{12}$ **12** $4\frac{3}{4}$

13 $7\frac{4}{5}$ **14** $2\frac{3}{5}$ **15** $6\frac{3}{5}$ **16** $9\frac{4}{9}$

17 $3\frac{4}{7}$ **18** $8\frac{5}{6}$ **19** $2\frac{2}{5}$ **20** $1\frac{5}{9}$

3 Improper fractions

Improper fractions are fractions that are "top heavy".
The numerator is greater than the denominator.

Mixed numbers have a whole number part and a fraction part.

Improper fractions can be written as mixed numbers.

$$\frac{9}{4} \begin{array}{l} \longleftarrow \textit{parts} \\ \longleftarrow \textit{fraction (quarters)} \end{array}$$

There are four quarters in each whole one.
We can put every four quarters together to make a whole one:

$$\frac{4}{4} = 1 \qquad \frac{4}{4} = 1 \qquad \frac{1}{4}\textit{left over}$$

$$\frac{9}{4} = 2 + \frac{1}{4} = 2\frac{1}{4}$$

a $\qquad \dfrac{19}{5} \qquad \begin{array}{l} \longleftarrow \textit{parts} \\ \longleftarrow \textit{fraction (fifths)} \end{array}$

Write as fifths. There are five fifths in each whole one.

$$\frac{19}{5} = \frac{5}{5} + \frac{5}{5} + \frac{5}{5} + \frac{4}{5}$$

$$= 3 + \frac{4}{5} = 3\frac{4}{5}$$

b $\qquad \dfrac{14}{3} = \dfrac{3}{3} + \dfrac{3}{3} + \dfrac{3}{3} + \dfrac{3}{3} + \dfrac{2}{3} = 4\dfrac{2}{3}$

c $\qquad \dfrac{11}{5} = \dfrac{5}{5} + \dfrac{5}{5} + \dfrac{1}{5} = 2\dfrac{1}{5}$

Exercise 10:3

Write these improper fractions as mixed numbers.

1	$\frac{17}{3}$	**2**	$\frac{41}{7}$	**3**	$\frac{11}{6}$	**4**	$\frac{9}{2}$	**5**	$\frac{63}{8}$
6	$\frac{27}{4}$	**7**	$\frac{25}{2}$	**8**	$\frac{57}{10}$	**9**	$\frac{19}{4}$	**10**	$\frac{14}{3}$
11	$\frac{41}{6}$	**12**	$\frac{82}{9}$	**13**	$\frac{77}{8}$	**14**	$\frac{49}{12}$	**15**	$\frac{44}{5}$
16	$\frac{61}{8}$	**17**	$\frac{23}{10}$	**18**	$\frac{19}{4}$	**19**	$\frac{28}{5}$	**20**	$\frac{93}{7}$

4 Ordering mixed numbers

Write these fractions in ascending order.

$$3\tfrac{1}{3} , 2\tfrac{3}{4} , 1\tfrac{3}{5} , 2\tfrac{2}{3}$$

To write mixed fractions in order:

      FIRST put them in order of the whole numbers
      NEXT order the mixed fractions with the **same** whole number in
           order of the fraction part.   *Compare these.*

FIRST: $3\tfrac{1}{3}$, $2\tfrac{3}{4}$, $2\tfrac{2}{3}$, $1\tfrac{3}{5}$ → $1\tfrac{3}{5}$, $2\tfrac{3}{4}$, $2\tfrac{2}{3}$, $3\tfrac{1}{3}$

NEXT: To compare $\tfrac{3}{4}$ and $\tfrac{2}{3}$, find the common denominator.

$$\frac{3}{4} \overset{\times 3}{\underset{\times 3}{=}} \frac{9}{12} \qquad\qquad \frac{2}{3} \overset{\times 4}{\underset{\times 4}{=}} \frac{8}{12}$$

4 × 3 = 12
3 × 4 = 12

So $\tfrac{3}{4}$ is larger than $\tfrac{2}{3}$

The final ascending order is: $3\tfrac{1}{3}$, $2\tfrac{2}{3}$, $2\tfrac{3}{4}$, $3\tfrac{1}{3}$

The descending order is: $3\tfrac{1}{3}$, $2\tfrac{3}{4}$, $2\tfrac{2}{3}$, $3\tfrac{1}{3}$

EXAMPLES

Write these fractions in ascending order: $1\frac{2}{5}$, $2\frac{1}{2}$, $1\frac{3}{8}$

FIRST: $1\frac{2}{5}$, $1\frac{3}{8}$, $2\frac{1}{2}$

Compare these.

NEXT: $\frac{2}{5}\stackrel{\times 8}{\underset{\times 8}{=}}\frac{16}{40}$, $\frac{3}{8}\stackrel{\times 3}{\underset{\times 3}{=}}\frac{15}{40}$

So $\frac{2}{5}\left(=\frac{16}{40}\right)$ is larger than $\frac{3}{8}\left(=\frac{15}{40}\right)$.

Final ascending order: $1\frac{3}{8}$, $1\frac{2}{5}$, $2\frac{1}{2}$

Exercise 10:4

Write these mixed numbers in ascending order.

1 $2\frac{1}{5}$, $2\frac{2}{6}$ **2** $5\frac{4}{5}$, $5\frac{7}{8}$ **3** $3\frac{4}{5}$, $3\frac{7}{10}$

4 $1\frac{7}{12}$, $1\frac{5}{6}$ **5** $6\frac{2}{5}$, $6\frac{1}{4}$ **6** $4\frac{2}{3}$, $4\frac{3}{4}$

7 $2\frac{4}{12}$, $1\frac{3}{8}$, $2\frac{3}{6}$ **8** $3\frac{7}{8}$, $3\frac{4}{5}$, $2\frac{2}{3}$

Write these mixed numbers in descending order.

9 $2\frac{3}{4}$, $3\frac{2}{3}$, $2\frac{1}{5}$ **10** $4\frac{5}{6}$, $4\frac{1}{4}$, $5\frac{7}{10}$

11 $4\frac{7}{10}$, $3\frac{8}{9}$, $3\frac{4}{7}$ **12** $2\frac{7}{12}$, $1\frac{6}{10}$, $2\frac{4}{7}$

5 Fractions of quantities

Jerry the mouse has eaten one-third of a 60 g piece of cheese.

What weight of cheese has he eaten?

We need to find $\frac{1}{3}$ of 60 g.

This is the same as **dividing** 60 g by three.

$60\text{ g} \div 3 = 20\text{ g}$

EXAMPLES

Find **a** $\frac{2}{3}$ of 72 **b** $\frac{7}{10}$ of £3.50

a To find $\frac{2}{3}$ of 72 first find $\frac{1}{3}$: $72 \div 3 = 24$

$\frac{2}{3}$ is **twice** $\frac{1}{3}$, so $\frac{2}{3}$ of 72 is $24 \times 2 = 48$

b To find $\frac{7}{10}$ of £3.50 first find $\frac{1}{10}$:

£3.50 $\div$ 10 = £0.35 (or 35p)

$\frac{7}{10}$ is **seven times** as much as $\frac{1}{10}$,
so $\frac{7}{10}$ of £3.50 is $7 \times £0.35 = £2.45$

Exercise 10:5

Find these amounts.
You must state the units with your answer.

1	$\frac{1}{5}$ of 30	**2**	$\frac{1}{6}$ of 9 kg	**3**	$\frac{1}{7}$ of £35
4	$\frac{1}{12}$ of 48 g	**5**	$\frac{1}{9}$ of 63 ml	**6**	$\frac{1}{10}$ of £4
7	$\frac{1}{3}$ of £72	**8**	$\frac{1}{4}$ of £28	**9**	$\frac{3}{10}$ of 48 g
10	$\frac{9}{15}$ of $90	**11**	$\frac{4}{5}$ of 3.5 g	**12**	$\frac{2}{5}$ of £5.75
13	$\frac{5}{9}$ of £38.43	**14**	$\frac{3}{4}$ of 15.8 km	**15**	$\frac{5}{6}$ of £15
16	$\frac{2}{3}$ of £5.34	**17**	$\frac{5}{6}$ of 54 g	**18**	$\frac{3}{8}$ of £4.80
19	$\frac{7}{9}$ of 63 litres	**20**	$\frac{4}{5}$ of 300 mg		

6 Writing parts as fractions

Jacob has to make a 56 km journey.
He has already travelled a distance of 14 km.

What fraction of his journey has he completed?

The denominator of the fraction is always the total or whole amount.

The fraction of his journey is is: $\dfrac{14 \text{ miles}}{56 \text{ miles}}$

Cancelling to its lowest terms:

$$\frac{14}{56} \, {\overset{\div 7}{\underset{\div 7}{=}}} \, \frac{2}{8} \, {\overset{\div 2}{\underset{\div 2}{=}}} \, \frac{1}{4}$$

He has completed $\frac{1}{4}$ of his journey.

On a train there are 160 men, 152 women and 88 children.

What fraction of the total number is made up of men?

Total number is 160 + 152 + 88 = 400

Fraction of men is $\dfrac{160}{400} = \dfrac{16}{40} = \dfrac{2}{5}$

Exercise 10:6

1 Adam has a test mark of 80.
Write this as a fraction of the total mark of 200.

2 There are 16 children and 50 adults on a coach.
What fraction of the coach passengers are children?

3 Davinder has driven 15 miles of a 75-mile journey.
What fraction of the journey has he completed?

4 Jodie has spent £10 of her £130 savings on a CD.
What fraction of her savings has she spent?

5 There is 200 ml of oil in a can. 30 ml is poured out.
What fraction remains?

6 There are 50 people on a train. 16 passengers get off.
What fraction of the passengers get off?

7 Of 120 cows in a field, 80 are brown.
What fraction of the cows are brown?

8 A coat worth £35 is reduced to £15.
What fraction is this of the original cost?

9 A bottle contains 140 ml of water. 60 ml is tipped out.
What fraction remains?

10 During June, which has 30 days, it rained on 5 days.
On what fraction of days in June did it rain?

7 Multiplying fractions

There is $\frac{3}{4}$ of a cake left.

Shona wants half of what is left.
What is half of three quarters?

The word "of " in maths tells us that we need
to multiply.

"half of three quarters" means $\frac{1}{2} \times \frac{3}{4}$

To multiply fractions we **do not** need the same
denominators.
Answers should be cancelled into their simplest form.

$$\frac{3}{4} \times \frac{1}{2} = \frac{3 \times 1}{4 \times 2} = \frac{3}{8}$$ ◄─── *Multiply the numerators.*
─── *Multiply the denominators.*

Write whole numbers   *Improper fraction –*
as a fraction over 1.   *cancel to a mixed number.*

EXAMPLE

a $3 \times \frac{4}{5} = \frac{3}{1} \times \frac{4}{5} = \frac{3 \times 4}{1 \times 5} = \frac{12}{5} = 2\frac{2}{5}$ *Cancel*

b $\frac{2}{3} \times \frac{6}{7} = \frac{2 \times 6}{3 \times 7} = \frac{12}{21} = \frac{4}{7}$

c $\frac{4}{5} \times \frac{5}{8} = \frac{4 \times 5}{5 \times 8} = \frac{20}{40} = \frac{2}{4} = \frac{1}{2}$

Exercise 10:7

Work out these multiplication problems.
Write down the first answer you get, then write your answer in its simplest form.

1 $\frac{1}{2} \times \frac{4}{5}$ **2** $\frac{3}{7} \times \frac{2}{6}$ **3** $\frac{2}{3} \times \frac{1}{4}$ **4** $\frac{5}{2} \times \frac{3}{10}$

5 $\frac{4}{7} \times \frac{2}{3}$ **6** $\frac{8}{9} \times \frac{3}{4}$ **7** $\frac{2}{3} \times 7$ **8** $\frac{1}{8} \times \frac{3}{4}$

9 $\frac{2}{5} \times \frac{7}{8}$ **10** $\frac{3}{4} \times 3$ **11** $\frac{2}{3} \times \frac{6}{7}$ **12** $\frac{6}{7} \times 14$

13 $\dfrac{2}{5} \times \dfrac{4}{3}$ **14** $\dfrac{3}{8} \times \dfrac{1}{4}$ **15** $\dfrac{3}{4} \times 11$ **16** $\dfrac{1}{4} \times \dfrac{5}{3}$

17 $\dfrac{3}{2} \times \dfrac{3}{2}$ **18** $\dfrac{3}{4} \times \dfrac{3}{16}$

19   There are 15 kg of cement in a bag. $\dfrac{5}{9}$ of it is used.
How many kilograms of cement are used?

20   A lawn makes up $\dfrac{11}{32}$ of a garden. $\dfrac{3}{4}$ of the lawn is to be re-seeded.
What fraction of the garden is to be re-seeded?

21   It takes $2\dfrac{1}{2}$ hours to paint a room. One quarter of this time is spent
painting the woodwork.
What fraction of an hour is spent painting the woodwork?

22   A piece of wood is $1\dfrac{1}{2}$ metres long. $\dfrac{3}{5}$ of it is cut off.
What fraction of a metre is cut off?

8   Dividing simple fractions

How many quarters are there in $\dfrac{2}{5}$?

This can be written as $\dfrac{2}{5} \div \dfrac{1}{4}$

Division is the inverse (opposite) of multiplication.

A fraction that is written upside down is the inverse (opposite) fraction.

Both inverses taken together make an easier
way of doing the problem.

Write the second fraction upside down.

$\dfrac{2}{5} \div \dfrac{1}{4}$ becomes $\dfrac{2}{5} \times \dfrac{4}{1}$

Change from ÷ to ×

So $\dfrac{2}{5} \div \dfrac{1}{4} = \dfrac{2}{5} \times \dfrac{4}{1} = \dfrac{8}{5} = 1\dfrac{3}{5}$

EXAMPLES

a $\dfrac{2}{3} \div 6 = \dfrac{2}{3} \div \dfrac{6}{1} = \dfrac{2}{3} \times \dfrac{1}{6} = \dfrac{2}{18} = \dfrac{1}{9}$

b $\dfrac{3}{4} \div \dfrac{4}{7} = \dfrac{3}{4} \times \dfrac{7}{4} = \dfrac{21}{16} = 1\dfrac{5}{16}$

Exercise 10:8

Work out these division problems.

Write down the first answer you get, then write your answer in its simplest form.

1 $\dfrac{2}{5} \div \dfrac{3}{4}$ **2** $\dfrac{4}{9} \div \dfrac{5}{12}$ **3** $\dfrac{4}{9} \div 5$

4 $\dfrac{1}{2} \div \dfrac{2}{3}$ **5** $\dfrac{3}{7} \div \dfrac{4}{5}$ **6** $\dfrac{1}{5} \div 2$

7 $\dfrac{1}{6} \div \dfrac{2}{5}$ **8** $\dfrac{3}{11} \div \dfrac{1}{3}$ **9** $\dfrac{7}{2} \div \dfrac{15}{2}$

10 $\dfrac{9}{3} \div \dfrac{15}{2}$ **11** $\dfrac{5}{9} \div 8$ **12** $\dfrac{9}{5} \div \dfrac{27}{10}$

13 $\dfrac{2}{3} \div 7$ **14** $6 \div \dfrac{3}{4}$ **15** $\dfrac{15}{2} \div \dfrac{15}{8}$

16 $\dfrac{15}{3} \div \dfrac{15}{9}$ **17** $\dfrac{8}{3} \div \dfrac{20}{9}$ **18** $\dfrac{9}{4} \div \dfrac{15}{8}$

19 6 kg of powder is put into $\frac{4}{5}$ kg bags.
How many bags are filled?

20 How many $\frac{1}{2}$-litre measures can you get from
a bottle containing $\frac{3}{5}$ litre?

21 A man sleeps for $7\frac{1}{2}$ h every 24 hours.
For what fraction of the day is he asleep?

22 $13\frac{1}{2}$ kg of tea is put into $\frac{3}{4}$ kg packets.
How many packets are needed?

ACTIVITIES

1 Sticks

This pattern is made from 24 sticks.

a There are 14 squares in this pattern.
Can you find them?

b Take away just 8 sticks so that you have 2 squares left.

c What is the least number of sticks needed to make squares?
Copy and complete the table.
Extend it for more sticks.

Squares	1	2	3	4	5
Sticks	4	7			

2 Digits

Write down any number between 1 and 9 (inclusive).
Follow these instructions, and carry out these three sums.

a Multiply your number by 3. Write down your answer.

b Add one to your answer to **a** and write down this answer.

c Add one to your answer to **b** and write down this answer.

Find the **total** of your answers to **a**, **b** and **c**.

Now add together the digits of your total.

If you not get a single digit answer, then add the digits of your answer together again.

Repeat this for several numbers.
What do you notice?

What happens if you subtract one instead of adding one?

3 Letters as numbers

CROSS
+ROADS
———————
DANGER
———————

This sum works when each letter has a number:

1 2 3 4 5 6 7 8 9
D O S E A R G N C

The sum is:

  9 6 2 3 3
+ 6 2 5 1 3
———————————
1 5 8 7 4 6

FOUR
+FIVE
———————
NINE
———————

becomes

2 9 8 0
+ 2 4 7 6
—————————
5 4 5 6

Write down the number that goes with each letter.

Now solve these.
Find numbers to replace each letter so that the problems work.

THERE
+ HERE
———————
TRUMP
———————

SPEND
− MORE
———————
MONEY
———————

AAAA
+ BBBB
———————
CDDDE
———————

FOUR
TWO
+ ONE
———————
SEVEN
———————

Try making your own. Start with something simple.
You don't need to make up real words!

4 Counters

A game for 2 or more players.

Arrange some counters into piles
It does not matter how many piles, nor how many how many counters are in each pile.

The players take turns to take as many counters as they wish from one of the piles.
They may choose to take all the counters in a pile, removing the pile completely.

The winner is the player that takes the very last counter.

5 Final digits

These are the multiples of 4:

4   8   12   16   20   24   ...

The final digits are

4   8   2   6   0   4   8   2   6   ...

a   What do you notice about the final digits?

b   Investigate the final digits of multiples of 6. What do you notice?

c   Investigate patterns for other multiples.

d   Explore the final digits of:

square numbers
prime numbers
odd numbers
triangle numbers

11 Ratio and proportion

KEY WORDS

* ratio • simplest form • simplifying • fractions
* cancelling • smallest • largest • quantity • amount
* unit • unitary • multiply • divide • division • share
* proportion • direct proportion • inverse proportion

1 Diagnostic exercises

Exercise 11:1a

Write these ratios in their simplest form:

1 9 cars to 12 buses

2 25 houses to 5 flats

3 6 potatoes to 18 sprouts

Simplify these ratios:

4 35 : 10		**5** 12 : 42		**6** 21 : 70	
7 1 mm : 5 cm		**8** 10 days : 2 weeks		**9** £1 : 40p	

10 It takes 8 seconds to fit one part to a radio.
How long will it take to fit 12 parts to a radio at the same rate?

11 Orange cordial is mixed in the ratio of 1 part cordial to 8 parts water.
How much cordial should be added to 400 ml of water?

12 Seven train tickets cost £59.50.
How much would five similar tickets cost?

13 Four men can paint a hall in 10 days.
How long would it take five men, if each man works at the same rate?

14 The ratio of boys to girls in a class is 3 : 4. There are 16 girls in the class. How many boys are there?

15 An amount of £330 is to be divided between Adam and Claire in the ratio 5 : 6.
How much will each receive?

Exercise 11.1b

Write as a ratio in its simplest form:

1 4 red apples to 6 green apples

2 40 clocks to 80 watches

3 2 pens to 8 pencils

Simplify these ratios:

4 $8 : 4$ **5** $21 : 35$ **6** $32 : 40$

7 $8 \text{ kg} : 32 \text{ g}$ **8** $90\text{p} : £1.10$ **9** $600 \text{ m} : 2 \text{ km}$

10 A train ticket costs £20.
How much would 15 similar train tickets cost?

11 Car windscreen wash is made in the ratio of 1 part wash to
10 parts water.
How much water should be added to 10 ml of windscreen wash?

12 A walker covers a distance of 16 km in 4 hours.
At the same rate, how long will it take her to walk 12 km?

13 A car travels at 30 mph and completes one part of a journey in
4 hours. How long will the return journey take at a speed of 40 mph?

14 The ratio of the number of people attending a school event on
Thursday and Friday was 4 : 5. On Thursday 120 people attended.
What was the attendance on Friday?

15 A bag of biscuits of weight 80 g is to be divided between two dogs, Bad
and Rover, in the ratio 5 : 3.
How much will each dog receive?

2 Simplifying ratios

4 red counters

2 blue counters

The number of counters of each colour can be written as a ratio:

red : blue
4 : 2

This can be simplified in the same way as fractions, by cancelling the numbers.

$\div 2$ $\div 2$

4 : 2 becomes the ratio   2 : 1

This tells you that for every 2 red counters there is 1 blue counter.

a Write as a ratio in its simplest form:

$\qquad$ 18 boys to 8 girls

$\qquad\qquad$ 18 : 8

$\div 2$ 9 : 4

b Simplify the ratio 24 : 32

Find the highest common factor of the numbers (see page 95).

Both 24 and 32 can be divided by 8.

$\qquad\qquad$ 24 : 32

$\div 8$ 3 : 4

Exercise 11:2

Write these ratios in their simplest form:

1 14 scouts to 32 guides $\qquad$ **2** 18 shoes to 27 socks

3 3 bolts to 12 screws $\qquad$ **4** 8 pins to 16 badges

5 10 coins to 15 notes $\qquad$ **6** 26 bikes to 6 mopeds

7 36 trees to 54 bushes $\qquad$ **8** 10 numbers to 4 letters

Simplify these ratios:

9 12 : 30 $\quad$ **10** 35 : 25 $\quad$ **11** 18 : 12 $\quad$ **12** 20 : 36

13 15 : 5 $\quad$ **14** 21 : 28 $\quad$ **15** 36 : 63 $\quad$ **16** 14 : 12

17 180 : 270 $\quad$ **18** 9 : 36 $\quad$ **19** 45 : 120 $\quad$ **20** 28 : 42

3 Simplifying ratios with units

Before we can simplify a ratio we have to make
sure the units for both quantities are the same.

The weight of one tin of beans is 1.5 kg.
The weight of another tin of beans is 500 g.

We can write these weights
as a ratio: 1.5 kg : 500 g.

To simplify this ratio, first change the weights
into the same units: grams.

$$1.5 \text{ kg} = 1.5 \times 1000 = 1500 \text{ g} \qquad 1 \text{ kg} = 1000 \text{ g}$$

So 1.5 kg : 500 g is the same as 1500 g : 500 g

$\div 100$ $= 15 : 5$ No need to write
$\div 5$ $= 3 : 1$ the units now, as
they are the same.

EXAMPLES

a   Simplify the ratio   2 mm : 5 cm

         becomes   2 mm : 50 mm

       $\div 2$ 1 : 25

b   Ali's package costs £1.60 to post.
Ben's package costs 30p to post.
Write the postage costs as a ratio in its simplest form.

              £1.60 : 30p

       becomes   160p : 30p

       $\div 10$ 16 : 3

Exercise 11:3

Write these ratios in their simplest form.

1	7 days : 3 weeks	**2**	£3 : 75p	**3**	3 cm : 90 mm
4	70 mg : 1 g	**5**	825 mm : 25 cm	**6**	25 m : 100 cm
7	35 cm : 50 mm	**8**	£1.50 : £5	**9**	£7 : 60p
10	800 m : 1 km	**11**	750 g : 1 kg	**12**	50 cm : 1 m
13	5 mm : 3 cm	**14**	30 cm : 2 m	**15**	4 kg : 200 g
16	24p : £1	**17**	450 cm : 3 m	**18**	£5 : 30p
19	1 m : 25 cm	**20**	£1.50 : 30p		

4 Unitary ratios

A unitary ratio is a ratio where one of the quantities is 1.

A pen costs £1.50. A pen with a gold-plated top
costs 7 times as much.
How much does a gold-plated pen cost?

The ratio of the cost of the pens is 1 : 7
The first pen cost £1.50
so the second pen costs

$$7 \times £1.50 = £10.50$$

In a car wash tank 1 part cleaning fluid is
added to 20 parts of water.
The tank contains 100 litres of water.
How much cleaning fluid should be added?

The ratio of cleaning fluid to water is 1 : 20
Twenty times as much water is used,
so the number of litres of cleaning fluid is

$$100 \div 20 = 5.$$

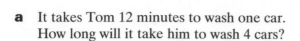

a It takes Tom 12 minutes to wash one car.
How long will it take him to wash 4 cars?

$$12 \times 4 = 48 \text{ minutes}$$

b The ratio of children to adults on a train is 1 : 5.
There are 250 adults on the train.
How many children are there?

$$250 \div 5 = 50 \text{ children}$$

Exercise 11:4

1 ✓ It takes a snail 14 minutes to travel 1 metre.
How many minutes will it take to travel 5 metres at the same rate?

2 A car travels 9 miles on one litre of petrol.
How far could it travel on 30 litres?

3 A shop sells garden tables and chairs in the ratio 1 : 5.
In one week it sells 45 chairs.
How many tables should they have sold?

4 A chocolate bar costs 28p.
How much will 12 of these chocolate bars cost?

5 Two lengths are in the ratio 1 : 4.
The longer length is 44 cm.
Find the shorter length.

6 The ratio of the number of dogs to cats owned by
the pupils in a school is 1 : 5. There are 75 cats.
How many dogs are there?

7 A carton contains 8 tennis balls.
How many tennis balls will there be in 16 cartons?

8 In an office the ratio of men to women is 1 : 7.
28 women work in the office.
How many men work there?

9 There are 6 eggs in each box.
How many eggs are there in 400 boxes?

10 The ratio of right-handed people to left-handed people
in an office is 4 : 1.
Eight people are left-handed.
How many are right-handed?

5 Direct proportion

6 chairs cost £54 in total.
What is the cost of 4 chairs?

We first need to work out the cost of just
one chair.

>Six chairs cost £54
>One chair costs £54 ÷ 6 = £9

Use this to find the cost of 4 chairs.

>£9 × 4 = £36

EXAMPLE

The total cost of six identical CDs is £84.
What is the cost of five of these CDs?

One CD costs £84 ÷ 6 = £14
So five CDs cost £14 × 5 = £70

Exercise 11:5

1 Seven pencils cost 56p.
How much will five pencils cost?

2 A boiler uses 500 kg of coal in 4 weeks.
How long will 1500 kg last?

3 A car takes 4 hours to travel 320 km.
How long would it take to travel 400 km?

4 Eight ostrich eggs cost £4.80.
Find the cost of a dozen ostrich eggs.

5 A carpet of area 12 m^2 cost £108.
What is the cost of 18 m^2 of this carpet?

6 An aeroplane travels 4200 km in 6 hours.
How far will it travel in 8 hours?

7 A motorcycle travels 72 km on 6 litres of petrol.
How far does it travel on 10 litres?

8 A machine fills 810 bottles in 6 hours.
How many could it fill in 5 hours?

9 A pile of 200 sheets of card is 12 cm thick.
How thick is a pile of 500 sheets of card?

10 You can buy 25 metres of material for £40.
How many metres of the material could you buy for £56?

6 Inverse proportion

Eight machines are used for 3 hours to stamp out metal parts.
The following day the factory needs to make the same number of metal parts, but only 6 machines are working.
How long will it take the 6 machines to make the parts?

We first need to find the total number of hours spent on the job by all the 8 machines.

8 machines × 3 hours = 24 machine hours.

So 8 machines spend 24 machine hours on the job.
We can now find the time it would take 6 machines:

24 ÷ 6 = 4 hours.

Nine people put up a fence in 10 days.
Working at the same rate, how long would 12 people take?

The total number of days for one person to put up the fence would be

9 × 10 = 90 days.

So 12 people would take 90 ÷ 12 = 7   days

Exercise 11:6

In this exercise assume that all rates remain constant.

1 Six machines do a job in 16 hours.
How long would it take if only four machines were used?

2 Five men take 14 days to do some work on a house.
How long would 7 men take to repeat the job on another house?

3 Eight 32 kg boxes can be carried safely on a truck.
How many 64 kg boxes can be carried?

4 Five pumps can water a field in 6 hours.
How long would it take 4 pumps?

5 A bag of counters is shared out so 8 children receive 9 counters each.
The counters are collected in, then shared out again equally between 12 children.
How many counters does each child have?

6 It takes 6 women a total of 30 days to complete a contract.
How long would it take 15 women to complete a similar contract?

7 A farmer needs two combine harvesters for 12 days on his farm.
How long would the same job take with 3 combine harvesters?

8 Pots are packed into 25 cases containing 12 pots each.
The same batch is to be packed into new cases, each containing 10 pots.
How many new cases are needed?

9 A cyclist took 4 hours to do a journey at an average speed of 6 mph.
On the return journey her average speed was 8 mph.
How long did the return journey take?

10 Three goats eat a bag of feed every 16 days.
How long will it take four goats to eat the same amount?

7 Using ratios

This recipe for Bread and Butter Pudding
serves 4 people.
We need to change the recipe to make
enough for 10 people.

$$\begin{array}{l} x2.5 \\ 4 \rightarrow 10 \qquad 10 \div 4 = 2.5 \end{array}$$

We will have to multiply each quantity by 2.5

Bread and Butter Pudding Recipe

6 slices of bread	6 × 2.5	=	15 slices of bread
2 eggs	2 × 2.5	=	5 eggs
1 pint of milk	1 × 2.5	=	2.5 pints of milk
150 g raisins	150 × 2.5	=	375 g raisins
10 g margarine	10 × 2.5	=	25 g margarine

Here is another type of problem using ratios.

The ratio of boys to girls in a class is 4:5.
There are 15 girls in the class.
How many boys are there?

boys : girls
4 : 5

What is the multiplier?

×?

boys : girls
? : 15

5 becomes 15, and 5 × 3 = 15

boys : girls
4 : 5

*We need to multiply the
boys by the same number.*

×3   ×3

12 : 15

There are 12 boys in the class.

EXAMPLES

Two lengths are in the ratio 7 : 3.
The shorter length is 42 cm.
Find the longer length.

Longer : Shorter
7 : 3
? : 42

*The multiplier is
42 ÷ 3 = 14*

$7 \times 14 = 98$

The longer length is 98 cm.

Exercise 11:7

Change these recipes for the number of people shown.

1 **Chocolate Eclairs**
   (for 10 people)

   80 g choux pastry
   250 ml double cream
   100 g melted chocolate

   Change for 6 people.

2 **Braised Oxtail**
   (for 4 people)

   20 g lard
   800 g oxtail joints
   4 small onions
   4 carrots
   2 tablespoons flour
   500 ml beef stock

   Change for 10 people.

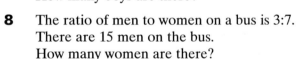

3 Macaroni Cheese
(for 3 people)

150 g Macaroni
30 g butter
30 g flour
360 ml milk
120 g cheddar cheese
15 g breadcrumbs

Change for 5 people.

4 Farmhouse Paté
(for 6 people)

200 g bacon
150 g belly pork
150 g pig's liver
80 g chicken liver
1 egg
1 onion

Change for 15 people.

Answer these questions.

5 In one day a cafe sold teas and coffees in the ratio 4 : 5.
It sold 60 coffees.
How many teas were sold?

6 The ratio of the number of blue
flowers to red flowers in a garden is
11 : 7. There are 132 blue flowers.
How many red flowers are there?

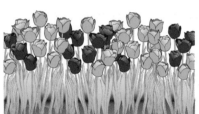

7 The ratio of boys to girls in a year
group is 6 : 7.
There are 140 girls in the group.
How many boys are there?

8 The ratio of men to women on a bus is 3:7.
There are 15 men on the bus.
How many women are there?

9 In a rectangle the ratio of the width to the length is 7 : 12.
The length is 36 cm.
Find the width.

10 Two boxes contain powder in the ratio 3 : 10.
The smaller box contains 9 kg.
What weight does the larger box contain?

11 In every 100 silicon chips made at a factory, 6 are faulty.
How many are expected to be faulty in a batch of 500?

12 At a garage an average of 3 cars out of 10 failed the MOT test.
During one week 60 cars are tested.
How many are expected to fail?

13 The ratio of men to women on an outward bound course is 9 : 2.
There are 4 women on the course.
What is the total number of people on the course?

14 The ratio of cars to vans passing a point on a road in one hour was 9:4.
There were 24 vans.
How many cars were there?

15 Three in every ten trains are late.
On one particular day 18 trains were late.
How many trains were on time?

8 Dividing in ratios

James and Sobia are going to
divide a bag of 35 sweets between
them in the ratio 3 : 2.
How many sweets does Sobia get?

This means that

for every 3 sweets that James gets
Sobia gets 2 sweets.

$3 + 2 = 5$

The sweets are divided into groups of: 5 sweets

$35 \div 5 = 7$ *This is one share.*

James will have $3 \times 7 = 21$ sweets.   *3 shares*

Sobia will have $2 \times 7 = 14$ sweets.   *2 shares*

We can check the result: $21 + 14 = 35$ sweets   *What we started with.*

So Sobia gets 14 sweets.

EXAMPLE

80p is divided between Asha and Bob in the ratio 3 : 7.
How much does each receive?

Asha receives 3 shares and Bob receives 7 shares.

$3 + 7 = 10$ shares

One share is $80p \div 10 = 8p$

Asha receives $3 \times 8p = 24p$

Bob receives $7 \times 8p = 56p$ *Check: 24p + 56p = 80p*

Exercise 11:8

1   Divide £6.50 in the ratio 1 : 4

2   Divide 96 kg in the ratio 3 : 5

3   Divide 660 in the ratio 5 : 6

4   Divide £6 in the ratio 7 : 13

5   Divide 108 litres in the ratio 6 : 3

6   Divide 224 g in the ratio 4 : 3

7   24 litres of oil is divided into two cans in the ratio 5 : 7.
How much oil is in the larger can?

8   Bill and Ben are going to share £6.75 in the ratio 4 : 5.
How much will Bill receive?

9   A sack of potatoes weighing 108 kg is divided into two bags in the
ratio 2 : 7.
What weight of potatoes is in the smaller bag?

10   Amy and Jamilla share prize money of £30.24 in the ratio 3 : 4.
How much does Jamilla receive?

ACTIVITIES

1 I'm thinking of a number . . .

A game for two players.

One person thinks of a number between 1 and 100.
The other tries to guess what that number is.
You can only ask questions that have answers "yes" or "no".

For each game, write down how many questions you need to ask before finding the number.

Some questions get you to the number faster than others. Describe a sequence of questions you could use.

What is the minimum number of questions you will need ask to be sure of finding the number?

2 Light bars

You will need a calculator for this activity.

The number 4 on a calculator uses 4 light bars.

The number 17 on a calculator uses 6 light bars.

The number 317 on a calculator uses 11 light bars.

a Copy and complete the table to show the number of light bars used for the first nine digits.

Digit	1	2	3	4	5	6	7	8	9
Light bars			4					

b Which numbers can be made using 7 light bars?

c Find the largest and the smallest number that can be made with 10 light bars.

d Investigate the largest and smallest numbers for other numbers of light bars.

e Which two-digit numbers use most light bars?
Which use the fewest?

3 Flowers

The flowers in the diagram are made from red and yellow counters.

For 1 yellow counter you need 6 red counters.

For 2 yellow counters you need 10 red counters.

For 3 yellow counters you need 14 red counters.

How many red counters will you need for 5 yellow counters?

How many red counters will you need for 10 yellow counters?

4 Half time

In a football match the final score was $1-1$.

What could the half-time score have been?

There are a number of alternatives:

$0-0, 1-0, 0-1, 1-1$

So there are four possible half-time alternatives for a final score of $1-1$.

a What about a final score of $2-2$?
Find all the possible half-time scores for a final score of $2-2$.

b Predict the possible number of half-time scores for a final result of $3-3$.

5   Palindromes

A palindrome is a number that is the same read front to back ... or back to front!

For example,   323   141   222

To make a palindrome, take any number and add it to its reverse.

```
    76
  + 67
  ────
   143        If you don't get a palindrome,
   341        add this to its reverse.
  ────        We get a palindrome!
   484
  ────
```

Write down several numbers, and see if you can make a palindrome number out of them.

Start with 3-digit numbers, but then try with 4-digit numbers, then 5-digit numbers, etc.

12 Percentages

You will use these words in this chapter.

1 Diagnostic exercises

Unemployment now 7.5%

Exercise 12:1a

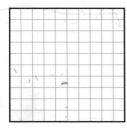

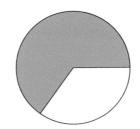

1 What percentage of the grid is shaded?

2 Estimate the percentage of the circle that is shaded.

3 Change 3% to a fraction.

4 Change 80% to a fraction.

5 Change 24% to a decimal.

6 Change 8% to a decimal.

7 Change $\frac{3}{5}$ to a percentage.

8 Change 0.37 to a percentage.

9 Change $\frac{11}{20}$ to a percentage.

10 30% of the CDs sold in a shop are dance music. What percentage of the CDs sold are **not** dance music?

11 At a school there are 180 pupils in a year group. 45% of the year are boys. How many boys are there in the year group?

12 The price of a bike falls 15% from £180. What is the reduced price of the bike?

13 3 out of every 20 radios produced at a factory have a fault. What percentage of the radios are faulty?

14 Change $8\frac{1}{2}\%$ to a fraction.

15 Change 0.135 to a percentage.

16 Calculate the total cost of a mountain bike advertised for £150 plus VAT at $17\frac{1}{2}\%$.

Exercise 12:1b

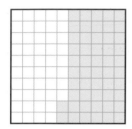 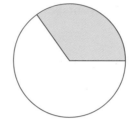

1 What percentage of the grid is shaded?

2 Estimate the percentage of the circle that is shaded.

3 Change 6% to a fraction.

4 Change 85% to a fraction.

5 Change 72% to a decimal.

6 Change 9% to a decimal.

7 Change $\frac{3}{10}$ to a percentage.

8 Change 0.06 to a percentage.

9 Change $\frac{19}{20}$ to a percentage.

10 At lunch time pupils can have school dinner, sandwiches, or go home. 65% have a school dinner and 20% have sandwiches. What percentage of the pupils go home?

11 In a school of 800 pupils, 35% are members of a school club. How many pupils are members of a school club?

12 The monthly fee for cable TV rises by 5%. It was £20. What is the new monthly fee?

13 A holiday resort has a record of having rain on only 1 in every 20 days. What is the percentage rainfall for the resort?

14 Change $6\frac{1}{4}\%$ to a fraction.

15 Change $\frac{9}{80}$ to a percentage.

16 Calculate the new price of a cooker which is normally priced at £360, but is reduced by $12\frac{1}{2}\%$ in a sale.

2 Recognising percentages

A percentage is a fraction of 100.

There are 100 squares on the grid.

30 of them are shaded.

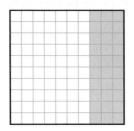

$\dfrac{30}{100}$ or 30% of the squares are shaded.

Here are some common percentages:

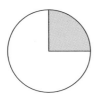 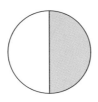

$\dfrac{1}{4}$ or 25% $\dfrac{1}{2}$ or 50% $\dfrac{3}{4}$ or 75%

a   What percentage of the grid is shaded?

There are 45 squares out of 100 shaded.

This is $\dfrac{45}{100}$ or 45%.

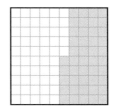

b   Estimate the percentage of the circle that is shaded.

The shading is more than 25%

but less than 50%

It is approximately 35%.

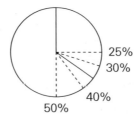

25%
30%
40%
50%

EXAMPLES

Exercise 12:2

Write down the percentage of each grid that is shaded.

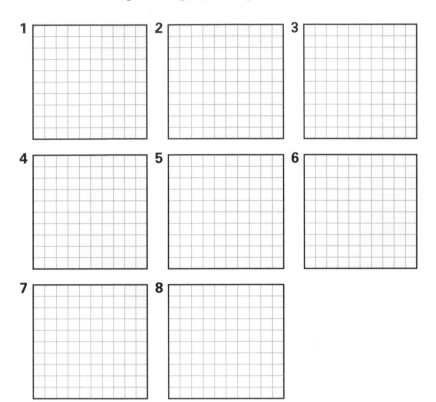

Estimate the percentage of each circle that is shaded.

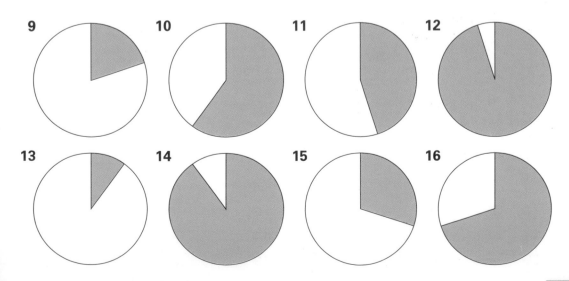

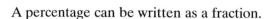

3 Conversion from percentages

A percentage can be written as a fraction.

37% means 37 out of 100.

As a fraction this is $\dfrac{37}{100}$

Always check if fractions can be cancelled to a simpler form:

60% is $\dfrac{60}{100}$,

$$\underset{\div 10}{\overset{\div 10}{\dfrac{60}{100}}} = \underset{\div 2}{\overset{\div 2}{\dfrac{6}{10}}} = \dfrac{3}{5}$$

A percentage can be written as a decimal.

$$\overset{\begin{array}{cc} 1 & 1 \\ \end{array}}{\underset{}{10\ 100}}$$

37% is the same as $\dfrac{37}{100}$, which as a decimal is 0 . 3 7

So 37% = 0.37

8% is the same as $\dfrac{8}{100}$, which as a decimal is 0.08

EXAMPLES

Change to **a** a fraction **b** a decimal

20%   **a** $20\% = \dfrac{20}{100} = \dfrac{1}{5}$ **b** 20% = 0.20

5%   **a** $5\% = \dfrac{5}{100} = \dfrac{1}{20}$ **b** 5% = 0.05

Exercise 12:3

Change the percentage to   **a**   a fraction   **b**   a decimal

1	5%	**2**	70%	**3**	45%	**4**	35%	**5**	10%
6	95%	**7**	15%	**8**	90%	**9**	40%	**10**	2%
11	65%	**12**	20%	**13**	12%	**14**	22%	**15**	30%
16	66%	**17**	7%	**18**	38%	**19**	24%	**20**	32%

4 Conversion to percentages

A decimal can be changed to a percentage.

To change 0.58 to a percentage:

$\qquad$ 0.58 of 100 means $0.58 \times 100 = 58\%$

To change 0.07 to a percentage:

$\qquad$ 0.07 of 100 means $0.07 \times 100 = 7\%$

A fraction can be changed to a percentage.

To change $\dfrac{2}{5}$ to a percentage:

$\qquad \dfrac{2}{5}$ of 100 means $\dfrac{2}{5} \times \dfrac{100}{1} = \dfrac{200}{5}$

$\qquad 200 \div 5 = 40$

So $\dfrac{2}{5} = 40\%$

$$5 \overline{)200} \quad {}^{40}$$

To change $\dfrac{9}{20}$ to a percentage:

$\qquad \dfrac{9}{20}$ of 100 means $\dfrac{9}{20} \times 100 = \dfrac{900}{20}$

$\qquad$ So $\dfrac{9}{20} = 45\%$

$$20 \overline{)900} \quad {}^{45}$$

EXAMPLES

Change to a percentage:

a $\dfrac{9}{100}$ **b** 0.04 **c** $\dfrac{1}{5}$

a $\dfrac{9}{100} \times 100 = \dfrac{900}{100} = 9\%$

b $0.04 \times 100 = 4\%$

c $\dfrac{1}{5} \times 100 = \dfrac{100}{5} = 20\%$

Exercise 12:4

Convert into a percentage:

1	$\dfrac{4}{5}$	2	$\dfrac{7}{10}$	3	0.03	4	$\dfrac{3}{20}$	5	0.41
6	$\dfrac{99}{100}$	7	$\dfrac{1}{20}$	8	0.2	9	0.81	10	$\dfrac{5}{10}$
11	$\dfrac{3}{10}$	12	0.91	13	$\dfrac{3}{5}$	14	$\dfrac{20}{100}$	15	0.52
16	0.09	17	$\dfrac{7}{20}$	18	0.55	19	$\dfrac{3}{50}$	20	0.01

5 Sum to 100%

When something has been divided up into percentage parts, then all those parts should sum to 100%. That is, they should add up to make 100%.

In a class, 60% of the pupils are girls.
What percentage are boys?

To find the boys: $100 - 60 = 40\%$.

In a box there are red, black and blue pens.
10% are red pens, 55% are blue pens.
What percentage are black pens?

$$10 + 55 = 65\%$$

$$100 - 65 = 35\%$$

The percentage of black pens is 35%

EXAMPLE

70% of the children at a school stay for lunch.
What percentage do **not** stay?

$$100 - 70 = 30\% \text{ do not stay for lunch}$$

Exercise 12:5

1   43% of the sales at a garage are new cars.
    What percentage of the sales are for second-hand cars?

2   A petrol engine wastes 55% of the energy in the petrol.
    What percentage is used?

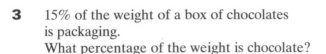

3 15% of the weight of a box of chocolates
is packaging.
What percentage of the weight is chocolate?

4 A carpet covers 70% of a floor.
What percentage of the floor is not covered?

5 82% of a blend of tea comes from India,
the rest comes from Sri Lanka.
What percentage of the tea comes from Sri Lanka?

3 90% of the lemon squash in a jug is water.
What percentage is not water?

7 85% of the pupils taking a test have passed.
What percentage have failed?

8 A newspaper contains news items, advertisements and letters.
26% of the newspaper is advertisements and 12% is letters.
What percentage is news items?

9 42% of the population of a village are men, and 36% are women.
Find the percentage who are children.

10 25% of a travel agent's customers booked a UK holiday and 48%
booked a holiday in other European countries.
What percentage booked a holiday outside Europe?

11 93% of people in the UK are estimated to have at least one television
set. What percentage of people do not have a television set?

12 Gas, electricity or oil are used for heating homes.
In a survey 73% of people used gas and 24% used electricity.
What percentage used oil?

6 Percentages of quantities

Finding a percentage of a quantity is like finding a fraction of a quantity.

There are 800 pupils at a school. 55% of them are girls.
How many girls are there?

55% is the same as $\dfrac{55}{100}$

55% of 800 $= \dfrac{55}{100} \times 800 = \dfrac{44\,000}{100}$

$44\,000 \div 100 = 440$

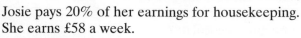

Josie pays 20% of her earnings for housekeeping.
She earns £58 a week.
How much housekeeping does she pay?

$$20\% \text{ of } £58 = \frac{20}{100} \times 58 = \frac{1160}{100}$$

$$1160 \div 100 = 11.60$$

She pays £11.60 for housekeeping.

Exercise 12:6

1 Find 10% of 50.   **2** Find 50% of 32.   **3** Find 20% of 30.

4 Find 60% of 50.   **5** Find 6% of £7.00   **6** Find 5% of £20.

7 A man weighs 90 kg. He loses 3% of his weight.
How many kilograms has he lost?

8 A tin of peas weighs 30 g.
70% of the can is water.
What weight of water is in the can?

9 Liam is given a discount of 7% on a sale of £200.
How much is the discount?

10 The price of a £10 000 car has been increased by 8%.
What amount has been added to the price of the car?

11 The staff have received a bonus of 5% of £100 000.
How much is the bonus?

12 A woman has covered 75% of a journey of 20 km.
How far has she driven so far?

7 Percentage increase and decrease

Quantities can be changed by a percentage.

A percentage increase makes the quantity larger by
adding on a percentage of the quantity.

A percentage decrease makes the quantity smaller by
taking off a percentage of the quantity.

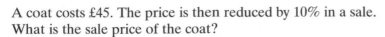

A coat costs £45. The price is then reduced by 10% in a sale.
What is the sale price of the coat?

$$10\% \text{ of } £45 \text{ is } \frac{10}{100} \times 45 = \frac{450}{100} = £4.50 \quad \textbf{This is the reduction.}$$

So the sale price of the coat is £45 − £4.50 = £40.50

EXAMPLE

The number of bookings at a holiday site have gone up by 15% this year. Last year there were 120 bookings.
How many bookings are there now?

$$15\% \text{ of } 120 = \frac{15}{100} \times 120 = 18$$

So the number of bookings now is 120 + 18 = 138

Exercise 12:7

1   Increase £420 by 65%

2   Increase 800 kg by 46%

3   Decrease 240 m by 15%

4   Increase £40 by 35%

5   Decrease £3.50 by 20%

6   Increase 48 g by 17%

7   A £48 jacket is reduced by 30% in a sale.
What is the sale price of the jacket?

8   A man pays 20% tax on his earnings of £8000.
How much money has he left after tax?

9   The price of a £650 holiday is reduced by 5% if you book early.
What is the reduced price?

10   The 40 000 population of a town
has increased this year by 6%.
What is the population now?

11   A 600 ml bottle of screen wash is sold in a
special offer bottle with 25% extra included.
How much screen wash is in the special offer
bottle?

12   Due to traffic, the time taken to get to school in
the morning has increased by 30% in a year.
It took 40 minutes last year.
How long does it take this year?

8 Writing as percentages

Sometimes you need to write one figure as a percentage of another.

As percentages are always out of one hundred it is easier to compare figures if they are written as a percentage.

Katy has two test results: Maths 34 out of 40, English 12 out of 15.
Write these two results as percentages.

Write the results as fractions, then change these fractions into percentages.

$$\text{Maths: } 34 \text{ out of } 40 = \frac{34}{40} \quad \frac{34}{40} \times 100 = \frac{3400}{40} = 85\%$$

$$\text{English: } 12 \text{ out of } 15 = \frac{12}{15} \quad \frac{12}{15} \times 100 = \frac{1200}{15} = 80\%$$

Maths: 85%, English: 80%

EXAMPLE

10% of a class were late one morning. This was 3 pupils.
How many pupils are there in the class?

10% is $\frac{1}{10}$ of the whole class.

$\frac{10}{10}$ or 100% represents the whole class.

This is 10 times as much.
$3 \times 10 = 30$ pupils in the class.

Exercise 12:8

1 During the 30 days of September it rained 12 days.
   On what percentage of the days did it rain?

2 Ben gained 57 out of 60 marks for a test.
   What was his percentage mark?

3 What is 126 as a percentage of 840?

4 In a road survey 30 out of 300 vehicles were vans.
   What percentage were vans?

5 In a box of 250 chalk sticks, 90 are white.
   What percentage are coloured?

6 What percentage of £1 is 5p?

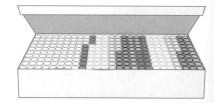

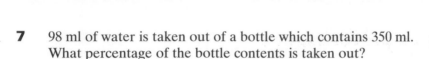

7 98 ml of water is taken out of a bottle which contains 350 ml. What percentage of the bottle contents is taken out?

8 The population of a village has increased by 100 from 2000. Write 100 out of 2000 as a percentage.

9 In a box there are 19 large eggs, and 31 medium eggs. What percentage of eggs in the box are large eggs?

10 A bag of counters is to be divided equally between 20 pupils. What percentage of the counters will each pupil receive?

9 Percentage fractions

Percentages are not only whole numbers.
Percentages can also include fractions, for example $12\frac{1}{2}\%$.

To convert percentages to and from decimals and fractions you need only convert the percentage into a decimal.

$12\frac{1}{2}\%$ becomes 12.5%. As a decimal: $12.5 \times 100 = 0.125$

0.0825 becomes $0.0825 \times 100 = 8.25\%$ or $8\frac{1}{4}\%$

$\dfrac{251}{400}$ becomes $\dfrac{251}{400} \times 100 = 62\frac{3}{4}\%$

To write a percentage as a fraction we need to change to an equivalent fraction.

$$12\frac{1}{2}\% = \frac{12\frac{1}{2}}{100} = \frac{25}{200} = \frac{1}{8}$$

Multiply by 2 since there are halves in the percentage.

This equivalent fraction can now be cancelled.

$33\frac{1}{3}\%$ is equivalent to $\frac{1}{3}$.

$66\frac{2}{3}\%$ is equivalent to $\frac{2}{3}$.

EXAMPLES

Write $87\frac{1}{2}\%$ as **a** a fraction **b** a decimal.

a $87\frac{1}{2}\% = \dfrac{87\frac{1}{2}}{100} = \dfrac{175}{200} = \dfrac{7}{8}$

b $87\frac{1}{2}\% = 87.5 \div 100 = 0.875$

Write as a percentage   **a** 0.025   **b** $\dfrac{17}{200}$

a $0.025 \times 100 = 2.5\%$ or $2\frac{1}{2}\%$

b $\dfrac{17}{200} \times 100 = \dfrac{1700}{200} = 8.5\%$ or $8\frac{1}{2}\%$

Exercise 12:9a

Change the percentage to   **a**   a fraction   **b**   a decimal.

1	$62\frac{1}{2}\%$	**2**	$9\frac{1}{2}\%$	**3**	$15\frac{1}{4}\%$	**4**	$31\frac{3}{4}\%$	**5**	$49\frac{1}{2}\%$
6	$51\frac{3}{4}\%$	**7**	$32\frac{1}{4}\%$	**8**	$86\frac{1}{2}\%$	**9**	$21\frac{3}{4}\%$	**10**	$9\frac{1}{4}\%$

Change to a percentage:

11	0.375	**12**	$\dfrac{9}{200}$	**13**	0.235	**14**	0.055	**15**	$\dfrac{1}{80}$
16	$\dfrac{3}{40}$	**17**	0.065	**18**	$\dfrac{9}{16}$	**19**	0.0125	**20**	0.1175

Percentage fractions are also be used in calculations.

The most common percentage fraction is $17\frac{1}{2}\%$, which is the current rate for Value Added Tax (VAT).

A television is advertised at a price of £250 plus VAT.
Calculate the total amount to be paid for the television.

$17\frac{1}{2}\%$ of £250 is $\dfrac{17\frac{1}{2}}{100} \times 250$

$\times 2$ $\div 5$

$= \dfrac{35}{200} \times 250 = \dfrac{7}{40} \times 250 = £43.75$

The VAT is £43.75, so this needs to be added on to the original price.

$£250 + £43.75 = £293.75$

Exercise 12:9b

Calculate:

1 $2\frac{1}{2}\%$ of 2400

2 $6\frac{1}{4}\%$ of £400

3 $33\frac{1}{3}\%$ of £4.50

4 $11\frac{1}{2}\%$ of £150

5 $17\frac{1}{2}\%$ of 280 g

6 $10\frac{1}{4}\%$ of 1600 cm

7   Lisa's £12 400 salary increased by $5\frac{1}{2}\%$.
What is the increase in her salary?

8   A restaurant meal costs £85.20 plus $17\frac{1}{2}\%$ VAT.
What is the total cost of the meal?

9   A car normally costs £12 400.
It is offered at a discount
of $12\frac{1}{2}\%$. What is the reduced price of the car?

10   Mortgage repayments of £280 are increased by $4\frac{1}{2}\%$.
What are the new repayments?

ACTIVITIES

1 Number squares

1	2	3	4	5	6	7	8	9	10
11	12	13	14	15	16	17	18	19	20
21	22	23	24	25	26	27	28	29	30
31	32	33	34	35	36	37	38	39	40
41	42	43	44	45	46	47	48	49	50
51	52	53	54	55	56	57	58	59	60
61	62	63	64	65	66	67	68	69	70
71	72	73	74	75	76	77	78	79	80
81	82	83	84	85	86	87	88	89	90
91	92	93	94	95	96	97	98	99	100

4		6
24		26

This is a 3-sided number square.

a What is the total of the 4 squares in the corners?

b Will any other 3-sided number square give you the same total for the 4 squares in the corners?

c Draw another 3-sided number square.
What can you find out about the total of the 4 squares in the corner?

Can you find an easy way of finding this total using only the number in the top left hand corner?

d Investigate other 3-sided number squares.

e What can you find out about 4-sided number squares?

2 Uminoes

This is a game based on dominoes, for 2 to 6 players.
First you need to make the cards to play the game.

Cut out 60 cards (uminoes),
3 cm by 6 cm.

Draw a line down the centre of each card,
dividing them into two squares
(do *not* cut them into two pieces!).

Next write out the fractions that you are
going to use in the game.
Here is a list of common fractions:

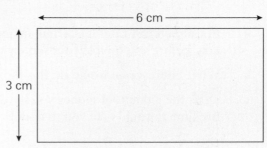

$$\frac{1}{2}, \frac{1}{4}, \frac{3}{4}, \frac{1}{3}, \frac{2}{3}, \frac{1}{5}, \frac{2}{5}, \frac{3}{5}, \frac{4}{5}, \frac{1}{6}, \frac{5}{6}, \frac{1}{8}, \frac{3}{8}, \frac{5}{8}, \frac{7}{8}, \frac{1}{10}, \frac{3}{10}, \frac{5}{10}, \frac{7}{10}, \frac{9}{10}$$

For each fraction in your list, write out the equivalent decimal and
percentage.

For example $\frac{1}{2} \rightarrow 0.5, 50\%$

$\frac{2}{5} \rightarrow 0.40, 40\%$

Now write two values on each umino, either fractions, decimals or
percentages.
You may write the same value on several uminoes if you wish, or even two
fractions on one umino (but not the identical fraction).

To play the game:

Turn all the uminoes face down, shuffle, and share them out equally.
One player starts by putting an umino down.
The next player checks to see if they can match a fraction on either end of
the umino (or the line of uminoes) with one of theirs.
If so, put it down on the end.

Continue to take turns.
The winner is the first to run out of uminoes.

3 Double your money

Banks pay you interest which is added to your account.

This interest can be added every year.

For example, for £1000 in an account earning 6% interest:
interest at the end of the year is 6% of £1000 = £60
so the new amount is £1060

Interest at the end of the next year would be
6% of £1060, and so on.

a For an interest rate of 6% and an amount of £1000, how long will it take before you double your money to £2000?

b What interest rate would do this for you in half the time?

c Does the amount of money you have in the bank have any effect on the time it would take you to double this amount?

4 Division patterns

You need a calculator.

To change a fraction to a decimal you divide:

$$\frac{4}{5} = 4 \div 5 = 0.8$$

Some fractions give repeating decimals.

$$\frac{1}{3} = 0.33333\ldots$$

$$\frac{2}{3} = 0.66666\ldots$$

a With your calculator investigate the decimals for all the fractions

$$\frac{1}{2}, \frac{1}{3}, \frac{1}{4}, \frac{1}{5}, \text{ up to } \frac{1}{30}.$$

Try $\frac{1}{33}, \frac{1}{36}, \frac{1}{37}, \frac{1}{44}, \frac{1}{54}, \frac{1}{60}, \frac{1}{66},$ and $\frac{1}{72}.$

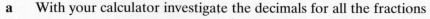

b

13 Measurement

You will use these words in this chapter.

KEY WORDS

• measure • measurement • positive • negative • minus
numbers • less than • more than • less than zero • more
than zero • days of the week • months of the year • calendar
• millennium • century • decade • year • leap year
• 12-hour clock • 24-hour clock • am • pm • noon
• midday • midnight • quarter past • half past • quarter to
• metric units • imperial units • millimetres • centimetres
• metres • kilometres • milligrams • grams • kilograms
• tonne • millilitres • litres • mass • weight • conversion
factors • approximate • equivalent • foot • inch
• pounds (weight) • pints • yard • mile

1 Diagnostic exercises

Exercise 13:1a

1 Write down a number that is less than −3.

2 The temperature falls 4 degrees from −2 °C.
What is the new temperature?

3 What is the difference in temperature between −4 °C and 5 °C?

4 What is the date two weeks after September 30th?

5 What is the year two centuries before 1940?

6 What is the day two weeks after Tuesday 30th April?

7 Write 3.50 pm in 24-hour clock time.

8 Mary got up at 6.50 am and left for school 45 minutes later.
At what time did she leave for school?

9 A bus leaves the main bus stop at 0935, and arrives at its final
destination 55 minutes later.
At what time does it arrive at its destination?

10 A bus calls at Prestwich precinct every 20 minutes. The first bus is there at 7.35 am.
At what time will the fourth bus be there?

11 Measure this line in centimetres.

_____

12 Which metric unit would you use to measure the weight of a cup?

13 Which metric unit would you use to measure the length of a car?

14 Change 3.5 tonnes into kilograms.

15 Change 450 centimetres into metres.

16 A pen has mass 25 g. What is the mass, in kilograms, of 1500 pens?

17 What is 16 litres approximately in pints?

18 A package weighs 8 kg. What is its approximate weight in pounds?

Exercise 13:1b

1 Write down a number that is less than −5.

2 A temperature rises 8 degrees from −2 °C. What is the new temperature?

3 What is the difference in temperature between −3 °C and 4 °C?

4 What is the date three weeks after October 7th?

5 What is the year six decades before 1990?

6 What is the day three weeks after Monday 30th June?

7 Write 10.05 pm in 24-hour clock time.

8 A cake is put in the oven at 1355 hours.
It needs to stay in the oven for $1\frac{1}{4}$ hours.
At what time should it be taken out?

9 A train leaves the station at 0635, and arrives at its final destination $2\frac{3}{4}$ hours later.
At what time does the train arrive at its destination?

10 A tram calls at Bury at 1345, and at Bowker Vale at 1403.
How long does it take to travel between the two stations?

11 Measure this line in centimetres.

_____

12 Which metric unit would you use to measure the amount of water in a kitchen sink?

13   Which metric unit would you use to measure the width of a pencil?

14   Change 6 kilometres into metres.

15   Change 8500 milligrams into grams.

16   How many 25 cm lengths can be cut from a 2 metre roll of string?

17   What is 15 cm approximately in inches?

18   A roll of wallpaper is 12 metres long.
         What is this approximately in yards?

2 Temperature

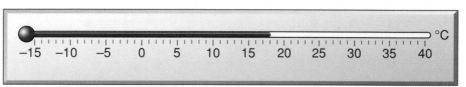

This is a thermometer.
Thermometers are used to measure temperature.

0 °C is freezing point.
The temperature can sometimes be **less than** zero.

$$20° \to 15° \to 10° \to 5° \to 0° \to -5° \to -10°$$
positive numbers   **negative numbers**

Negative numbers are less than 0.
A negative number is less than a **positive** number.

Find the missing numbers in this number sequence.

7, 5, 3, 1, ___ , ___
     $\nwarrow$ $\nwarrow$
     -2 -2

This number series is going down by 2 each time.
We can keep going below zero.

7   5   3   1   **−1**   **−3**   ...

We can show negative numbers on a number line:

Write down a number that is less than −2.

Numbers less than −2 are −3, −4, −5, −6, ...
We can write down any of these.

EXAMPLES

a The temperature falls by 5 degrees from 3 °C.
What is the new temperature?

b The temperature rises by 10 degrees from −6 °C.
What is the new temperature?

c What is the difference in temperature between −4 °C and 2 °C?

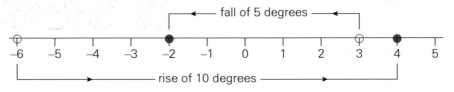

a A fall of 5 degrees from 3 °C gives −2 °C.

b A rise of 10 degrees from −6 °C gives 4 °C

c From −4 °C to 2 °C:

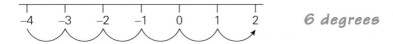

6 degrees

Exercise 13:2

1 The temperature falls 3 °C from −4 °C.
What is the new temperature?

2 The temperature changes from −7 °C to −3 °C.
By how many degrees has it changed?

3 The temperature rose 5 °C from −3 °C.
What was the new temperature?

4 The temperature was 2 °C and then fell by 5 °C.
What was the new temperature?

5 What is the difference in temperature between −3 °C and 2 °C?

6 The temperature changed from 6 °C to −3 °C.
By how many degrees did the temperature change?

7 The temperature was −2 °C and it fell by 8 °C.
What was the new temperature?

8   The temperature was −8 °C and it rose by 15 °C.
       What was the new temperature?

9   What is the difference in temperature between −10 °C and −3 °C?

10 The temperature rose 7 °C from −4 °C.
       What is the new temperature?

11 On the outside of a satellite the temperature
       changed from 35 °C to −24 °C.
       By how many degrees had the temperature
       fallen?

12 During a desert dawn the temperature
       rises by 14 °C from −8 °C.
       What is the temperature after dawn?

3 Calendars

A calendar shows the days and weeks in a year.

You need to know:

> 1 millennium = 1000 years
> 1 century = 100 years
> 1 decade = 10 years
> 1 year = 12 months = 52 weeks = 365 days
> 1 leap year = 366 days

A leap year occurs every **four** years: 1996, 2000, 2004, 2008, etc.

AD means years after year 0.
BC means years before year 0.

This is part of the calendar for the year 2001.

JANUARY 2001 - DECEMBER 2001

JANUARY 2001
S M T W T F S
1 2 3 4 5 6
7 8 9 10 11 12 13
14 15 16 17 18 19 20
21 22 23 24 25 26 27
28 29 30 31

FEBRUARY 2001
S M T W T F S
1 2 3
4 5 6 7 8 9 10
11 12 13 14 15 16 17
18 19 20 21 22 23 24
25 26 27 28

MARCH 2001
S M T W T F S
1 2 3
4 5 6 7 8 9 10
11 12 13 14 15 16 17
18 19 20 21 22 23 24
25 26 27 28 29 30 31

APRIL 2001
S M T W T F S
1 2 3 4 5 6 7
8 9 10 11 12 13 14
15 16 17 18 19 20 21
22 23 24 25 26 27 28
29 30

MAY 2001
S M T W T F S
1 2 3 4 5
6 7 8 9 10 11 12
13 14 15 16 17 18 19
20 21 22 23 24 25 26
27 28 29 30 31

JUNE 2001
S M T W T F S
1 2
3 4 5 6 7 8 9
10 11 12 13 14 15 16
17 18 19 20 21 22 23
24 25 26 27 28 29 30

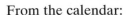

From the calendar:

a How many days are there after 16th January up to and including 3rd February?

b What is the date 20 days after 20th February?

c What is the date on the second Monday of July?

Remember: when you count on, do **not** count the day you start on.

a Counting days from 16th January to 3rd February: 18 days

JANUARY 2001						
S	M	T	W	T	F	S
	1	2	3	4	5	6
7	8	9	10	11	12	13
14	15	16	17	18	19	20
21	22	23	24	25	26	27
28	29	30	31			

FEBRUARY 2001						
S	M	T	W	T	F	S
				1	2	3
4	5	6	7	8	9	10
11	12	13	14	15	16	17
18	19	20	21	22	23	24
25	26	27	28			

b 12th March

c The last date, 30th June, is on a Saturday. Counting the calendar into July:

S	M	T	W	T	F	S	S	M
1	**2**	3	4	5	6	7	8	**9**

The second Monday in July is the 9th.

Exercise 13:3

Use the 2001 calendar to answer these questions.

1 What date is the third Tuesday in March?

2 What is the date 18 days after January 25th?

3 What is the year three centuries before 1980?

4 How many days are there after 6th February up to and including 22nd March?

5 What is the date on the third Friday of July?

6 What was the year 3 millennium before 2000AD?

7 What is the date exactly 6 weeks before 15th May?

8 What year is three centuries before 100AD?

9 What date is the third Friday in May?

10 On what day was Christmas Day in the year 2000?

11 What year is 3 decades after 1955?

12 How many days are there after 7th June up to and including 28th March?

13 What is the date exactly 8 weeks after 13th February?

14 What year is 4 decades before 1962?

15 What is the date 30 days after 30th January?

4 Time

You need to know:

> 1 day = 24 hours
> 1 hour = 60 minutes
> 1 minute = 60 seconds
> Midnight is 12 o'clock during the night
> Midday is 12 o'clock during the day

The time on this clock is half past three.

On a 12-hour clock this could be
> 3.30 am in the morning, or
> 3.30 pm in the afternoon

On a 24-hour clock this could be
> 0330 hours or
> 1530 hours

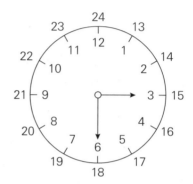

a Change 8.20 pm to a 24-hour clock time
8.20 pm is 2020 hours

b Change 0210 hours to a 12-hour clock time
0210 hours is 2.10 am

c Find the time $3\frac{1}{4}$ hours after 1330 hours.
$\frac{1}{4}$ hour after 1330 is 1345.
3 hours on is 1645

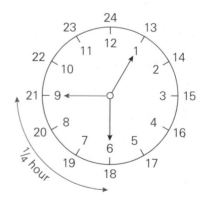

d Work out how long it is between 0735 and 1015.
From 0735 to **0815** is 25 + 15 = 40 minutes
From 0815 to 1015 is 2 hours
Total time difference is 2 hours 40 minutes.

Note: If the question is in 24-hour time, give the answer in 24-hour clock time.

Exercise 13:4

1 Change these 12-hour clock times to 24-hour clock times.

    a 10.30 am   **b** 3.40 pm   **c** 8.10 am   **d** 12.40 pm

    e 8.45 pm   **f** 9.35 am   **g** 3.15 pm   **h** 1.50 am

2 Change these 24-hour clock times to 12-hour clock times.

    a 0855   **b** 2335   **c** 1320   **d** 0730

    e 1225   **f** 0330   **g** 2225   **h** 0054

3 Find:

    a $1\frac{1}{2}$ hours before 10.35 pm   **b** $2\frac{1}{4}$ hours before 0515 hours

    c $4\frac{1}{4}$ hours after 2.20 pm   **d** $2\frac{1}{4}$ hours before 2020 hours

    e $3\frac{3}{4}$ hours after 2.40 am   **f** 12 hours after 1740 hours

4 Work out how long it is between these times.

    a 1505 h to 1942 h   **b** 1.30 pm to 4.45 pm

    c 9.25 am to 6.40 pm   **d** 1455 h to 2015 h

    e 10.30 am to 1.40 pm   **f** 0135 h to 2305 h

5 A train leaves at 1045 h and arrives at its destination at 1455 h.
    How long does the journey take?

6 A school lunchtime lasts for 50 minutes.
    It starts at 12.45 pm. What time does it finish?

7 A video recorder was set to come on at 1020, and go off at 1155.
    How long was the video recording?

8 The sun set at 1840 and rose again at 0510.
    How long was the night?

5 Timetables

We can use timetables to plan journeys on buses
and trains.

Most timetables use 24-hour clock times.

This is a train timetable for trains between Wigan Wallgate and Kirkby.

Wigan Wallgate – Kirkby						Mondays to Saturdays			
Wigan Wallgate	0648	0748	0933	1103	1303	1403	1603	1718	1818
Pemberton	0652	0752	0937	1107	1307	1407	1607	1722	1822
Orrell	0656	0756	0941	1111	1311	1411	1611	1726	1826
Upholland	0659	0759	0944	1114	1314	1414	1614	1729	1829
Rainford	0703	0803	0948	1118	1318	1418	1618	1733	1833
Kirkby	0714	0814	0959	1129	1329	1429	1629	1744	1844

EXAMPLES

a What time does the 0752 from Pemberton arrive in Rainford?

Wigan Wallgate	0748
Pemberton	**0752**
Orrell	0756
Upholland	0759
Rainford	**0803**
Kirkby	0814

It arrives at 0803.

b You need to be in Upholland by 3.00 pm.
What time is the latest train you could catch from Wigan Wallgate?

3.00 pm is 1500 hours
The latest train to arrive at Upholland **before** 1500 is the 1414.
This 1414 train leaves Wigan Wallgate at 1403.
So the latest train you could catch is the 1403.

Wigan Wallgate	**1403**
Pemberton	1407
Orrell	1411
Upholland	**1414**

Exercise 13:5

Use the train timetable for Wigan Wallgate to Kirkby.

1 How many stations do the trains stop at between Wigan Wallgate and Kirkby?

2 What time does the 1603 from Wigan arrive at Orrell?

3 How long does it take the 0933 from Wigan to get to Upholland?

4   A train arrives on time at Kirkby at 0959.
What time did it leave Upholland?

5   How long does the 0652 from Pemberton take to get to Rainford?

6   You need to meet a friend at Kirkby at 1800.
What is the latest time you could catch a train from Orrell?

7   You have to arrive in Rainford at 12 noon.
What time is the latest train you could catch from Pemberton?

Use this bus timetable to answer these questions.

Mondays to Fridays										
Bolton, Bus Station								0705		0735
Farnworth, King Street			0630		0654	0709	0724	0739	0754
New Bury, Tennyson Road			0636		0700	0715	0730	0745	0800
Little Hulton, Spa Hotel			0642		0706	0721	0736	0751	0806
Little Hulton, Cleggs Lane			0646		0711	0726	0741	0756	0811
Walkden Centre		0635	0652	0702	0717	0732	0747	0802	0817
Worsley, Court House		0642	0659	0711	0726	0741	0756	0811	0826
Monton Green		0648	0707	0719	0734	0749	0804	0819	0834
Eccles, College Croft		0655	0715	0727	0742	0757	0812	0827	0842
Pendleton, Shopping Centre	arr.	0707	0727	0739	0754	0809	0824	0839	0854
Pendleton, Shopping Centre	dep.	0709	0729	0741	0756	0811	0826	0841	0856
Victoria Bridge		0719	0739	0751	0806	0821	0836	0851	0906
Manchester, Cannon Street		0725	0745	0757	0812	0827	0842	0857	0912

8   How many buses run all the way from Farnworth to Manchester?

9   At what time does the 0811 from Worsley Court House arrive at Victoria Bridge?

10   How long does it take the 0735 from Bolton to get to Monton Green?

11   For how long do the buses wait at Pendleton Shopping Centre?

12   At what time does the 0819 from Monton Green arrive in Manchester?

13   You need to be in Pendleton at 0800. What time is the latest bus you could catch from Worsley?

14   How long does it take the 0751 from Little Hulton to get to Pendleton?

15   You need to meet a friend in Eccles at 0800. What time is the latest bus you could catch from Walkden Centre?

6 Taking measurements

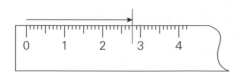

*In centimetres this
is 2.8 cm*

*In millimetres this
is 20 + 8 = 28 mm*

You need to know these metric units of measurement:

Length:	**Mass/weight:**	**Capacity:**
millimetres (mm)	grams (g)	millilitres (ml)
centimetres (cm)	kilograms (kg)	litres (l)
metres (m)	tonnes (t)	
kilometres (km)		

Exercise 13:6

Measure these lines in centimetres, giving your answer as a decimal if appropriate.

Measure these lines in millimetres.

Which unit would you use to measure:

13 The distance across a town.   **14** The height of a house.

15 The weight of a car.   **16** The weight of a baby.

17 The dose of medicine on a spoon.

18 The length of a pencil.

1 _____   2 _____

3 _____   4 _____

5 _____   6 _____

7 _____   8 _____

9 _____   10 _____

11 _____   12 _____

19 The weight of a pencil.

20 The amount of water in a bath.

7 Metric units

You need to know these **conversion factors** to change from one metric unit to another.

Length:
1 kilometre (km) = 1000 metres (m)
1 metre (m) = 100 centimetres (cm)
1 metre (m) = 1000 millimetres (mm)
1 centimetre (cm) = 10 millimetres (mm)

Weight:
1 kilogram (kg) = 1000 grams (g)
1 gram (g) = 1000 milligrams (mg)
1 tonne (t) = 1000 kilograms (kg)

Capacity:
1 litre (l) = 1000 millilitres (ml)

All these are conversion factors which we can use to change a measurement from one metric unit to another.

To change a small unit to a larger unit we **divide**.
To change a large unit to a smaller unit we **multiply**.

a Change 7000 g into kg

small unit → larger unit so divide. *Conversion factor: 1 kg = 1000 g*

7000 ÷ 1000 = 7 kg

b Change 2.34 m into cm

large unit → smaller unit so multiply. *Conversion factor: 1 m = 100 cm*

2.34 × 100 = 234 cm

c A nail has mass 3.6 g.
What is the total mass, in kilograms, of 1500 nails?

We start off in grams: 3.6 g × 1500 = 5400 g
Then change to kilograms: 5400 ÷ 1000 = 5.4 kg

Exercise 13:7

Change these units:

1	7 cm into mm	**2**	54 km into m	**3**	8 m into cm
4	83 mg into g	**5**	0.7 l into ml	**6**	2420 g into kg
7	2.4 kg into g	**8**	4.2 kg into m	**9**	1800 ml into litres
10	427 cm into m	**11**	3.7 t into kg	**12**	0.04 litres into ml
13	800 mg into g	**14**	300 kg into t	**15**	800 ml into litres

16 Seeds are planted 20 cm apart to make a row of plants 25 metres long. How many seeds are needed?

17 A farmer has $3\frac{1}{2}$ tonnes of potatoes. They are to be packed into 2 kg bags. How many bags can be filled?

18 How many 25 g servings of breakfast cereals are there in a box containing 2 kg?

19 How many 15 cm lengths can be cut from a 4-metre roll of string?

8 Imperial/metric equivalents

In the UK we use *imperial* measurements as well as metric measurements. Imperial measurements are still used in the USA, and were used in this country before metric measurements were introduced.

Two measurements that are approximately the same are said to be **equivalent** ($\approx$).

You need to know these common metric and imperial equivalents.

1 kg $\approx$ 2.2 pounds (weight)

1 litre $\approx$ 1.75 pints

1 foot $\approx$ 30 centimetres
1 inch $\approx$ 2.5 centimetres
1 yard $\approx$ 1 metre
1 km $\approx$ $\frac{5}{8}$ mile

To change 48 kilometres to miles.

Use 1 km $\approx$ $\frac{5}{8}$ mile, so multiply by $\frac{5}{8}$ for kilometres $\rightarrow$ miles

$$48 \times \frac{5}{8} = \frac{240}{8} = 30 \text{ miles}$$

To change 80 miles to kilometres:

Use 1 km ≈ $\frac{5}{8}$ miles,

but as we want to change miles → kilometres, do the reverse: ÷ $\frac{5}{8}$

$$80 \div \frac{5}{8} = 80 \times \frac{8}{5} = \frac{640}{5} = 128 \text{ kilometres}$$

For more on dividing by fractions, see page 137.

For more on dividing by fractions, see page 137.

EXAMPLE

Which is heavier: a 4 kg bag of cement, or a 8 lb bag of cement?

> Change kg to lb: 1 kg ≈ 2.2 pounds
> 4 kg = 2.2 × 4 = 8.8 lbs
> 8.8 lbs is heavier than 8 lb.
> So the 4 kg bag is heavier.

Exercise 13:8

Change into approximate equivalents:

1 40 miles into kilometres   **2** 5 metres into yards

3 18 inches into centimetres   **4** 15.75 pints into litres

5 36 inches into centimetres   **6** 15 litres into pints

7 4.5 metres into yards   **8** 60 miles into kilometres

9 45 centimetres into inches   **10** 32 kilometres into miles

11 16 litres into pints   **12** 11 lbs into kilograms

13 $5\frac{1}{2}$ yards into metres   **14** 17.6 lbs into kilograms

15 24 inches into centimetres

16 A speed limit in Spain is 120 kilometres per hour.
What is this in miles per hour?

17 A man weighs 80 kilograms.
What is his weight in pounds (lbs)?

18 What is heavier: a package of weight 3 kg or
a package of weight 5 lb?

19 A tank contains 40 litres of oil. The oil is to
be emptied into 2-pint containers.
How many containers will be needed?

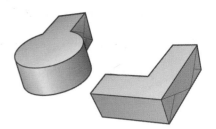

20 A pole is estimated to be 27 feet in height.
How high is this in metres?

ACTIVITIES

1   Timing minutes

You will need a stopwatch or timer.

How long is a minute?

We all know that a minute is 60 seconds long, but how long is that?

Start the timer. Your partner must tell you when they think the minute is up.
Make a note of how long their "minute" actually was, and then swap over.

Then try 2 minutes, 3 minutes.

Is your estimate closer to the actual time when it is a short time, or when it is
a long time?

2   Clock capers

A game for two players.

Rules

a   The first player picks an odd number
and an even number.

b   The players then take turns to pick
another number. They must also pick
odd and even numbers in turn odd,
then even, then odd numbers, and so
on.

c   You may not pick a number on the
clock face that has already been
picked

d   You may not pick a number in the
same quarter on the clock face as
the last number you picked.

You lose if you cannot pick a number!

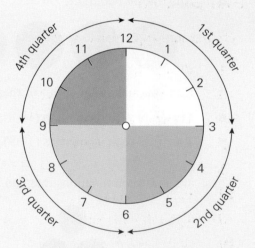

3   Numbered counters

You have six numbered counters.

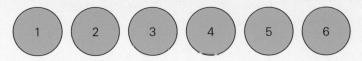

These counters can be arranged in a triangle so that the total along each side is 9:

a   Arrange the counters in a triangle so that the total along each edge of the shape is 10.

Then try 11 and 12.

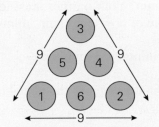

b   Add another counter.

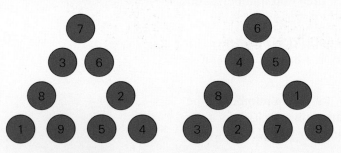

Can you make shapes out of these?

c   Try again with 8 counters (1−8).

d   Try again with 9 counters (1−9).

These are some combinations that can be made with 9 counters:

Find another two combinations.

e   Try arranging the counters in a square, instead of a triangle.

4   Dates of birth

Use this calculation to find someone's date of birth.
Write down your answer at each stage, to use in the next stage.

a   Start with the day of the month you were born on

b   Multiply this by 20, add 3, and then multiply by 5.

c   Add to your answer the number of the month you were born in

d   Multiply by 20, add 3, and multiply by 5.

e   Add to your answer the number formed by the last two digits of the year in which you were born.

f   Take away the number 1515 from your answer.

The answer should be the date of birth.

5   Perimeters

You will need some squared paper.

The shapes have perimeters of 10 units:

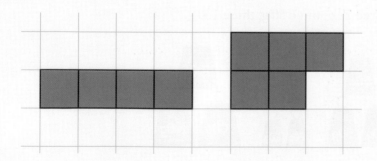

a   Draw some more shapes with perimeters of 10 units.

b   Draw some shapes which have perimeters of 12 units.

c   Investigate shapes which have perimeters of lengths.

d   How many shapes can you draw for a given perimeter?

6 Areas

You will need squared paper.

These shapes each
have area four
square units.

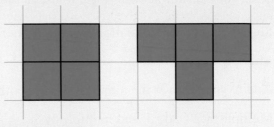

How many other shapes can you draw that have an area of four square units?

a Draw some more shapes with areas of 5 square units.

b Draw some shapes with areas of 6 square units.

c Investigate shapes with other areas.

d How many shapes can you draw for a given area?

7 Balances

a The left hand pan of this balance has a weight
of 250 g on it.

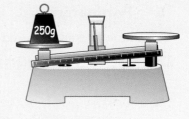

You have these weights:

three 10 g, three 20 g, three 50 g, three 100 g.

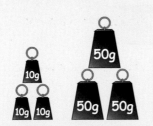  

Write down the combinations of weights you could put on the right-hand pan
to balance the scales.

> You could start with
> 100 g + 100 g + 50 g
> 10 g + 20 g + 20 g + 50 g + 50 g + 100 g

Write down as many combinations as you can that would add up to
give 250 g.

b You are given one extra of each of the weights.

You now have 16 weights in total.

Write down as many combinations as you can that add up to 250 g.

8 Rectangles

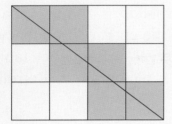

The diagram shows a rectangle with dimensions 4 by 3.

A diagonal line is drawn across the rectangle.
This diagonal line passes through 6 of the squares, which have been shaded.

a If a rectangle is drawn with dimensions 5 by 3, how many squares will need to be shaded after the diagonal has been drawn in?

b How would the answer be different if the rectangle was a square, perhaps of dimensions 4 by 4?

c Investigate the number of squares that will need shading for different dimensions of rectangle .

d Predict the number of squares that need to be shaded, given the size of the rectangle.

14 Tables, graphs and charts

You will use these words in this chapter.

1 Diagnostic exercises

Exercise 14:1a

1 Look at the Venn diagram.

   a How many numbers start with 2?

   b Which numbers are odd numbers, but do not start with 2?

   c Copy the Venn diagram and add the numbers 17 and 27 to it.

Numbers that start with 2   Odd numbers

26   21   31

24   55

2 Look at the Carroll diagram.

   a How many numbers have 3 or 4 tens?

   b Which numbers end in 5?

   c Copy the diagram and add the numbers 45 and 50

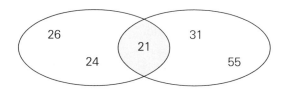

	Numbers that end in 5	Numbers that do *not* end in 5
Numbers that have 3 or 4 tens	35	37 48
Numbers that have 5 or 6 tens	55 65	63

3 **a** Copy and complete the frequency table for the information shown below.

b Draw a bar chart for this information.

The number of pins in a box.

41	38	42	39	40	39	38	41	42	39	40	40
40	39	39	41	41	42	41	38	40	40	38	39
42	40	40	40	39	38	41	41	38	39	41	

Number of pins	Tally	Frequency
38		
39		
40		
41		
42		

Total _____

4 **a** Copy and complete the frequency table for the information shown below.

b Draw a bar chart for this information.

Mileage for a fleet of cars

27	45	33	40	55	65	54	46	42	27	37	19
39	24	40	40	54	48	56	43	66	51	32	51
30	31	38	41	49	42						

Mileage (miles)	Tally	Frequency
10−19		
20−29		
30−39		
40−49		
50−59		
60−69		

Total _____

5 The pictogram shows the number of tyres fitted to cars at a car tyre shop.

Mon ⦿ ⦿ ⦿ ⦿ ⦿ ◖

Tue ⦿ ⦿ ⦿ ⦿ ◖

Wed ⦿ ⦿ ⦿ ⦿ ◟

Thu ⦿ ⦿ ⦿ ⦿ ⦿ ⦿ ◟

Fri ⦿ ⦿ ⦿ ⦿ ⦿ ◟

Key: ⦿ represents 4 tyres

a On which day was the greatest number of tyres fitted?

b How many tyres were fitted on

(i) Tuesday   (ii) Thursday?

c Draw the symbols you would use to show 14 tyres fitted.

6 The bar chart shows the number of pupils who were late in a week in several forms.

a Which form had the greatest number of late pupils?

b Which form had the least number of late pupils?

c How many pupils were late in form 8A?

d How many more pupils were late in form 8B than in form 8E?

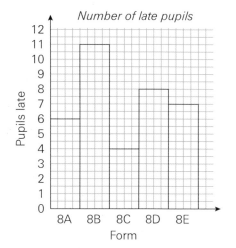

Number of late pupils

7 This pie chart shows energy use in the home.

a For which purpose is the most energy used?

b How many times more energy is used for heating than cooking?

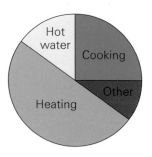

Exercise 14:1b

1

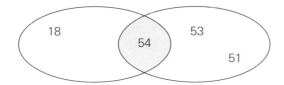

Even numbers   Numbers that
                                 start with 5

18   54   53

51

a How many numbers start with 5?

b Which numbers are even numbers?

c Copy the Venn diagram and add the numbers 50 and 60 to it.

2

	Odd	Even	
Numbers greater than 50	73 91	82	
Numbers 50 or less	49	36 24	

a How many even numbers less than 50 are there?

b Which numbers are odd?

c Copy the Carroll diagram and add the numbers 7 and 85 to it.

3 **a** Complete the frequency table for the information shown below.

b Draw a bar chart for this information.

The number of packets of crisps in a box

24   26   26   24   27   23   25   24   27   23   25   24
26   25   25   27   25   24   24   26   26   24   25   23
23   25   25   25   23   26   23   24   27   26   25

Number of packets of crisps	Tally	Frequency
23		
24		
25		
26		
27		

Total _____

4   **a**   Complete the frequency table for the information shown below.

   b   Draw a bar chart for this information.

The numbers of counters in bags

51   45   32   61   49   64   34   57   65   68   53   38   60   73
87   74   45   66   60   47   55   33   42   52   43   45   59   54
41   75   56   30   54   40   48   59   46   52   50   67

Number of counters	Tally	Frequency
30−39		
40−49		
50−59		
60−69		
70−79		
80−89		

Total   _____

5   The pictogram shows the number of pizzas delivered by a telephone pizza delivery shop.

Mon 🍕 🍕 🍕 🍕

Tue 🍕 🍕 🍕 🍕 🍕

Number of pizzas delivered   Wed 🍕 🍕 🍕 🍕 🍕

Thu 🍕 🍕 🍕 🍕

Fri 🍕 🍕 🍕 🍕 🍕

Key: 🍕 represents 5 pizzas

   a   On which day was the least number of pizzas delivered?

   b   How many pizzas were delivered on

   (i) Tuesday   (ii) Thursday?

   c   Draw the symbols you would use to show 18 pizzas delivered.

198

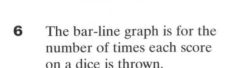

6 The bar-line graph is for the number of times each score on a dice is thrown.

   a Which score was thrown the least?

   b How many times was a score more than 3 thrown?

   c How many times was a score of 1 or 2 thrown?

   d How many times was the dice thrown?

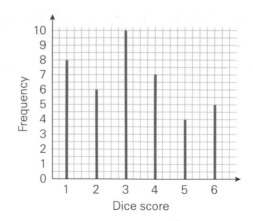

7 The pie chart shows the results of a survey of favourite pets.

   a Which pet is the most popular?

   b What pet is the favourite with a quarter of the children?

   c 32 children give answers in the survey. Estimate how many children gave a dog as their favourite.

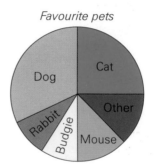

Favourite pets

2 Venn diagrams

Venn diagrams are used to sort information.
Adrian and Sadia like Maths but not Science.
Paul, Remi and Joe like Science but not Maths.
Tim and Ben like both Maths and Science.

For those who like both Maths and Science.

For those who like only Science.

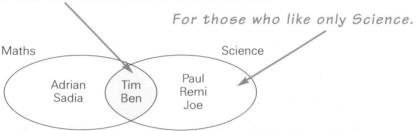

Put these values in the Venn diagram:

13   23   34   36   49   52   76   79   87   92

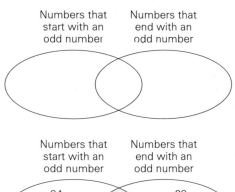

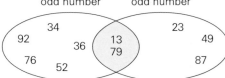

Exercise 14:2

For each question copy the Venn diagram and write the information in the spaces on the diagram.

1   Even numbers   Numbers that start with 4

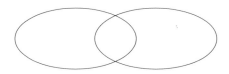

14, 34, 41, 42, 43, 45,
48, 52

2   Odd numbers   Numbers that start with 3

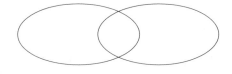

23, 32, 34, 35, 38, 39
43, 51

3   Multiples of 3   Even numbers less than 20

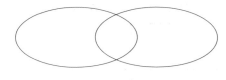

3, 6, 8, 9, 10, 12, 15,
16, 18

4   Factors of 12   Factors of 16

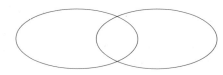

1, 2, 3, 4, 6, 8,
12, 16

5   Tennis   Squash

Julie and Kevin like tennis.
Azhar and Beejal like squash.
Tina and Martin like both tennis
and squash.

6   Numbers that   Even
        start with 9   numbers

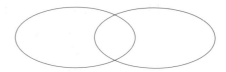

8, 74, 84, 88
91, 94, 95, 98, 99

7   Factors of   Factors of
        30   75

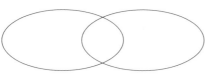

All numbers.

8   Multiples of   Factors
        3 less than 25   of 24

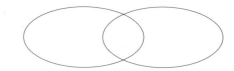

1, 2, 3, 4, 6, 8, 9
12, 15, 18, 21, 24

3 Carroll diagrams

A Carroll diagram helps when sorting in two different ways.

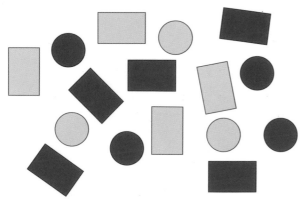

There are two shapes here.
There are also two colours.

A Carroll diagram can show how
many there are of each.

	Red	Blue
Rectangle	5	4
Circle	4	3

	Odd	Even
Numbers that have 4 tens	43 49	46 42
Numbers that have 7 tens	71 77	70 78

a How many even numbers are there?

	Odd	Even
Numbers that have 4 tens	43 49	46 42
Numbers that have 7 tens	71 77	70 78

4 numbers.

b Which numbers have 7 tens and are also odd?

	Odd	Even
Numbers that have 4 tens	43 49	46 42
Numbers that have 7 tens	71 77	70 78

The numbers 71, 77.

c Which numbers have 4 tens?

	Odd	Even
Numbers that have 4 tens	43 49	46 42
Numbers that have 7 tens	71 77	70 78

43, 49, 42, 46.

Exercise 14:3

For each question copy the Carroll diagram and write the information in the correct spaces.

1 23, 22, 27, 33, 35, 32, 26, 39, 34, 28

	Odd	Even
Numbers that have 2 tens		
Numbers that have 3 tens		

2 72, 70, 77, 93, 96, 94 71, 75, 95, 98, 99

	Odd	Even
Numbers that have 7 tens		
Numbers that have 9 tens		

3 33, 54, 38, 37, 57, 50, 59, 83, 56, 51, 34

	Odd	Even
Numbers that have a digit 3		
Numbers that have 5 tens		

4

	Circles	Triangles
Blue		
Red		

5 *Pupils taking history and geography*

	History	Geography
Martin	✔	
Amy	✔	✔
Louise		✔
Ali	✔	✔
Jane		✔
John	✔	✔
Lisa		✔
Michael	✔	

	Boys	Girls
History		
Geography		

6 44, 19, 11, 20, 34, 33, 21, 99, 22, 48

	Numbers that have 2 digits the same	Numbers that have 2 digits that are different
Even		
Odd		

7 10, 3, 1, 2, 4, 5, 6, 15, 12, 20, 25

	Factors of 12	Multiples of 5 less than 28
Even		
Odd		

4 Frequency tables and charts

When we have a lot of information we need to put it in a table so the information can be **summarised** more easily.
These tables are called **frequency** tables.
The frequency table can be drawn as a bar chart.

The information below show the number of mice in a litter.

```
3 4 5 4 4 2 1 5 4 2 6 5
3 1 5 3 4 6 5 3 1 1 3 5
6 4 2 2 5 4 3 4 6 3 5 5
```

This is how 5 is shown in tallies.

Tallies can be used to count the numbers accurately.

Number	Tally	Frequency
1	I	
2	I I	
3	LHHT	
4	I	
5	I I I	
6		
	Total	_____

This is how the table looks after the first row of information has been written in.

Now complete the tallies. Then add them up and write in the frequency column the total for each number.

Number	Tally	Frequency
1	I I I I	4
2	I I I I	4
3	LHHT I I	7
4	LHHT I I I	8
5	LHHT I I I I	9
6	I I I I	4
	Total	36

Add the total of frequencies

Count the tallies and add the number here as a frequency

This table can now be drawn as a bar chart.

The heights of the columns show the frequencies from the table.

Notice there is no gap between the columns.

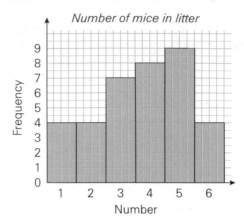

Exercise 14:4

For each question:

    a   draw a frequency table for the information

    b   draw a bar chart to represent the information in your table.

The frequency tables for the first two questions are drawn for you.

1   *The number of minutes late to school of a group of latecomers*

```
2  1  4  3  1  2  2  4  1  4  1  1
4  5  2  1  6  4  4  5  2  1  3  3
1  1  5  6  2  2  1  3  4  1  6  5
```

Minutes late	Tally	Frequency
1		
2		
3		
4		
5		
6		
	Total _____	

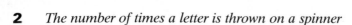

2   *The number of times a letter is thrown on a spinner*

E	B	F	C	F	B	A	E	D
D	B	D	D	A	D	B	C	A
F	B	E	D	B	A	D	B	B
E	C	A	F	D	A	E	F	

Letter	Tally	Frequency
A		
B		
C		
D		
E		
F		

Total _____

3   *Numbers thrown on a dice*

4	5	3	3	5	5	6	5	2	4	1	3	3	1
5	3	6	4	2	3	6	1	2	2	2	5	3	1
4	6	3	4	2	6	1	5	1	4	2	3		

4   *The number of car breakdowns in a car hire company*

4	5	5	5	7	3	4	4	5	6	2	4
3	3	4	5	6	7	4	3	7	6	2	5
5	4	7	6	6	3	5	6	4	2	3	

5   *The number of pens brought to a test by pupils*

2	4	0	3	3	1	3	4	3	2	1	0	1	3	4
2	2	3	2	4	2	0	4	0	3	2	1	3	4	3

6   *The ages of pupils entered for a Junior Maths quiz*

9	13	11	13	9	14	11	10	12	12	14	13	11	10
12	9	12	11	10	13	12	11	14	14	11	11	13	10
9	13	12	11	13	10	10	13	12	9	14	10		

7   *The tries scored by rugby teams in a local league*

2	4	3	2	1	3	3	5	2	1	4	3	1	1
4	3	4	5	0	2	2	3	2	3	3	2	5	1
1	4	2	0	3	3	4	5	1	1	3	2		

8   *The vowels in a paragraph of writing*

a	e	i	a	o	o	e	i	a	i	u	a	a	a
u	e	u	e	o	i	e	o	o	u	a	e	e	i
i	a	e	o	o	u	a	u	e	e	i	a		

9   *The number of letters delivered to each house*

5 6 2 2 5 3 1 4 6 5 3 2 3 2 4 1 3 2 5 1 2
4 6 2 2 1 2 3 2 4 5 1 4 2 3 2 3 3 2 5 1 2
5 6 4 4 3 1 2 6

10   *The ages of pupils in a school Arts club*

12 11 14 15 12 14 13 16 12 16 13 12 16 13 11
12 12 16 14 11 13 14 15 14 12 16 11 15 15 11
13 14 15 12 15 15 13 11 12 11

5   Grouped frequency tables and charts

When we have a lot of information we need to put it in a table so the information can be **summarised** more easily.
When there is a lot of *different* information it is useful to group the information together in a table.
These tables are called **grouped frequency** tables.

Percentage marks of pupils in a test

51 40 79 55 30 65 74 75 53 66 53 44 85 67 20
70 11 51 90 80 19 60 73 45 74 50 69 51 93 78
72 58 34 65 75 55 73 82 55 38 58 80 25 78 48
70 57 85 49 60

This information is tallied in groups called **class intervals**.

Marks	Tally	Frequency
10−19	I I	2
20−29	I I	2
30−39	I I I	3
40−49	⌢⌢⌢⌢⌢	5
50−59	⌢⌢⌢⌢⌢ ⌢⌢⌢⌢⌢ I I	12
60−69	⌢⌢⌢⌢⌢ I I	7
70−79	⌢⌢⌢⌢⌢ ⌢⌢⌢⌢⌢	10
80−89	⌢⌢⌢⌢⌢	5
90−99	I I	2
	Total	50

These are called class intervals.

Add the total of the frequencies.

The table can now be drawn as a bar chart.

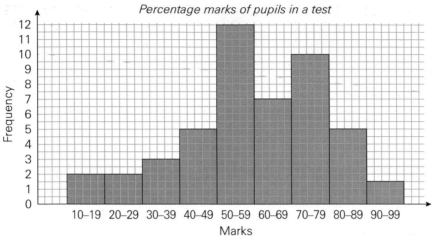

The heights of the columns show the frequencies from the table.

Note there is no gap between the columns.

Exercise 14:5

For each question

a   draw a grouped frequency table for the information.

b   draw a bar chart to represent the information in your table.

The frequency tables for the first two questions have been drawn for you.

1   *Points scored in a competition*

8	19	9	5	12	16	23	13	23	11	7
6	19	18	24	15	4	3	21	13	19	22
11	2	23	24	17	16	14	10	16	20	18

Points	Tally	Frequency
0−4		
5−9		
10−14		
15−19		
20−24		
	Total	_____

2   *Number of people in a supermarket at certain times*

355	222	214	163	263	261	294	127	172	209	286	233
268	167	132	144	232	195	190	283	243	239	155	235
177	53	41	139	331	305	241	240	203	212	183	153
249	181	247	87	342	101	279	160	255			

Number of people	Tally	Frequency
0–49		
50–99		
100–149		
150–199		
200–249		
250–299		
300–349		
350–399		

Total _____

3   *The number of letters delivered to certain streets*

Use class intervals of 0–9, 10–19, etc.

49	8	64	35	28	33	24	16	12	47	43	37	19	7
53	43	31	21	5	61	26	12	26	40	18	28	38	57
10	17	3	55	29	24	20	5	31	48	63	65		

4   *Number of people waiting at bus stops on a bus route*

Use class intervals of 0–4, 5–9, etc.

| 11 | 9 | 16 | 25 | 0 | 24 | 19 | 6 | 13 | 14 | 7 | 19 | 23 | 0 | 4 |
| 26 | 12 | 8 | 15 | 30 | 3 | 18 | 11 | 7 | 21 | 27 | 1 | 5 | 10 | 13 |

5   *The number of pins in boxes*

Use class intervals of 81–85, 86–90, etc.

96	107	115	108	98	90	112	109	97	104	107	100
106	102	105	95	102	89	114	118	84	103	106	117
101	87	92	98	111	93	105	104	93	107	119	

6   *Weight (in grams) of fish caught*

Use class intervals of 0–4, 5–9, etc.

3	21	13	26	22	11	2	23	24	17	18	16
14	10	25	20	18	15	4	24	18	6	8	19
11	7	23	13	23	16	9	12	19	26	5	

7 *Speeds of cars (in mph)*

Use class intervals of 21−30, 31−40, etc.

50	75	38	79	35	43	55	56	65	39	46	50	61	46	54
44	66	56	54	28	72	76	58	53	53	67	48	44	57	57
83	63	25	64	52	51	36	61	30	45	55	70	68	41	35

8 *The amount of liquid in bottles, in ml*

Use class intervals of 30−39, 40−49, etc.

91	65	50	75	89	44	68	81	36	63	85	77	65	38
60	45	50	70	77	53	42	81	93	31	84	65	51	59
45	74	77	69	63	77	49	60	92	58	55	76		

6 Pictograms

Pictograms are used to show information using symbols.
Often the symbol will represent more than one item of information.

House number

Key: represents 5 cartons of milk

a Which house used the least milk?
House number 5

b How many cartons were delivered to house number 3?

One full carton symbol:	5 cartons
A 3/5 carton symbol:	3 cartons
Total:	8 cartons

c How many cartons were delivered altogether?

$$20 + 10 + 8 + 12 + 10 = 60 \text{ cartons.}$$

Exercise 14:6

1   The pictogram shows the items bought by a class during their break.

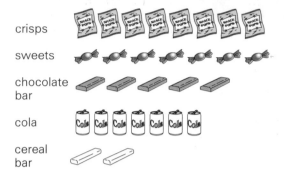

crisps

sweets

chocolate
bar

cola

cereal
bar

Key: 1 picture represents 1 item

a   Which two items had the same amount bought?

b   Which items sold the least?

c   How many sweets were bought?

d   How many cans of cola were bought?

2   The pictogram shows the number of video players sold by an electrical store.

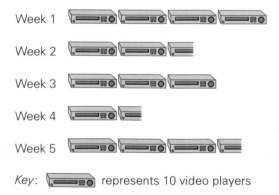

Week 1

Week 2

Week 3

Week 4

Week 5

Key: represents 10 video players

a   How many video players were sold in

(i) week 1   (ii) week 2   (iii) week 5?

b   In which week was the greatest number of video players sold?

c   How many video players were sold in weeks 4 and 5 together?

3 The pictogram shows the number of deliveries made to a shopping centre on each day of the week.

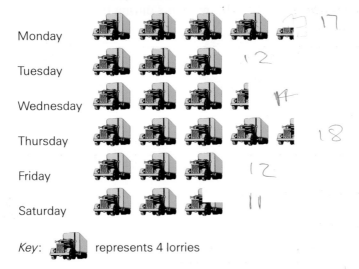

Monday   *17*

Tuesday   *12*

Wednesday   *14*

Thursday   *18*

Friday   *12*

Saturday   *11*

Key: represents 4 lorries

a On which day were most deliveries made?

b On which day were the least deliveries made?

c How many deliveries were made on

(i) Tuesday   (ii) Thursday   (iii) Saturday?

4 The pictogram shows the number of homeworks given to five students in a week.

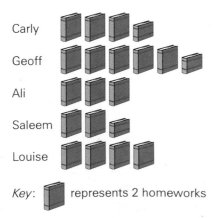

Carly

Geoff

Ali

Saleem

Louise

Key: represents 2 homeworks

a Who had the most homework?

b Who had the least homework?

c Find the total number of homeworks given to the five pupils.

For the next four questions draw a pictogram of the information shown in the table.

5 *Hours of television watched*

BBC1	BBC2	ITV	Ch4	Ch5
6	2	8	3	1

Use a television screen symbol in your pictogram.

6 *Goals scored in a season by six players.*

Tom	Jerry	Fernandez	Philip	David	Remi
12	15	20	14	18	9

Use a football symbol to show 4 goals.

7 *Money raised for charities*

Year 7	Year 8	Year 9	Year 10	Year 11
£350	£250	£200	£150	£100

Use a coin symbol to show £50.

8 *Pupils with birthdays on each day*

Mon	Tue	Wed	Thu	Fri	Sat	Sun
25	14	20	18	28	17	20

Use a birthday cake symbol to show 4 pupils.

7 Using graphs and diagrams

Bar chart	Bar-line graph	Line graph
Goals scored by Stanthorne netball team	*Scores on a spinner*	*Level of water in a barrel*

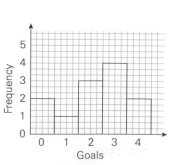

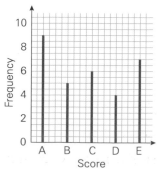

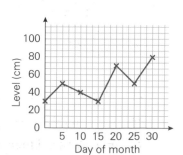

1 This is a bar-line graph of the number of times each score on a dice is thrown.

    a Which score is thrown the least?

    b Which score was thrown the most?

    c Which two scores were thrown an equal number of times?

    d How any times was a score less than 4 thrown?

    e How many times was the dice thrown altogether?

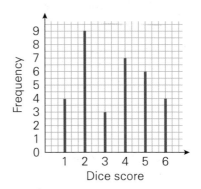

2 This is a graph of temperatures over several hours.

    a Write down the temperature after (i) 1 hours (ii) 2 hours (iii) 3 hours.

    b Write down the times at which the temperature was 15 °C.

    c State the time and temperature at the points of the graph which are the (i) highest (ii) lowest.

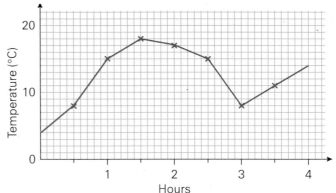

3 The bar chart shows the number of babies born in a hospital ward over several months.

    a During which month were the greatest number of babies born?

    b During which two months were the same number of babies born?

    c How many fewer babies were born in February than in March?

    d How many babies were born altogether in April and May?

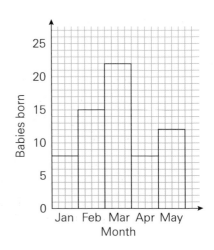

4 This is a graph of a hospital patient's temperature.

   a What was the maximum temperature?

   b What was the minimum temperature?

   c What was the temperature at 0600 hours on Tuesday?

   d By how many degrees did the temperature fall between 1400 hours on Monday and 1400 hours on Tuesday?

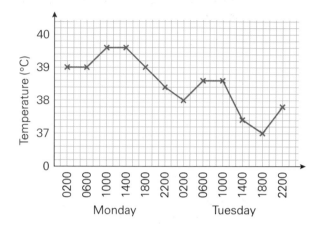

5 The bar chart shows the amounts collected for charity by six form groups.

   a Which form groups collected the smallest amount?

   b Which was the largest amount collected by any form group?

   c How much more was collected by 7Y than 7M?

   d What was the total amount collected?

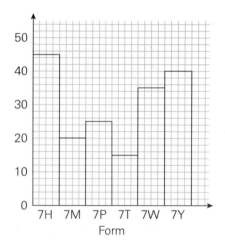

6 The graph shows the monthly television sales in a shop, over a period of time.

   a What were the sales in (i) February (ii) May?

   b In which month were 55 televisions sold?

   c How many televisions were sold from January to March?

   d By how much did the sales fall from March to May?

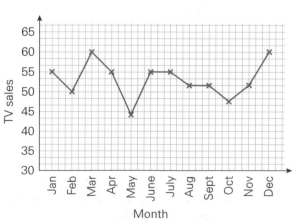

7 This is a graph of the flying times from Manchester to various places in the world.

    a To which place is the flying time longest?

    b To which place is the flying time shortest?

    c How long does it take to get to (i) Palma (ii) Antigua?

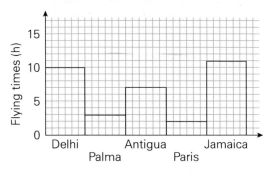

8 The bar-line graph shows scores thrown on an 8-sided spinner.

    a Which score was thrown the least?

    b How many times was a score of 3 thrown?

    c Which two scores were thrown the same number of times?

    d How many times was a score of 6 or more thrown?

    e How many times was the spinner thrown?

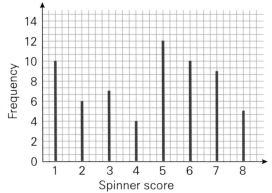

9 The graph shows the cost of a holiday at different times of the year.

    a Which are the most expensive weeks to go on holiday?

    b What is the cost of a holiday in (i) the 2nd week of June (ii) the 1st week of August?

    c When is the cost (i) £640 (ii) £580?

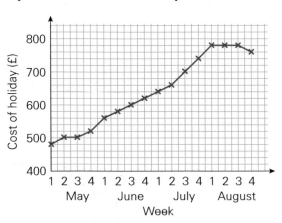

10 The bar chart shows the lengths of fish caught in a competition.

   a How many fish between 4 cm and 8 cm long were caught?

   b How many fish under 8 cm were caught?

   c How many fish more than 12 cm were caught?

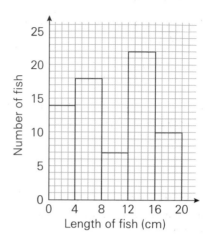

8 Pie charts

A pie chart shows how information is **classified** or divided into different categories.

16 people were asked to name their favourite subject.

Their answers were:

   Maths, English, Maths, PE,
   Art, Science, English, Maths,
   PE, Maths, Maths, Art,
   Science, English, Maths, English

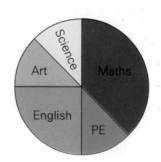

This information is shown on a pie chart:

There are 8 sectors, so each sector represents 2 people.

For Maths there are 2 + 2 + 2 = 6 people.
For Science there are 2 people.

Exercise 14:8

1 The results of a survey of the car colours are shown as a pie chart.

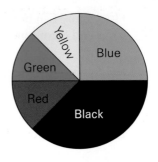

  a Which colour was the most common?

  b Which colour was twice as common as red?

  c There were 80 cars in the survey. How many were (i) green (ii) black?

2 Parents were asked to give the destination of their summer holiday.

  a Which destination was most popular?

  b Which destination was twice as popular as the USA?

  c There were 40 parents involved in the survey. For how many was the destination given as (i) UK (ii) Africa?

3 A school secretary spent £20 on stamps. The pie chart shows how the stamps were used.
Use the pie chart to write down the total cost of stamps used for:

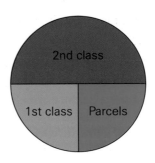

  a 2nd class postage

  b parcels

  c 1st class postage.

4 A group of youths were asked to name their favourite sport.

  a Which part of the pie chart shows of the sports named?

  b Which is the least popular sport?

  c Which sport is half as popular as football?

5 The pie chart shows the different results in an examination.

   a Which type of result was awarded most often?

   b Which type of result was awarded least often?

   c Results were awarded to 100 students. How many received a result of "credit"?

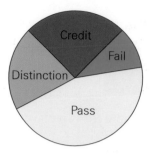

6 The pie chart shows how time is spent in school.

   a Which activity is most time spent on?

   b Which activity is least time spent on?

   c How many more times longer is spent in lessons than in registration?

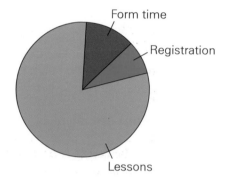

7 The pie chart shows sales of four different types of sugar.

   a Which type of sugar sold the least?

   b What fraction of the sugar sales is castor sugar?

   c How many times more granulated sugar was sold than brown sugar?

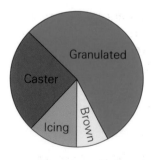

8 Businessmen arriving at an airport were asked their destination.
The results are shown in the pie chart.

   a What destination was most popular?

   b What fraction of the destinations was America?

   c To which two destinations were the same number of businessmen travelling?

ACTIVITIES

1   The dock

HOME				START				DOCK

This is a game for two players.

Place a counter at START.

Take turns to throw a dice.

If you throw 1, 2 or 3 move one square to the left.
If you throw 4, 5 or 6 move one square to the right.
If you arrive at HOME then you are safe.
If you arrive at DOCK then you lose the game.

Try the game several times.

a   What changes can you make to improve the chance of you getting to HOME safely?

b   Change the rules of the dice, and investigate the probability of your getting home safely.

2   To fifteen

Make nine cards, numbered 1 to 9.

Set out the nine cards, face up.

Two players take turns to choose any one of the cards remaining.
The winner is the first player to put down a set of *three* cards totalling 15.

3 Distance charts

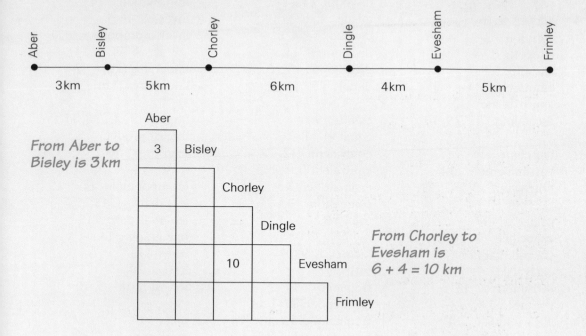

From Aber to Bisley is 3 km

From Chorley to Evesham is 6 + 4 = 10 km

a Fill in the rest of the distances in the chart.

b Draw distance charts for these diagrams:

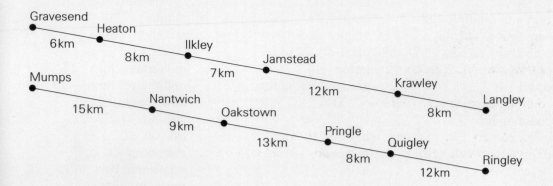

1 Number

Diagnostic exercises: 1.1

Question	Section	Explanation
1,2,3,4	2	Number values
5,6	3	Numbers to words (up to 4 digits)
7	4	Larger numbers to words (more than 4 digits)
8,9	5	Words to numbers (up to 4 digits)
	6	Words to larger numbers (more than 4 digits)
10,11	7	Comparing number sizes
	8	Estimating numbers
12,13	9	Rounding numbers

EXERCISE 1:1a

1 20 **2** 300 **3** 2000 **4** 40
5 Nine hundred and seven
6 One thousand and thirty-two
7 Twelve thousand and fifty-eight
8 3407 **9** 104 300
10 4900, 4907, 5012, 5100
11 796, 799, 868, 878, 987
12 **a** 420 **b** 780 **c** 1710 **d** 940
13 **a** 1500 **b** 900 **c** 6000 **d** 700

EXERCISE 1:1b

1 700 **2** 8000
3 60 **4** 400
5 Three hundred and ten
6 Five thousand, five hundred and seven
7 Eleven thousand, three hundred and one
8 5019
9 350 305
10 1996, 2640, 2644, 3686
11 687, 706, 732, 745, 760
12 **a** 440, **b** 260, **c** 3810, **d** 550
13 **a** 3400, **b** 800, **c** 5800, **d** 400

EXERCISE 1:2

1 $6 \times 100 + 3 \times 10 + 4 \times 1$
2 $9 \times 100 + 2 \times 10 + 7 \times 1$
3 $1 \times 100 + 3 \times 10 + 6 \times 1$
4 $4 \times 100 + 5 \times 10 + 1 \times 1$
5 $8 \times 1000 + 3 \times 100 + 6 \times 10 + 9 \times 1$
6 $7 \times 1000 + 1 \times 100 + 0 \times 10 + 2 \times 1$
7 $4 \times 1000 + 5 \times 100 + 1 \times 10 + 6 \times 1$
8 $8 \times 1000 + 3 \times 100 + 0 \times 10 + 3 \times 1$
9 $9 \times 1000 + 4 \times 100 + 1 \times 10 + 2 \times 1$
10 $3 \times 1000 + 0 \times 100 + 5 \times 10 + 6 \times 1$
11 $7 \times 1000 + 5 \times 100 + 0 \times 10 + 3 \times 1$
12 $2 \times 1000 + 0 \times 100 + 0 \times 10 + 4 \times 1$

EXERCISE 1:3

1 90 **2** 3 **3** 20 **4** 500
5 10 **6** 800 **7** 2000 **8** 7
9 7000 **10** 100 **11** 10 **12** 6000

EXERCISE 1:4

1 Two hundred and eighty-five
2 Four hundred and five
3 Two hundred and seventy
4 Six hundred and fifty-eight
5 Five thousand and sixteen
6 Four thousand, six hundred and seven
7 Four thousand and fifty
8 One thousand, eight hundred and fifty
9 One thousand, four hundred and seven
10 Three thousand and eighty-nine
11 Two thousand and seven
12 Nine thousand and eight hundred
13 Seven thousand, four hundred and seven
14 Five thousand and forty-four
15 Two thousand, nine hundred and thirty
16 Eight thousand, three hundred and sixty-one

EXERCISE 1:5

1 Five thousand six hundred and forty-seven
2 Four thousand one hundred and thirty-five
3 Eighty-nine thousand, three hundred and fourteen
4 Seventy-two thousand, three hundred and eighty
5 Sixty-four thousand, three hundred and thirty-eight
6 Fifty thousand and six hundred
7 One hundred and ninety thousand, two hundred and eighty
8 Two hundred and fifty-six thousand and thirty-five

9 One million, one hundred and twenty thousand and seven hundred

10 Two million, three hundred and forty thousand, eight hundred and seventy

11 Seven million, six hundred thousand, eight hundred and forty

12 Seventy-five million, twenty thousand and four hundred

EXERCISE 1:6

1 744	**2** 4282	**3** 7426	**4** 502
5 3970	**6** 1490	**7** 8909	**8** 876
9 2342	**10** 7027	**11** 2002	**12** 6406

EXERCISE 1:7

1 3 500 400	**2** 12 040	**3** 127 403
4 81 627	**5** 303 271	**6** 10 910
7 30700	**8** 13 004	**9** 20 550
10 10 600	**11** 1 100 001	**12** 821 400

EXERCISE 1:8

1 495, 562, 568, 587
2 201, 431, 713, 843
3 489, 498, 500, 501
4 599, 630, 723, 764
5 412, 533, 655, 711, 713
6 621, 673, 678, 690
7 93, 186, 198, 281, 373
8 6225, 6661, 6663, 6883
9 4587, 3645, 3640, 2996
10 6100, 6011, 5907, 5900
11 3100, 3003, 2890, 2752
12 8656, 8565, 8555, 7656
13 88 722, 87 800, 78 600, 68 560
14 78 600, 48 560, 47 500, 8850,
15 100 000, 99 400, 98 800, 78 640,

EXERCISE 1:9

1 2 < 6	**2** 7 > 3	**3** 9 = 9
4 3 < 5	**5** 6 > 2	**6** 4 = 4
7 14 < 15	**8** 5 < 9	**9** 12 > 10
10 8 > 3	**11** 2,3,4,5,6,7,8,9	
12 0,1,2,3,4	**13** 7,8,9,10	
14 7,8,9,10	**15** 0,1,2	
16 0,1,2,3,4,5,6,7	**17** 0,1,2,3,4,5	
18 9,10	**19** 5,6,7,8,9,10	
20 0,1,2,3,4,5,6		

EXERCISE 1:10

As these are estimates, allow ±3 on these answers.

1 19	**2** 31	**3** 40	**4** 25
5 42	**6** 15	**7** 50	**8** 22
9 35	**10** 45	**11** 28	**12** 52

EXERCISE 1:11

1 90	**2** 60	**3** 60	**4** 80
5 60	**6** 30	**7** 20	**8** 30
9 70	**10** 90	**11** 70	**12** 30
13 800	**14** 700	**15** 800	**16** 600
17 500	**18** 500	**19** 700	**20** 300
21 400	**22** 300	**23** 800	
24 300	**25** 4000	**26** 4000	
27 56 000	**28** 13 000	**29** 18 000	
30 65 000	**31** 56 000	**32** 125 000	
33 40 000	**34** 89 000	**35** 551 000	

ACTIVITIES

1 **Reverse numbers** You should always get 1089.

2 **Two-digit sums** You should always get 22.

3 **Max–min** You should find that many of your attempts arrive at the same answer, such as 6174.

4 **Consecutive numbers** It is not possible to make the numbers 4, 8 or 16. Some numbers have more than one way of writing them.
It is worth noting that all odd numbers have at least one way of writing them with a pair of consecutive numbers.

5 **The 100 race** This is a game of strategy. You should work out the best way to win.

6 **Crossing the river** Another game of strategy.
A possible, but not necessarily unique answer, is:
Across: both children
Back: one child
Across: one adult
Back: one child
Then repeat for the next adult.

7 **Colours**

a

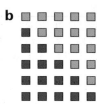

b

$1 + 2 + 3 + 4 + 5 + 1 + 2 + 3 + 4 + 5$
$= 6 + 6 + 6 + 6 + 6 = 30$

c 19 columns, 20 rows

8 Change The way to a solution is to list the combinations in a structured way.
For example for 7p:
5p + 2p
5p + 1p + 1p
2p + 2p + 2p + 1p
2p + 2p + 1p + 1p + 1p
2p + 1p + 1p + 1p + 1p + 1p
1p + 1p + 1p + 1p + 1p + 1p + 1p

9 Cash deposits
a £50.97 **b** £57.15 **c** £99.88
d £76.07 **e** £139.30

2 Addition

Diagnostic exercises

Question	Section	Explanation
1	2	Addition without carrying
2,9,10	3	Addition with carrying
3	4	Far more carrying
4,12	5	Adding with hundreds
5	6	Adding with thousands
6,11	7	Finding totals
7	8	Mental addition – single digits
8	9	Mental addition – two-digit numbers

EXERCISE 2:1a

1 57	**2** 73	**3** 121	**4** 721
5 8365	**6** 1342	**7** 27	**8** 93
9 45p	**10** 151	**11** 4200	**12** 802

EXERCISE 2:1b

1 95	**2** 83	**3** 151	**4** 820
5 6431	**6** 3083	**7** 25	**8** 160
9 84 g		**10** £66	
11 11 344 miles		**12** 383	

EXERCISE 2:2

1 98	**2** 49	**3** 59	**4** 94
5 67	**6** 69	**7** 84	**8** 78
9 59	**10** 97	**11** 97	**12** 99
13 £90	**14** 96	**15** 97 cm	**16** 97

EXERCISE 2:3

1 51	**2** 92	**3** 66	**4** 91
5 91	**6** 92	**7** 81	**8** 93
9 82	**10** 85	**11** 91	**12** 53
13 82	**14** 92p	**15** 62	**16** 62

EXERCISE 2:4

1 111	**2** 145	**3** 131	**4** 123
5 123	**6** 121	**7** 112	**8** 163
9 125	**10** 122	**11** 133	**12** 116
13 131 g		**14** 154	
15 112 min		**16** 155 litres	

EXERCISE 2:5

1 672	**2** 545	**3** 408	**4** 810
5 930	**6** 390	**7** 644	**8** 645
9 481	**10** 433	**11** 483	**12** 521
13 525 km		**14** 905 m	
15 721 mm		**16** 758	

EXERCISE 2:6

1 3922	**2** 3519	**3** 2707	**4** 11 674
5 12 953	**6** 13 471	**7** 8000	**8** 14 792
9 15 687		**10** 12 803	
11 6887		**12** 13 585	
13 9871 litres		**14** 9940	
15 7568 mm^3		**16** 14 853	

EXERCISE 2:7

1 2663	**2** 3842	**3** 3983	**4** 5155
5 4955	**6** 5904	**7** 4680	**8** 2560
9 7194	**10** 2371	**11** 6012	**12** 5839
13 1515 miles		**14** 1123	
15 £2249		**16** 6422	

EXERCISE 2:8

1 30	**2** 26	**3** 25	**4** 24
5 28	**6** 20	**7** 22	**8** 22
9 27	**10** 22	**11** 31	**12** 32
13 37	**14** 46	**15** 34	**16** 47

EXERCISE 2:9

1	138	**2**	117	**3**	201	**4**	158
5	118	**6**	157	**7**	186	**8**	111
9	149	**10**	185	**11**	196	**12**	146
13	122	**14**	£169	**15**	156	**16**	213 kg

ACTIVITIES

1 **Darts**
   a 94   **b** 65   **c** 71

2 **Combinations** The solution should be obtained using a structured approach. Listing should not be random.

3 **Coins** You could use coins to assist you in finding the combinations, but always write down the coins you use to make each amount. Work systematically, as in Activity 8 in Chapter 1.

4 **Maximum and minimum** Largest number 43, smallest number 12.

5 **Operation grid**
   b the lowest score is $+ 2 - 1 - 2 + 5$
      $= +4$
   c the highest score is $+ 5 + 7 - 2 + 5$
      $= +15$

6 **Estimates** This task can also be tackled as a mental calculation exercise by asking someone to read the numbers to you.

3 Subtraction

Diagnostic exercises

Question	Section	Explanation
1,9	2	Subtraction without borrowing.
2,7	3	Borrowing tens
3,10	4	Borrowing hundreds
4,11	5	Borrowing more than once
5,8	6	Borrowing from zero
6,12	7	Borrowing from several zeros

EXERCISE 3:1a

1	21	**2**	56	**3**	373	**4**	3737
5	572	**6**	5337	**7**	2126	**8**	4631
9	44	**10**	2193	**11**	£6954	**12**	4306

EXERCISE 3:1b

1	13	**2**	38	**3**	1082	**4**	2266
5	224	**6**	6733	**7**	3407	**8**	1627
9	52	**10**	4276	**11**	£4616	**12**	1597

EXERCISE 3:2

1	17	**2**	12	**3**	42	**4**	34
5	33	**6**	22	**7**	30	**8**	25
9	44	**10**	33	**11**	44	**12**	21
13	34	**14**	31	**15**	14	**16**	33

EXERCISE 3:3

1	19	**2**	36	**3**	16	**4**	38
5	28	**6**	37	**7**	37	**8**	27
9	39	**10**	38	**11**	58	**12**	36
13	28	**14**	£38	**15**	28		

EXERCISE 3:4

1	1068	**2**	98	**3**	273	**4**	1081
5	1903	**6**	72	**7**	4718	**8**	5891
9	820	**10**	282	**11**	902	**12**	1098
13	281	**14**	£434	**15**	209	**16**	3800

EXERCISE 3:5

1	2828	**2**	2479	**3**	1791	**4**	182
5	6882	**6**	2479	**7**	1791	**8**	182
9	176	**10**	1828	**11**	268	**12**	1967
13	176	**14**	£2790	**15**	488	**16**	2788

EXERCISE 3:6

1	268	**2**	995	**3**	458	**4**	2882
5	1574	**6**	572	**7**	351	**8**	4657
9	4367	**10**	157	**11**	5139	**12**	346
13	356 g	**14**	3556	**15**	275	**16**	1469

EXERCISE 3:7

1	3565	**2**	1818	**3**	4612	**4**	4820
5	4382	**6**	3842	**7**	2558	**8**	2643
9	2864	**10**	2767	**11**	3799	**12**	7695
13	1675	**14**	£5543	**15**	6687	**16**	4822

ACTIVITIES

1 **Tower of Hanoi**
   Three discs: 7 moves.
   Four discs: 15 moves.
   Five discs: 31 moves.
   The number of moves is determined by the rule $2^n - 1$.

2 **Taking counters**
   A game of strategy.

3 Making 100
There is no unique list of solutions.
Other solutions include:
$12 + 3 + 4 + 5 - 6 - 7 + 89$,
$1 + 23 - 4 + 5 + 6 + 78 - 9$,
$123 + 45 - 67 + 8 - 9$,
$98 + 1 + 2 + 3 + 4 + 5 - 6 - 7$,
$1 + 2 + 34 - 5 + 67 - 8 + 9$,
$12 - 3 - 4 + 5 - 6 + 7 + 89$,
$123 - 4 - 5 - 6 - 7 + 8 - 9$,
$98 - 76 + 54 + 3 + 21$,
$1 + 23 - 4 + 56 + 7 + 8 + 9$

4 Hockey tournament
The rule is $x(x - 1)$ where x is the number of teams. You need to start by looking at a tournament with a small number of teams.

4 Times tables

Diagnostic exercises

Question	Section	Explanation
1,2,3	2	Multiplication by 2,5, and 10
4,5,13	3	Multiplication by 2,3,4,5, and 10
6,7,8,14	4	Multiplication by numbers up to 10
9,10,15	5	Division by numbers up to 5
11,12,16	6	Division by numbers up to 10

EXERCISE 4:1a

1 12	**2** 15	**3** 40	**4** 28
5 24	**6** 42	**7** 32	**8** 54
9 9	**10** 9	**11** 8	**12** 7
13 24	**14** 56	**15** 8	**16** 8

EXERCISE 4:1b

1 16	**2** 30	**3** 70	**4** 16
5 27	**6** 48	**7** 56	**8** 36
9 8	**10** 10	**11** 4	**12** 9
13 24	**14** 36	**15** 7	**16** 5

EXERCISE 4:2a

1 6	**2** 35	**3** 40	**4** 10
5 10	**6** 40	**7** 30	**8** 12
9 60	**10** 15	**11** 10p	**12** 15 miles
13 80	**14** 8	**15** 30 years	

EXERCISE 4:2b

1 15	**2** 70	**3** 14	**4** 25
5 10	**6** 60	**7** 18	**8** 20
9 40	**10** 45	**11** 70 s	**12** 16 litres
13 45 kg	**14** 40p	**15** 40	

EXERCISE 4:3a

1 12	**2** 14	**3** 32	**4** 30	**5** 21
6 60	**7** 24	**8** 45	**9** 20	**10** 90
11 16	**12** 25 p	**13** 27	**14** 80	**15** 24

EXERCISE 4:3b

1 16	**2** 15	**3** 60	**4** 36	**5** 35
6 18	**7** 40	**8** 28	**9** 21	**10** 50
11 20 kg	**12** 32	**13** 24	**14** 70p	**15** 24

EXERCISE 4:4a

1 54	**2** 64	**3** 36	**4** 24	**5** 63
6 56	**7** 72	**8** 27	**9** 49	**10** 54
11 32	**12** 56	**13** 48	**14** 30p	**15** 81

EXERCISE 4:4b

1 32	**2** 48	**3** 45	**4** 56	**5** 28
6 42	**7** 35	**8** 72	**9** 24	**10** 54
11 36	**12** 36	**13** 63	**14** 40p	**15** 49

EXERCISE 4:5a

1 8	**2** 5	**3** 8	**4** 7	**5** 8
6 7	**7** 4	**8** 5	**9** 9	**10** 5
11 5 m	**12** 8	**13** £8	**14** 4	**15** 3 h

EXERCISE 4:5b

1 4	**2** 3	**3** 4	**4** 10	**5** 6
6 6	**7** 6	**8** 9	**9** 8	**10** 6
11 9 kg	**12** 5	**13** 7 min	**14** 12	**15** 7

EXERCISE 4:6a

1 6	**2** 7	**3** 6	**4** 5	**5** 8
6 7	**7** 4	**8** 5	**9** 9	**10** 7
11 £8	**12** 9	**13** 6	**14** 4	**15** 8

EXERCISE 4:6b

1 3	**2** 7	**3** 8	**4** 9	**5** 6
6 5	**7** 8	**8** 4	**9** 9	**10** 5
11 4	**12** 9	**13** 7	**14** 4	**15** 8

ACTIVITIES

1 Handshakes Start with a small number of people and work out the result, then increase the number of people shaking hands. The rule is $h(h - 1)$, where h is the number of people shaking hands.
For 4 people: $4 \times 3 = 12$;
for 5 people: $5 \times 4 = 20$
For 50 people: $50 \times 49 = 2450$ handshakes.

2 Lines A game of strategy.

3 Magic squares

8	1	6
3	5	7
4	9	2

2	9	4
7	5	3
6	1	8

9	2	7
4	6	8
5	10	3

3	10	5
8	6	4
7	2	9

5	12	7
10	8	6
9	4	11

10	3	8
5	7	9
6	11	4

11	6	7
4	8	12
9	10	5

11	12	7
6	10	14
13	8	9

4	9	8
11	7	3
6	5	10

4 The wall
This is a game of strategy. To win you
need to get to a point on the side which is
just three moves away from the top.

5 The restaurant
1 £6.90   2 £3.00   3 £2.80   4 £4.80
5 £10.00   6 £5.30   7 £7.70   8 £4.80
9 £11.10   10 £7.10

5 Multiplication

Diagnostic exercises

Question	Section	Explanation
1,2	2	Multiplication by single digits
3,4	3	Multiplication with one carry
5,6	4	Multiplication with more carries
7,8	5	Multiplication by 10, 100, 1000
9,10	6	Multiplication by multiples of 10
11	7	Multiplying two 2-digit numbers
12	8	Multiplication by a 2 digit number

EXERCISE 5:1A

1 160	**2** 120	**3** 2412
4 3296	**5** 3255	**6** 14 502
7 3420	**8** 50 200	**9** 9920
10 69 000	**11** 416	**12** 3408

EXERCISE 5:1b

1 135	**2** 320	**3** 1296
4 3128	**5** 4878	**6** 32 368
7 604 000	**8** 1320	**9** 6390
10 164 000	**11** 364	**12** 8505

EXERCISE 5:2

1 108	**2** 282	**3** 72
4 161	**5** 260	**6** 360
7 177	**8** 672	**9** 280
10 445	**11** 352	**12** 402
13 252	**14** 234	**15** £405
16 196		

EXERCISE 5:3

1 492	**2** 3618	**3** 1696
4 1414	**5** 2580	**6** 2060
7 4032	**8** 2191	**9** 568
10 5445	**11** 1572	**12** 2121
13 1272	**14** 2065p	**15** 6336
16 3584		

EXERCISE 5:4

1 1512	**2** 1519	**3** 2056
4 1062	**5** 2322	**6** 3668
7 1435	**8** 4944	**9** 1104
10 2988	**11** 2506	**12** 2272
13 3720	**14** 1404	**15** 2352
16 2196		

EXERCISE 5:5

1 8600	**2** 680 000	**3** 850
4 6700	**5** 4310	**6** 10 100
7 82 000	**8** 2820	**9** 596 000
10 870	**11** 3000	**12** 672 000
13 14 000	**14** 15 000	**15** 2700
16 7000	**17** 487 000	**18** 20 000

EXERCISE 5:6

1 1040	**2** 132 000	**3** 14 800
4 8460	**5** 18 500	**6** 7440
7 305 000	**8** 24300	**9** 244 000
10 109 600	**11** 780	**12** 8540
13 3600	**14** 2 247 000	**15** 2700
16 292 000	**17** 1260	**18** £264 000

EXERCISE 5:7

1	1672	**2**	1482	**3**	2173
4	4698	**5**	4056	**6**	5494
7	2144	**8**	2117	**9**	1848
10	3626	**11**	5429	**12**	2772
13	2368	**14**	3060	**15**	3588
16	4418	**17**	6708	**18**	1298
19	4704	**20**	4161		

EXERCISE 5:8

1	48 706	**2**	36 624	**3**	81 153
4	46 248	**5**	70 668	**6**	20 664
7	11 788	**8**	131 112	**9**	9633
10	171 160	**11**	51 742	**12**	20 748
13	25 284 g	**14**	£7095	**15**	76 092
16	54 925				

ACTIVITIES

1 **The darts game** A game of strategy. To win, avoid reducing the score to an even number from 10 − 18, or to less than 9.

2 **Multiplication routes**
  a $4 \to 3 \to 2$ **b** $5 \to 3 \to 2 \to 5$
  c $3 \to 4 \to 6$ **d** $3 \to 4 \to 9$

3 **That number again!** You should always get 4.

4 **Number times** To find the largest product always put the two largest numbers in the tens. To find the smallest product put the two smallest numbers in the tens.

6 Division

Diagnostic exercises

Question	Section	Explanation
1,2	2	Single digit division (no remainders)
3,4	3	Single digit division (with remainders)
5,6	4	Single digit division as a decimal
7,8	5	Division by 10, 100, 1000
9,10	6	Division by multiples of 10
11	7	Division by a 2-digit number
12	8	Rounding remainders

EXERCISE 6:1a

1	201	**2**	301	**3**	1713r1
4	1492r3	**5**	1789.5	**6**	769.875
7	700	**8**	85	**9**	457
10	40	**11**	154	**12**	8

EXERCISE 6:1b

1	321	**2**	710	**3**	1309r1
4	1336r2	**5**	706.8	**6**	1614.25
7	900	**8**	450	**9**	87
10	800	**11**	173	**12**	8

EXERCISE 6:2

1	423	**2**	421	**3**	911	**4**	613
5	310	**6**	624	**7**	802	**8**	801
9	802	**10**	511	**11**	631	**12**	410
13	1010	**14**	723	**15**	511	**16**	601
17	512			**18**	921 km		
19	£301			**20**	401		

EXERCISE 6:3

1	3107r1	**2**	858r2	**3**	812r1
4	752r1	**5**	365r3	**6**	815r1
7	845r1	**8**	1290r2	**9**	711r2
10	1908r2	**11**	712r4	**12**	418r5
13	526r5	**14**	820r7	**15**	11 224r2
16	3540r4	**17**	3	**18**	221
19	4	**20**	3		

EXERCISE 6:4

1	1908.5	**2**	981.75	**3**	904.8
4	667.125	**5**	978.25	**6**	579.625
7	46 308.5	**8**	767.4	**9**	432.75
10	1756.8	**11**	7693.5	**12**	739.5
13	28 213.5 mm	**14**	1649.25		
15	1951.2 g	**16**	1084.375		

EXERCISE 6:5

1	709	**2**	9	**3**	650	**4**	4
5	70	**6**	50	**7**	800	**8**	200
9	59	**10**	150	**11**	82	**12**	40
13	1400	**14**	17	**15**	4300	**16**	250
17	250	**18**	£40	**19**	900	**20**	720

EXERCISE 6:6

1	22	**2**	2600	**3**	160	**4**	6
5	280	**6**	240	**7**	93	**8**	130
9	12	**10**	980	**11**	530	**12**	370
13	109	**14**	25	**15**	1900	**16**	122
17	210	**18**	147	**19**	1200	**20**	82

EXERCISE 6:7

1 32	**2** 33	**3** 55	**4** 36
5 33	**6** 68	**7** 370	**8** 64
9 89	**10** 60	**11** 64	**12** 99
13 77	**14** 371	**15** 344	**16** 621
17 355	**18** £532	**19** 347	**20** £213

EXERCISE 6:8

1 7	**2** 7	**3** 8	**4** 5
5 10	**6** 8	**7** 7	**8** 5

ACTIVITIES

1 Number chain
For numbers less than 100 the number with the longest chain is 65. For numbers between 100 and 200 the number with the longest chain is 129.

2 Remainders
The remainder you get when you divide by 9 should be the same number as you get for your single digit answer.

3 Sliding counters
It may be practical to try this with counters on a cardboard grid. Move the counters around in loops until the blue counter arrives at the opposite corner. Keep a record of the moves you have made.

4 Number maze
The numbers in the squares are

a 8 14 42 **c** 6 3 12
   16 22 30   18 45 3
   11 66 6   10 90 9

7 Decimals

Diagnostic exercises

Question	Section	Explanation
1–6	2	Decimal values
7–9	3	Using decimals in estimation
10,11	4	Ordering decimals
12,13	5	Adding decimals
14,15	6	Subtracting decimals
16–18	7	Multiplying decimals
19	8	Multiplication and division by 10,100, and 1000
20	9	Dividing decimals

EXERCISE 7:1a

1 0.9 **2** 0.43 **3** 4.3
4 $\frac{7}{10}$ **5** $\frac{42}{100}$ **6** $8\frac{3}{100}$
7 96.5 g **8** 6.1–6.2 kg
9 2.65 **10** 0.004, 0.04, 0.4
11 6.10, 6.52, 65.4, 66.3
12 9.464 **13** 694.285 **14** £2.94
15 3.93 m **16** 57.8 **17** 0.042
18 0.52 **19** 0.005 **20** 1.52

EXERCISE 7:1b

1 0.5 **2** 0.029 **3** 5.07
4 $\frac{37}{100}$ **5** $\frac{3}{10}$ **6** $4\frac{42}{1000}$
7 3.65 **8** 6.75 **9** 7.35
10 0.012, 0.132, 0.232
11 0.04, 0.85, 4.0, 5.8
12 19.494 **13** 33.02 **14** £3.07
15 0.495 mm **16** 20.185
17 0.72 **18** 1.44
19 0.0142 **20** 0.569

EXERCISE 7:2

1 $\frac{33}{100}$ **2** $\frac{4}{10}$ **3** $\frac{135}{1000}$ **4** $\frac{9}{100}$
5 $\frac{1}{10}$ **6** $\frac{49}{100}$ **7** $\frac{31}{1000}$ **8** $\frac{6}{10}$
9 $\frac{7}{100}$ **10** $2\frac{9}{10}$ **11** $5\frac{303}{1000}$ **12** $6\frac{9}{1000}$
13 0.3 **14** 0.16 **15** 0.017
16 0.7 **17** 0.07 **18** 0.2
19 0.153 **20** 0.37 **21** 0.321
22 7.56 **23** 3.4 **24** 5.057

EXERCISE 7:3

1 6.6–6.7 cm **2** 3.2–3.3
3 1.44–1.46 kg **4** 7.47–7.48 m
5 4.6–4.7 **6** 0.02–0.04 litres
7 7.7–7.9 **8** 3.36–3.38 m
9 8.1–8.3 **10** 2.1–2.2 Amps
11 2.3–2.4 **12** 5.3–5.7 mm
13 8.1–8.3 °C **14** 5.7–5.8
15 4.26–4.27 kg

EXERCISE 7:4

1 0.51, 0.52, 0.59
2 0.022, 0.032, 0.049
3 6.009, 6.039, 6.109
4 9.099, 9.909, 9.990
5 0.23, 0.32, 2.3, 3.2
6 1.09, 9.09, 9.90, 10.9
7 0.343, 0.243, 0.023
8 0.8, 0.0888, 0.008
9 5.009, 5.0079, 5.0069

10 4.4, 0.44, 0.4, 0.04
11 1.26, 0.56, 0.526, 0.126
12 1.01, 1.0, 0.110, 0.011

EXERCISE 7:5

1	11.86	**2**	14.3	**3**	7.06
4	10.43	**5**	17.46	**6**	3.355
7	2.001	**8**	17.84	**9**	7.903
10	24.785	**11**	53.53	**12**	43.64
13	£4.09			**14**	28.18 kg
15	11.905 litres			**16**	33.025 s

EXERCISE 7:6

1	0.07	**2**	1.07	**3**	0.94	**4**	2.8
5	0.98	**6**	3.07	**7**	0.65	**8**	3.6
9	0.33	**10**	3.14	**11**	2.23	**12**	3.62
13	0.053	**14**	0.118	**15**	0.013		
16	0.396	**17**	0.837	**18**	0.93		
19	0.12	**20**	8.99	**21**	2.95 litres		
22	4.06 m	**23**	£4.85	**24**	0.36		

EXERCISE 7:7a

1	33.06	**2**	35.35	**3**	62	**4**	15.13
5	49	**6**	12.34	**7**	6.18	**8**	51.84
9	1.704			**10**	35.368		
11	42.21			**12**	5.255		
13	88.911			**14**	0.04		
15	0.936			**16**	43.68		
17	£57.92			**18**	19.224 m		
19	£92.70			**20**	12.32 litres		

EXERCISE 7:7b

1	12.8	**2**	48.6	**3**	0.824	**4**	102.2
5	3.22	**6**	4.48	**7**	0.109	**8**	0.1944
9	0.603	**10**	2.04	**11**	0.96	**12**	0.665
13	0.0816	**14**	0.020 32	**15**	0.034 35		
16	0.042	**17**	0.595	**18**	10.5 cm		

EXERCISE 7:8a

1	34.2	**2**	1230	**3**	651	**4**	3.1
5	2750	**6**	590	**7**	3.34	**8**	16
9	214.5	**10**	1244	**11**	639	**12**	9
13	0.7	**14**	0.8	**15**	22	**16**	£85.00
17	£283.50			**18**	3 m		

EXERCISE 7:8b

1	8.97	**2**	0.213	**3**	0.221	**4**	0.42
5	0.275	**6**	0.029	**7**	0.79	**8**	0.0015
9	2.131			**10**	0.0049		
11	0.041			**12**	0.0003		
13	0.004			**14**	0.000 02		
15	0.103			**16**	0.15 kg		
17	£3.28			**18**	0.05 litres		

EXERCISE 7:9

1	1.458	**2**	1.5842	**3**	0.893
4	2.654	**5**	1.6128	**6**	1.3632
7	3.4708	**8**	7.137	**9**	4.442 75
10	1.900 94	**11**	11.0855	**12**	1.102 75
13	25.867 75	**14**	95.442	**15**	88.8425
16	2.3875 kg	**17**	0.96 litres	**18**	1.575 m

ACTIVITIES

1 **Three point one** A game of strategy. Avoid getting a total of 2.6 or more as this allows your partner sufficient to win.

2 **Estimating a square root** Working to two decimal places is sufficient. Use a calculator to check your answers.

3 **Fencing** A square will enclose the greatest area. You can draw a table to show the maximum area that can be enclosed from different lengths.

4 **Post office**
a £1.75 **b** 70p **c** 39p
d 80p **e** £2.55

8 Number properties and sequences

Diagnostic exercises

Question	Section	Explanation
1–5	2	Number names
6,7	3	Common multiples and factors
8,9	4	Special numbers
10	5	Sequences of diagrams
11–13	6	Number sequences
14–15	7	Finding rules
16	8	Using rules

EXERCISE 8:1a

1	3, 9, 11	**2**	2, 6, 8	**3**	3, 6, 9
4	2, 3, 6	**5**	1, 2, 5, 10	**6**	14
7	2			**8**	49
9	$2 \times 3 \times 3 \times 5$				
10	**a**				
	b 11, 13				
11	15, 17	**12**	57, 55	**13**	11, 16
14	+5	**15**	$\times 2 + 2$	**16**	$\times 3 + 1$; 61

EXERCISE 8:1b

1 3, 7, 15   **2** 6, 8, 12   **3** 8, 12
4 3, 15   **5** 1, 2, 4, 8, 16
6 12   **7** 4   **8** 36
9 $2 \times 2 \times 2 \times 3$
10 a

```
        4                        5
  . . . . . .          . . . . . . .
  . . . . . .          . . . . . . .
  . . . . . .          . . . . . . .
```

    b 14, 17
11 30, 36
12 13, 11   **13** 26, 31   **14** $+ 4$
15 $\times 3 - 1$ **16** $\times 2 - 1$

EXERCISE 8:2

1 23   **2** 18   **3** 30   **4** 33
5 a 18, 40, 74   **b** 23, 37, 51, 65
6 8, 16, 24, 32, 40
7 5, 10, 15, 20, 25, 30
8 6, 12, 18, 24, 30, 36, 42
9 a 8, 24, 40   **b** 15, 30, 40   **c** 24, 30
10 a 1, 2, 3, 6, 9, 18
    b 1, 2, 3, 5, 6, 10, 15, 30
    c 1, 2, 4, 5, 10, 20
    d 1, 2, 4, 13, 26, 52
11 a 1, 2, 3, 6
    b 1, 3, 7, 21
    c 1, 2, 3, 4, 6, 12
    d 1, 2, 3, 6, 7, 14, 21, 42
12 a 2, 8   **b** 2, 6, 12   **c** 2, 6, 10, 15

EXERCISE 8:3

1 a 12, 24, 36, …   **b** 24, 48, 72, …
    c 24, 48, 72, …   **d** 40, 80, 120, …
    e 12, 24, 36, …   **f** 36, 72, 108, …
2 a 24   **b** 20   **c** 9   **d** 48   **e** 30   **f** 72
3 a 1, 3   **b** 1, 7   **c** 1, 3   **d** 1, 2, 3, 6
    e 1, 7   **f** 1, 3, 5, 15
4 a 2   **b** 4   **c** 5   **d** 8   **e** 8   **f** 7

EXERCISE 8:4

1 a 41, 43, 47   **b** 71, 73, 79
2 17, 19
3 a 2, 5, 13   **b** 3, 7, 11
    c 17, 23, 29   **d** 3, 11, 17
4 25, 36, 49
5 a 4, 49   **b** 9, 16
    c 9, 36   **d** 1, 4, 25, 64
6 15, 21, 28
7 55
8 a 2, 3   **b** 3, 7   **c** 2, 5   **d** 5
    e 2, 3   **f** 2, 7

9 a $2 \times 3 \times 3$ **b** $2 \times 2 \times 3 \times 5$
    c $2 \times 2 \times 5$ **d** $3 \times 3 \times 5$
    e $2 \times 2 \times 3 \times 3$ **f** $2 \times 5 \times 7$
10 a 16   **b** 49   **c** 81
11 11 cm   **12** 13

EXERCISE 8:5

Number answers only
1 6,10,14,18,22   **2** 4,7,10,13,16
3 4,6,8,10,12   **4** 4,8,12,16,20
5 6,10,14,18,22   **6** 8,13,18,23,28
7 1,3,5,7,9   **8** 2,3,4,5,6
9 1,3,6,10,15   **10** 0,2,4,6,8
11 6,11,16,21,26   **12** 1,4,9,16,25

EXERCISE 8:6

1 29, 34   **2** 29, 32   **3** 11, 13
4 18, 22   **5** 54, 79   **6** 18, 23
7 47, 55   **8** 8, 14   **9** 8, 5
10 20, 28   **11** 25, 18   **12** 28, 39
13 43, 59   **14** 36, 49   **15** 58, 83
16 44, 58   **17** 33, 45   **18** 70, 78
19 89, 115   **20** 27, 39

EXERCISE 8:7

1 a 5,6   **b** $- 1$
2 a 9,10   **b** $+ 3$
3 a 10,12   **b** $\times 2 - 2$
4 a 19,22   **b** $\times 3 + 1$
5 a 27,31   **b** $\times 4 + 3$
6 a 16,19   **b** $\times 3 - 2$
7 a 15,17   **b** $\times 2 + 3$
8 a 21,25   **b** $\times 4 - 3$
9 a 20,23   **b** $\times 3 + 2$
10 a 28,33   **b** $\times 5 - 2$
11 a 16,18   **b** $\times 2 + 4$
12 a 21, 24   **b** $\times 3 + 3$

EXERCISE 8:8

1 a $\times 3 - 1$ **b** 17, 29
2 a $\times 4 + 1$ **b** 41, 61
3 a $\times 2 - 2$ **b** 14, 28
4 a $\times 4 + 2$ **b** 30, 42
5 a $\times 2 + 4$ **b** 28, 44
6 a $\times 4 - 1$ **b** 39, 59
7 a $\times 5 + 2$ **b** 42, 52
8 a $\times 3 - 3$ **b** 33, 42
9 a $\times 4 + 4$ **b** 44, 84
10 a $\times 5 + 1$ **b** 41, 51
11 a $\times 4 - 2$ **b** 38, 58
12 a $\times 5 - 3$ **b** 72, 97

ACTIVITIES

1 Frogs The table below shows the number of moves needed for combinations of red and blue frogs.

Number of red frogs

Number of blue frogs		1	2	3	4	5
	1	3	5	7	9	11
	2	5	8	11	14	17
	3	7	11	15	19	23
	4	9	14	19	24	29
	5	11	17	23	29	35

a 8   **b** 15   **c** 5   **d** 11

2 Number maze Values to fill the squares are:

4	−4	−11	5	−1	−4
+2	+5	−6	8	1	−2
+9	−1	6	3	−1	7

3 Spinner game Copy the spinner out on to card and play the game to get a feel for the spinners, and how they are used. The first spinner is the worst to use, since the negative numbers are greatest (− 11). The last two spinners have the smallest negative numbers, at − 6, but the last spinner then has more positive numbers (+ 10) and is therefore the best one to use.

4 Number pyramids

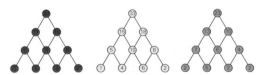

5 Cards The general rule is $\frac{1}{2}n(3n + 1)$, where n is the number of storeys. The table below shows the series.
For a house of cards 10 storeys high you will need 155 cards.

Number of storeys	1	2	3	4	5	6
Number of cards	2	7	15	26	40	57

6 Patterns Spot the pattern and extend it.

9 Fractions – addition and subtraction

Diagnostic exercises

Question	Section	Explanation
1−3	2	Simple fractions
4−6	3	Equivalent fractions
7	4	Comparing fractions
8	5	Ordering fractions
9−11	6	Cancelling fractions
12−13	7	Adding fractions
14−15	8	Subtracting fractions

EXERCISE 9:1a

1 $\frac{1}{4}$ **2** $\frac{3}{6}$ **3** $\frac{3}{5}$ shaded

4 $\frac{3}{12}$, $\frac{4}{16}$, $\frac{5}{20}$ **5** $\frac{2}{6}$ **6** $\frac{10}{35}$

7 $\frac{3}{8}$, $\frac{2}{5}$ **8** $\frac{1}{4}$, $\frac{5}{6}$ **9** $\frac{3}{4}$

10 $\frac{5}{6}$ **11** $\frac{8}{11}$ **12** $\frac{7}{8}$

13 $\frac{13}{16}$ **14** $\frac{4}{10}$ **15** $\frac{3}{6}$

EXERCISE 9:1b

1 $\frac{1}{3}$ **2** $\frac{3}{6}$ **3** $\frac{4}{7}$ shaded

4 $\frac{6}{15}$, $\frac{8}{20}$, $\frac{10}{25}$ **5** $\frac{3}{18}$

6 $\frac{16}{20}$ **7** $\frac{1}{4}$, $\frac{2}{5}$ **8** $\frac{3}{8}$, $\frac{3}{4}$

9 $\frac{3}{5}$ **10** $\frac{5}{6}$ **11** $\frac{5}{11}$

12 $\frac{7}{9}$ **13** $\frac{21}{32}$ **14** $\frac{2}{6}$ **15** $\frac{5}{8}$

EXERCISE 9:2

1 $\frac{1}{3}$ **2** $\frac{1}{6}$ **3** $\frac{2}{7}$ **4** $\frac{1}{8}$

5 $\frac{3}{8}$ **6** $\frac{3}{5}$ **7** $\frac{4}{5}$ **8** $\frac{2}{6}$

9 $\frac{4}{9}$ **10** $\frac{7}{12}$

11

12   **13**

14   **15**

16  **17**

18

19   **20**

23   **24**

25

EXERCISE 9:3

1 $\frac{2}{4}, \frac{3}{6}, \frac{4}{8}, \frac{5}{10}, \frac{6}{12}$ **2** $\frac{4}{6}, \frac{8}{12}$

3 $\frac{3}{4}, \frac{6}{8}$ **4** $\frac{3}{5}$ **5** $\frac{5}{6}$

6 $\frac{2}{6}$ **7** $\frac{6}{8}$ **8** $\frac{4}{10}$

9 $\frac{1}{5}, \frac{2}{6}, \frac{2}{3}, \frac{3}{4}$ **10** $\frac{1}{4}, \frac{1}{2}, \frac{7}{12}, \frac{7}{10}, \frac{5}{6}$

11 $\frac{2}{3}, \frac{9}{12}, \frac{4}{5}, \frac{7}{8}$ **12** $\frac{1}{4}, \frac{4}{12}, \frac{3}{8}, \frac{2}{5}, \frac{3}{6}$

EXERCISE 9:4

1 $\frac{3}{9}, \frac{4}{12}$ **2** $\frac{2}{10}, \frac{3}{15}, \frac{4}{20}$

3 $\frac{6}{8}, \frac{9}{12}, \frac{12}{16}$ **4** $\frac{10}{12}, \frac{15}{18}, \frac{20}{24}$

5 $\frac{4}{14}, \frac{6}{21}, \frac{8}{28}$ **6** $\frac{4}{6}, \frac{6}{9}, \frac{8}{12}$

7 $\frac{8}{10}, \frac{12}{15}, \frac{16}{20}$ **8** $\frac{8}{18}, \frac{12}{27}, \frac{16}{36}$

9 $\frac{8}{12}$ **10** $\frac{15}{27}$ **11** $\frac{12}{16}$ **12** $\frac{25}{30}$

13 $\frac{2}{5}$ **14** $\frac{6}{9}$ **15** $\frac{9}{12}$ **16** $\frac{3}{7}$

17 $\frac{49}{63}$ **18** $\frac{2}{8}$ **19** $\frac{24}{28}$ **20** $\frac{27}{90}$

21   **22**

EXERCISE 9:5

1 $\frac{2}{3}, \frac{3}{4}$ **2** $\frac{2}{7}, \frac{1}{3}$ **3** $\frac{3}{8}, \frac{4}{10}$ **4** $\frac{5}{7}, \frac{4}{5}$

5 $\frac{7}{9}, \frac{9}{10}$ **6** $\frac{5}{8}, \frac{3}{4}$ **7** $\frac{5}{7}, \frac{8}{12}$ **8** $\frac{7}{8}, \frac{2}{3}$

9 $\frac{2}{6}, \frac{3}{10}$ **10** $\frac{4}{5}, \frac{9}{12}$ **11** $\frac{8}{9}, \frac{7}{10}$ **12** $\frac{3}{5}, \frac{4}{7}$

EXERCISE 9:6

1 $\frac{3}{4}$ **2** $\frac{3}{4}$ **3** $\frac{8}{9}$ **4** $\frac{2}{3}$

5 $\frac{2}{3}$ **6** $\frac{1}{5}$ **7** $\frac{4}{5}$ **8** $\frac{2}{3}$

9 $\frac{1}{2}$ **10** $\frac{3}{4}$ **11** $\frac{1}{4}$ **12** $\frac{9}{16}$

13 $\frac{4}{5}$ **14** $\frac{4}{5}$ **15** $\frac{2}{5}$ **16** $\frac{4}{5}$

17 $\frac{7}{10}$ **18** $\frac{11}{30}$ **19** $\frac{13}{16}$ **20** $\frac{7}{8}$

EXERCISE 9:7

1 $\frac{1}{2}$ **2** $\frac{3}{5}$ **3** $\frac{5}{6}$ **4** $\frac{7}{9}$

5 $\frac{5}{8}$ **6** 1 **7** $\frac{7}{10}$ **8** $\frac{5}{6}$

9 $\frac{5}{16}$ **10** $\frac{11}{12}$ **11** $\frac{5}{8}$ **12** $\frac{7}{16}$

13 $\frac{25}{32}$ **14** $\frac{17}{32}$ **15** $\frac{19}{32}$ **16** $\frac{29}{32}$

17 $\frac{5}{8}$ **18** $\frac{15}{32}$

EXERCISE 9:8

1 $\frac{4}{9}$ **2** $\frac{2}{7}$ **3** $\frac{2}{5}$ **4** $\frac{7}{12}$

5 $\frac{3}{8}$ **6** $\frac{1}{9}$ **7** $\frac{3}{8}$ **8** $\frac{1}{16}$

9 $\frac{5}{8}$ **10** $\frac{1}{8}$ **11** $\frac{19}{32}$ **12** $\frac{1}{16}$

13 $\frac{3}{16}$ **14** $\frac{1}{4}$ **15** $\frac{5}{16}$ **16** $\frac{1}{8}$

17 $\frac{1}{8}$ **18** $\frac{3}{16}$

ACTIVITIES

1 **Calculator digits** Be sure to write out all the correct combinations that make each number.

2 **Uminoes** A game to make and play to help you recognise equivalent fractions.

3 Number trees The numbers 9, 17 and 25 have interesting family trees as they go on and on for ever!

4 Missing numbers

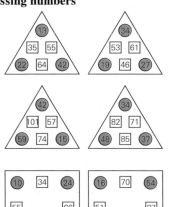

10 Fractions – multiplication and division

Diagnostic exercises

Question	Section	Explanation
1–3	2	Mixed numbers
4–6	3	Improper fractions
7,8	4	Ordering mixed numbers
9,10	5	Fractions of quantities
11,12	6	Writing parts as fractions
13,14	7	Multiplying fractions
15,16	8	Dividing fractions

EXERCISE 10:1a

1 $\frac{9}{4}$ **2** $\frac{13}{3}$ **3** $\frac{8}{5}$ **4** $2\frac{2}{3}$

5 $2\frac{3}{5}$ **6** $3\frac{2}{7}$ **7** $2\frac{5}{7}, 2\frac{8}{9}$

8 $2\frac{3}{4}, 3\frac{2}{5}, 3\frac{5}{6}$ **9** $\frac{1}{4}$ **10** $\frac{7}{10}$

11 6 mm **12** £7.50 **13** $\frac{5}{12}$

14 $\frac{20}{6} = 3\frac{1}{3}$ **15** $\frac{35}{12} = 2\frac{11}{12}$ **16** $\frac{7}{24}$

EXERCISE 10:1b

1 $\frac{7}{3}$ **2** $\frac{7}{2}$ **3** $\frac{23}{4}$ **4** $3\frac{1}{2}$

5 $2\frac{3}{4}$ **6** $3\frac{5}{8}$ **7** $3\frac{1}{4}, 3\frac{2}{5}$

8 $4\frac{4}{7}, 5\frac{2}{3}, 5\frac{3}{4}$ **9** $\frac{13}{25}$ **10** $\frac{5}{12}$

11 £0.50 **12** 48 kg **13** $\frac{12}{88} = \frac{3}{22}$

14 $\frac{12}{5} = 2\frac{2}{5}$ **15** $\frac{8}{15}$ **16** $\frac{3}{28}$

EXERCISE 10:2

1 $\frac{9}{2}$ **2** $\frac{23}{6}$ **3** $\frac{37}{5}$ **4** $\frac{17}{4}$

5 $\frac{26}{3}$ **6** $\frac{29}{3}$ **7** $\frac{8}{3}$ **8** $\frac{10}{3}$

9 $\frac{17}{7}$ **10** $\frac{29}{5}$ **11** $\frac{67}{12}$ **12** $\frac{19}{4}$

13 $\frac{39}{5}$ **14** $\frac{13}{5}$ **15** $\frac{33}{5}$ **16** $\frac{85}{9}$

17 $\frac{25}{7}$ **18** $\frac{53}{6}$ **19** $\frac{12}{5}$ **20** $\frac{14}{9}$

EXERCISE 10:3

1 $5\frac{2}{3}$ **2** $5\frac{6}{7}$ **3** $1\frac{5}{6}$ **4** $4\frac{1}{2}$

5 $7\frac{7}{8}$ **6** $6\frac{3}{4}$ **7** $12\frac{1}{2}$ **8** $5\frac{7}{10}$

9 $4\frac{3}{4}$ **10** $4\frac{2}{3}$ **11** $6\frac{5}{6}$ **12** $9\frac{1}{9}$

13 $9\frac{5}{8}$ **14** $4\frac{1}{12}$ **15** $8\frac{4}{5}$ **16** $7\frac{5}{8}$

17 $2\frac{3}{10}$ **18** $4\frac{3}{4}$ **19** $5\frac{3}{5}$ **20** $13\frac{2}{7}$

EXERCISE 10:4

1 $2\frac{1}{5}, 2\frac{2}{6}$ **2** $5\frac{4}{5}, 5\frac{7}{8}$

3 $3\frac{7}{10}, 3\frac{4}{5}$ **4** $1\frac{7}{12}, 1\frac{5}{6}$

5 $6\frac{1}{4}, 6\frac{2}{5}$ **6** $4\frac{2}{3}, 4\frac{3}{4}$

7 $1\frac{3}{8}, 2\frac{4}{12}, 2\frac{3}{6}$ **8** $2\frac{2}{3}, 3\frac{4}{5}, 3\frac{7}{8}$

9 $3\frac{2}{3}, 2\frac{3}{4}, 2\frac{1}{5}$ **10** $5\frac{7}{10}, 4\frac{5}{6}, 4\frac{1}{4}$

11 $4\frac{7}{10}, 3\frac{8}{9}, 3\frac{4}{7}$ **12** $2\frac{7}{12}, 2\frac{4}{7}, 1\frac{6}{10}$

EXERCISE 10:5

1	6	**2**	1.5 kg	**3**	£5
4	4 g	**5**	7 ml	**6**	40p
7	£24	**8**	£7	**9**	14.4 g
10	$54	**11**	2.8 g	**12**	£2.30
13	£21.35	**14**	11.85 km	**15**	£12.50
16	£3.56	**17**	45 g	**18**	£1.80
19	49 litres	**20**	240 mg		

EXERCISE 10:6

1 $\frac{80}{200} = \frac{2}{5}$ **2** $\frac{16}{66} = \frac{8}{33}$ **3** $\frac{15}{75} = \frac{1}{5}$

4 $\frac{10}{130} = \frac{1}{13}$ **5** $\frac{170}{200} = \frac{17}{20}$ **6** $\frac{16}{50} = \frac{8}{25}$

7 $\frac{80}{120} = \frac{2}{3}$ **8** $\frac{15}{35} = \frac{3}{7}$ **9** $\frac{80}{140} = \frac{4}{7}$

10 $\frac{5}{30} = \frac{1}{6}$

EXERCISE 10:7

1 $\frac{4}{10} = \frac{2}{5}$ **2** $\frac{6}{42} = \frac{1}{7}$ **3** $\frac{2}{12} = \frac{1}{6}$

4 $\frac{15}{20} = \frac{3}{4}$ **5** $\frac{8}{21}$ **6** $\frac{24}{36} = \frac{2}{3}$

7 $\frac{14}{3} = 4\frac{2}{3}$ **8** $\frac{3}{32}$ **9** $\frac{14}{40} = \frac{7}{20}$

10 $\frac{9}{4} = 2\frac{1}{4}$ **11** $\frac{12}{21} = \frac{4}{7}$ **12** $\frac{84}{7} = 12$

13 $\frac{8}{15}$ **14** $\frac{3}{32}$ **15** $\frac{33}{4} = 8\frac{1}{4}$

16 $\frac{5}{12}$ **17** $\frac{9}{4} = 2\frac{1}{4}$ **18** $\frac{9}{64}$

19 $8\frac{1}{3}$ kg **20** $\frac{33}{128}$ **21** $\frac{5}{8}$

22 $\frac{9}{10}$

EXERCISE 10:8

1 $\frac{8}{15}$ **2** $\frac{48}{45} = 1\frac{1}{15}$ **3** $\frac{4}{45}$

4 $\frac{3}{4}$ **5** $\frac{15}{28}$ **6** $\frac{1}{10}$

7 $\frac{5}{12}$ **8** $\frac{9}{11}$ **9** $\frac{14}{30} = \frac{7}{15}$

10 $\frac{18}{45} = \frac{2}{5}$ **11** $\frac{5}{72}$ **12** $\frac{90}{135} = \frac{2}{3}$

13 $\frac{2}{21}$ **14** $\frac{24}{3} = 8$ **15** $\frac{120}{30} = 4$

16 3 **17** $\frac{72}{60} = 1\frac{1}{5}$ **18** $\frac{72}{60} = 1\frac{1}{5}$

19 $7\frac{1}{2}$ **20** $\frac{6}{5} = 1\frac{1}{5}$ **21** $\frac{5}{16}$

22 18

ACTIVITIES

1 Sticks Use small sticks or counters to carry out this activity.

b

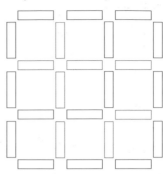

c Table: 4, 7, 10, 12, 15, 17, 20, 22, 24, ...

2 Digits The final answer should always be:

3 for addition of one.
6 for subtraction of one.

3 Letters as numbers

```
  1 2 3 4 3          7 0 8 3 9
    2 3 4 3            6 4 5 8
  ─────────          ─────────
  1 4 6 8 6          6 4 3 8 1


    8 8 8 8          9 5 2 8
    4 4 4 4            6 4 5
  ─────────            5 3 0
  1 3 3 3 2          ─────────
                     1 0 7 0 3
```

4 Counters A strategy game. Don't leave your partner with only one pile!

5 Final digits An investigation into the final digits of numbers. Be sure to write out exactly what you have found about the final digits in each case.

a The final digits are all multiples of 2 (even numbers)

b The final digits are all multiples of 2 (even numbers)

c List the multiples and patterns you find for each one.

d Square numbers: the final digits are all 0, 1, 4, 5, 6, or 9.
Prime numbers: the final digits are all odd numbers (with the exception of 2).
Odd numbers: the final digits are all odd numbers.
Triangle numbers: there is no pattern.

11 Ratio and proportion

Diagnostic exercises

Question	Section	Explanation
1−6	2	Simplifying ratios
7−9	3	Simplifying ratios with units
10,11	4	Unitary ratios
12	5	Direct proportion
13	6	Inverse proportion
14	7	Using ratios
15	8	Division in ratios

EXERCISE 11:1a

1 $3:4$ **2** $5:1$ **3** $1:3$ **4** $7:2$
5 $2:7$ **6** $3:10$ **7** $1:50$ **8** $5:7$
9 $5:2$ **10** 96 seconds **11** 50 ml
12 £42.50 **13** 8 days
14 12 boys **15** £150 and £180

EXERCISE 11.1b

1 $2:3$ **2** $1:2$ **3** $1:4$ **4** $2:1$
5 $3:5$ **6** $4:5$ **7** $250:1$ **8** $9:11$
9 $3:10$ **10** £300 **11** 100 ml
12 3 hours **13** 3 hours **14** 150
15 50 g to 30 g

EXERCISE 11:2

1 $7:16$ **2** $2:3$ **3** $1:4$ **4** $1:2$
5 $2:3$ **6** $13:3$ **7** $2:3$ **8** $5:2$
9 $2:5$ **10** $7:5$ **11** $3:2$ **12** $5:9$
13 $3:1$ **14** $3:4$ **15** $4:7$ **16** $7:6$
17 $2:3$ **18** $1:4$ **19** $3:8$ **20** $2:3$

EXERCISE 11:3

1 $1:3$ **2** $4:1$ **3** $1:3$ **4** $7:100$
5 $33:10$ **6** $25:1$ **7** $7:1$ **8** $3:10$
9 $35:3$ **10** $4:5$ **11** $3:4$ **12** $1:2$
13 $1:6$ **14** $3:20$ **15** $20:1$ **16** $6:25$
17 $3:2$ **18** $50:3$ **19** $4:1$ **20** $5:1$

EXERCISE 11:4

1 70 min **2** 270 miles **3** 9
4 £3.36 **5** 11 cm **6** 15 dogs
7 128 balls **8** 4 men
9 2400 eggs **10** 32 people

EXERCISE 11:5

1 40p **2** 12 weeks **3** 5 hours
4 £7.20 **5** £162 **6** 5600 km
7 120 km **8** 675 bottles
9 30 cm **10** 35 m

EXERCISE 11:6

1 24 hours **2** 10 days **3** 4 boxes
4 7.5 hours **5** 6 counters **6** 12 days
7 8 days **8** 30 cases
9 3 hours **10** 12 days

EXERCISE 11:7

1 48 g choux pastry
150 ml double cream
60 g melted chocolate

2 50 g lard
2000 g oxtail joints
10 small onions
10 carrots
5 tablespoons flour
1250 ml beef stock

3 250 g macaroni
50 g butter
50 g flour
600 ml milk
200 g cheddar cheese
25 g breadcrumbs

4 500 g bacon
375 g belly pork
375 g pigs liver
200 g chicken liver
3 eggs
3 onions

5 48 teas **6** 84 flowers
7 120 boys **8** 35 women
9 21 cm **10** 30 kg
11 30 **12** 18 cars
13 $18 + 4 = 22$ **14** 54 cars
15 42 trains

EXERCISE 11:8

1 £1.30, £5.20 **2** 36 kg, 60 kg
3 300, 360 **4** £2.10, £3.90
5 72 litres, 36 litres **6** 128 g, 96 g
7 14 litres **8** £3.00
9 24 kg **10** £17.28

ACTIVITIES

1 I'm thinking of a number
The questions should be directed at midpoints: eg from 1−100, start by asking whether the number is more than 50. If it is, then you target the middle of those numbers that are more: ask whether the number is more than 75. If it is not, then again target the middle of those that are less: that is 25.
It does not have to be the exact middle you use, just as long as it is a whole number!

2 Light bars

Digit	0	1	2	3	4	5	6	7	8	9
Light bars	6	2	5	5	4	5	6	4	7	6

b 12, 21, 13, 31, 15, 51, 8.
c 11 111, 23.
e Most: any 2-digit number using the number 8 and either one of the numbers 0, 6 or 9.
Fewest: 11

3 Flowers

Number of yellow counters	1	2	3	4	5
Number of red counters	6	10	14	18	22

The general rule is $2(2n + 1)$ or $4n + 2$ where n = number of yellow counters. For 10 yellow counters you will need 42 red counters.

4 Half-time   For a half-time score of n–n the number of possible half time scores is $(n + 1)^2$

5 Palindromes   Be sure to set out all working neatly.

12 Percentages

Diagnostic exercises

Question	Section	Explanation
1–2	2	Recognising percentages
3–6	3	Conversion from percentages
7–9	4	Conversion to percentages
10	5	Sum to 100%
11	6	Percentages of quantities
12	7	Percentage increase and decrease
13	8	Writing as percentages
14–16	9	Percentage fractions

EXERCISE 12:1a

1 45% **2** 65% **3** $\frac{3}{100}$ **4** $\frac{4}{5}$
5 0.24 **6** 0.08 **7** 60% **8** 37%
9 55% **10** 70% **11** 81 **12** £153
13 15% **14** $\frac{17}{200}$ **15** $13\frac{1}{2}$% **16** £176.25

EXERCISE 12:1b

1 52% **2** 35% **3** $\frac{3}{50}$ **4** $\frac{17}{20}$
5 0.72 **6** 0.09 **7** 30% **8** 6%
9 95% **10** 15% **11** 280 **12** £21
13 5% **14** $\frac{1}{16}$ **15** $11\frac{1}{4}$% **16** £315

EXERCISE 12:2

1 40% **2** 70% **3** 35% **4** 65%
5 57% **6** 82% **7** 24% **8** 19%
9 20% **10** 60% **11** 45% **12** 95%
13 10% **14** 90% **15** 30% **16** 70%

EXERCISE 12:3

1 a $\frac{1}{20}$ **b** 0.05 **2 a** $\frac{7}{10}$ **b** 0.7

3 a $\frac{9}{20}$ **b** 0.45 **4 a** $\frac{7}{20}$ **b** 0.35

5 a $\frac{1}{10}$ **b** 0.1 **6 a** $\frac{19}{20}$ **b** 0.95

7 a $\frac{3}{20}$ **b** 0.15 **8 a** $\frac{9}{10}$ **b** 0.9

9 a $\frac{2}{5}$ **b** 0.4 **10 a** $\frac{1}{50}$ **b** 0.02

11 a $\frac{13}{20}$ **b** 0.65 **12 a** $\frac{1}{5}$ **b** 0.2

13 **a** $\frac{3}{25}$ **b** 0.12 14 **a** $\frac{11}{50}$ **b** 0.22

15 **a** $\frac{3}{10}$ **b** 0.3 16 **a** $\frac{33}{50}$ **b** 0.66

17 **a** $\frac{7}{100}$ **b** 0.07 18 **a** $\frac{19}{50}$ **b** 0.38

19 **a** $\frac{6}{25}$ **b** 0.24 20 **a** $\frac{8}{25}$ **b** 0.32

EXERCISE 12:4

1	80%	**2**	70%	**3**	3%	**4**	15%
5	41%	**6**	99%	**7**	5%	**8**	20%
9	81%	**10**	50%	**11**	30%	**12**	91%
13	60%	**14**	20%	**15**	52%	**16**	9%
17	35%	**18**	55%	**19**	6%	**20**	1%

EXERCISE 12:5

1	57%	**2**	45%	**3**	85%	**4**	30%
5	18%	**6**	10%	**7**	15%	**8**	62%
9	22%	**10**	27%	**11**	7%	**12**	3%

EXERCISE 12:6

1	5	**2**	16	**3**	6
4	30	**5**	42p	**6**	£1
7	2.7 kg	**8**	21 g	**9**	£14
10	£800	**11**	£5000	**12**	15 km

EXERCISE 12:7

1	£693	**2**	1168 kg	**3**	204 m
4	£54	**5**	£2.80	**6**	56.16 g
7	£33.60	**8**	£6400	**9**	£617.50
10	42 400	**11**	750 ml	**12**	52 minutes

EXERCISE 12:8

1	40%	**2**	95%	**3**	15%	**4**	10%
5	64%	**6**	5%	**7**	28%	**8**	5%
9	38%	**10**	5%				

EXERCISE 12:9a

1 **a** $\frac{5}{8}$ **b** 0.625 2 **a** $\frac{19}{200}$ **b** 0.095

3 **a** $\frac{61}{400}$ **b** 0.1525 4 **a** $\frac{127}{400}$ **b** 0.3175

5 **a** $\frac{99}{200}$ **b** 0.495 6 **a** $\frac{207}{400}$ **b** 0.5175

7 **a** $\frac{129}{400}$ **b** 0.3225 8 **a** $\frac{173}{200}$ **b** 0.865

9 **a** $\frac{87}{400}$ **b** 0.2175 10 **a** $\frac{37}{400}$ **b** 0.0925

11 $37\frac{1}{2}\%$ 12 $4\frac{1}{2}\%$ 13 $23\frac{1}{2}\%$

14 $5\frac{1}{2}\%$ 15 $1\frac{1}{4}\%$ 16 $7\frac{1}{2}\%$

17 $6\frac{1}{2}\%$ 18 $56\frac{1}{4}\%$ 19 $1\frac{1}{4}\%$

20 $11\frac{3}{4}\%$

EXERCISE 12:9b

1	60	**2**	£25	**3**	£1.50
4	£17.25	**5**	49 g	**6**	164 cm
7	£682	**8**	£100.11	**9**	£10 850
10	£292.60				

ACTIVITIES

1 Number squares

  a 60

  b no

  c The total is $4n + 44$, where n is the number in the top left hand corner.

  d $4n + 44$ works for all other 3-sided number squares

  e The total of the four numbers in the corners can be found using $4n + 66$.

2 Uminoes A game that helps you practise with equivalent fractions, decimals and percentages.

3 Double your money

  a Year 1: £1060.00
   Year 2: £1123.60
   Year 3: £1191.02
   Year 4: £1262.48
   Year 5: £1338.23
   Year 6: £1418.52
   Year 7: £1503.63
   Year 8: £1593.85
   Year 9: £1689.48
   Year 10: £1790.85
   Year 11: £1898.30
   Year 12: £2012.20 → 12 years

  b In half the time 12% would only give you £1973.82. You would need a percentage rate of 13% to double your money in 6 years.

  c No.

4 Division patterns

   Once you have found a simple fraction that repeats, you can then find a repeating pattern for any other fraction with the same denominator.

   eg $\frac{1}{7} = 0.142\ 857\ 142...$

   so $\frac{2}{7}$ (etc) will also repeat.

Using your calculator you should be able to find that the following fractions give you a pattern of numbers which repeat:

$$\frac{1}{3}, \frac{1}{6}, \frac{1}{7}, \frac{1}{9}, \frac{1}{11}, \frac{1}{13}, \frac{1}{15}, \frac{1}{18}, \frac{1}{21}, \frac{1}{22},$$

$$\frac{1}{24}, \frac{1}{26}, \frac{1}{27}, \frac{1}{30}.$$

13 Measures

Diagnostic exercises

Question	Section	Explanation
1–3	2	Temperature
4–6	3	Calendars
7–8	4	Time
9–10	5	Timetables
11–13	6	Taking measurements
14–16	7	Metric units
17,18	8	Imperial/metric equivalents

EXERCISE 13:1a

1	−4, −5, −6,...		2	−6°C	
3	9°		4	14th October	
5	1740		6	Tuesday 14th May	
7	1550	8	7.35 am	9	1030
10	8.35	11	6.5 cm	12	grams
13	metres	14	3500 kg	15	4.5 m
16	37.5 kg	17	28 pints	18	17.6 lb

EXERCISE 13:1b

1	−6, −7, −8,...	2	6 °C
3	7°	4	28th October
5	1930	6	Monday 21st July
7	2205	8	1510
9	0920	10	18 minutes
11	5.5 cm	12	litres
13	millimetres	14	6000 m
15	8.5 g	16	8
17	6 inches	18	12 yards

EXERCISE 13:2

1	−7 °C	2	4 °C	3	2 °C
4	−3 °C	5	5 °C	6	9 °C
7	−10 °C	8	7 °C	9	7 °C
10	3 °C	11	59 °C	12	6 °C

EXERCISE 13:3

1	20th March	2	12th February
3	1680	4	44 days
5	20th July	6	1000 BC
7	3rd April	8	200 BC
9	18th May	10	Monday
11	1985	12	294 days
13	10th April	14	1922
15	1st March		

EXERCISE 13:4

1	a	1030	b	1540	c	0810	
	d	1240	e	2045	f	0935	
	g	1515	h	0150			
2	a	8.55 am	b	11.35 pm	c	1.20 pm	
	d	7.30 am	e	12.55 pm	f	3.30 am	
	g	10.25 pm	h	0.54 am			
3	a	2105/9.05 pm			b	0300/3.00 am	
	c	18.35/6.35 pm			d	1805/6.05 pm	
	e	0625/6.25 am			f	0540/5.40 am	
4	a	4 h 37 min			b	3 h 15 min	
	c	9 h 15 min			d	5 h 20 min	
	e	3 h 10 min			f	21 h 30 min	
5	4 h 10 min			6	1.35 pm		
7	1 h 35 min			8	9 h 30 min		

EXERCISE 13:5

1	5	2	1611
3	11 minutes	4	0944
5	11 minutes	6	1726
7	1107	8	6
9	0851	10	59 minutes
11	2 minutes	12	0857
13	0726	14	48 minutes
15	0732		

EXERCISE 13:6

Allow ±0.1 cm or ±1 mm either way for ruler inaccuracies.

1	4 cm	2	6 cm	3	2.5 cm
4	3.5 cm	5	1.8 cm	6	4.3 cm
7	40 mm	8	60 mm	9	25 mm
10	35 mm	11	18 mm	12	43 mm
13	kilometres	14	metres		
15	tonnes	16	kilograms		
17	millilitres	18	centimetres		
19	grams	20	litres		

EXERCISE 13:7

1	70 mm	2	54 000 m	3	800 cm
4	0.083 g	5	700 ml	6	2.42 kg
7	2400 g	8	4200 m	9	1.8 litres

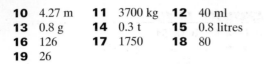

10	4.27 m	**11**	3700 kg	**12**	40 ml
13	0.8 g	**14**	0.3 t	**15**	0.8 litres
16	126	**17**	1750	**18**	80
19	26				

EXERCISE 13:8

1	64 km	**2**	5 yards	**3**	45 cm
4	9 litres	**5**	90 cm	**6**	26.25 pints
7	$4\frac{1}{2}$ yards	**8**	96 km	**9**	18 inches
10	20 miles	**11**	28 pints	**12**	5 kg
13	5.5 m	**14**	8 kg	**15**	60 cm
16	75 mph		**17**	176 lb	
18	3 kg = 6.6 lb		**19**	35	
20	9 m				

ACTIVITIES

1 Timing minutes How close can you get to the actual time?

2 Clock capers A game of strategy.

3 Numbered counters

a

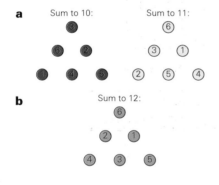

Sum to 10:   Sum to 11:

b Sum to 12:

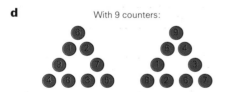

c 8 counters cannot be made into a triangle.

d With 9 counters:

It is possible to put together triangles using all the numbers 1 to 12.
The totals of the triangles are 28, 29, 30, 31, 32, 33, 34, 35, 36, 37.

4 Dates of birth You should always arrive back at the date of birth.

5 Perimeters Squared paper would be useful.

6 Areas Squared paper would be useful.

7 Balances Write out the different combinations in an ordered way.

8 Rectangles Start with a square and work up to a rectangle.

14 Tables, graphs and charts

Diagnostic exercises

Question	Section	Explanation
1	2	Venn diagrams
2	3	Carroll diagrams
3	4	Frequency tables and charts
4	5	Grouped frequency tables and charts
5	6	Pictograms
6	7	Using graphs and diagrams
7	8	Pie charts

EXERCISE 14:1a

1 a 3   **b** 21

c

Number that start with 2 / Odd numbers

26 24 | 27 21 | 31 17 55

2 a 3   **b** 35, 55, 65

c

	Numbers that end in 5	Numbers that do not end in 5
Numbers that have 3 or 4 tens	35 45	37 48
Numbers that have 5 or 6 tens	55 65	50 63

3

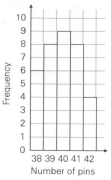

Number of pins	Frequency
38	6
39	8
40	9
41	8
42	4
Total	35

4

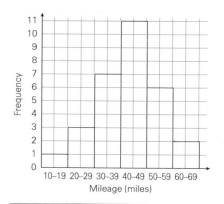

Mileage (miles)	Frequency
10−19	1
20−29	3
30−39	7
40−49	11
50−59	6
60−69	2
Total	30

5 a Thursday   **b** (i) 18 (ii) 25

c ◉◉◉◉◖

6 a 8B   **b** 8C   **c** 6   **d** 4

7 a Heating   **b** twice as much

EXERCISE 14:1b

1 a 3   **b** 18, 54

c

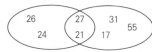

Number that start with 2 | Odd numbers

26 | 27 | 31
24 | 21 | 17 | 55

2 a 2   **b** 49, 73, 91

c

	Odd	Even
Numbers greater than 50	73 85 91	82
Numbers 50 or less	7 49	36 24

3

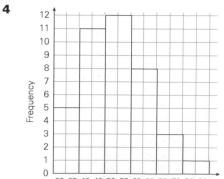

Number of packets	Frequency
23	6
24	8
25	10
26	7
27	4
Total	35

4

Number of counters	Frequency
30−39	5
40−49	11
50−59	12
60−69	8
70−79	3
80−89	1
Total	**40**

5 **a** Thursday   **b** (i) 25 (ii) 17
    c $3\frac{3}{5}$ pizza symbols
6 **a** 5   **b** 16   **c** 14   **d** 40
7 **a** Dog   **b** Cat   **c** 10–11

EXERCISE 14:2

1

2

3

4

5

6

7

8

EXERCISE 14:3

1

23 27	22 26
33 39 35	32 34

2

71 75 77	70 72
93 95 99	94 96 98

3

33 37 83	34 38
51 57 59	50 54 56

4

2	4
4	3

5

4	1
1	4

6

22 44	20 34 48
11 33 99	19 21

7

2 4 6 12	10 20
1 3	5 15 25

EXERCISE 14:4

1

Minutes late

Minutes late	Frequency
1	11
2	7
3	4
4	7
5	4
6	3
Total	**36**

2

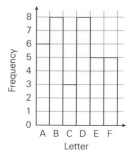

Letter	Frequency
A	6
B	8
C	3
D	8
E	5
F	5
Total	35

3

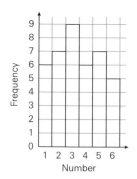

Number	Frequency
1	6
2	7
3	9
4	6
5	7
6	5
Total	40

4

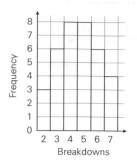

Break-downs	Frequency
2	3
3	6
4	8
5	8
6	6
7	4
Total	35

5

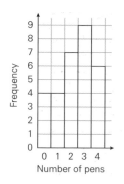

Number of pens	Frequency
0	4
1	4
2	7
3	9
4	6
Total	30

6

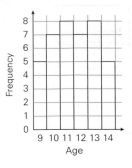

Age	Frequency
9	5
10	7
11	8
12	7
13	8
14	5
Total	40

8

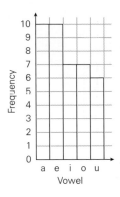

Vowel	Frequency
a	10
e	10
i	7
o	7
u	6
Total	40

7

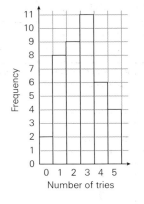

Number of tries	Frequency
0	2
1	8
2	9
3	11
4	6
5	4
Total	40

9

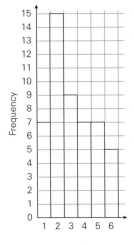

Number of letters	Frequency
1	7
2	15
3	9
4	7
5	7
6	5
Total	50

10

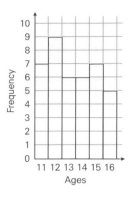

Ages	Frequency
11	7
12	9
13	6
14	6
15	7
16	5
Total	40

EXERCISE 14:5

1

Points	Frequency
0–4	3
5–9	5
10–14	7
15–19	10
20–24	8
Total	33

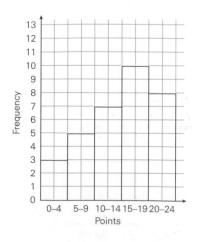

2

Number of people	Frequency
0–49	1
50–99	2
100–149	5
150–199	11
200–249	14
250–299	8
300–349	3
350–399	1
Total	45

3

Number of letters	Frequency
0–9	5
10–19	7
20–29	9
30–39	6
40–49	6
50–59	3
60–69	4
Total	40

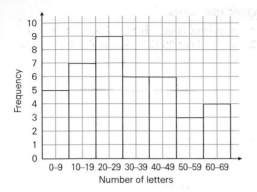

5

Pins	Frequency
81−85	1
86−90	3
91−95	4
96−100	5
101−105	8
106−110	7
111−115	4
116−120	3
Total	35

4

Number of people	Frequency
0−4	5
5−9	6
10−14	7
15−19	5
20−24	3
25−29	3
30−34	1
Total	30

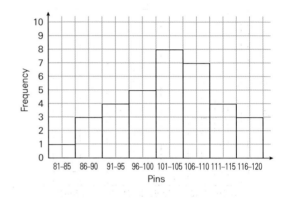

6

Weight of fish	Frequency
0−4	3
5−9	5
10−14	7
15−19	9
20−24	8
25−29	3
Total	35

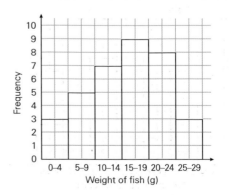

7

Speed (mph)	Frequency
21−30	3
31−40	5
41−50	10
51−60	13
61−70	9
71−80	4
81−90	1
Total	45

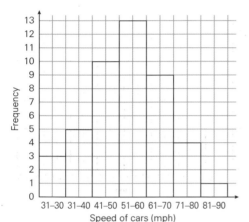

Speed of cars (mph)

8

Amount of liquid in bottles	Frequency
30−39	3
40−49	5
50−59	7
60−69	9
70−79	8
80−89	5
90−99	3
Total	40

Amount of liquid in bottles

EXERCISE 14:6

1 **a** sweets, cola **b** cereal bar **c** 7 **d** 7
2 **a** (i) 40 (ii) 25 (iii) 35 **b** Week 1 **c** 50
3 **a** Thursday **b** Saturday
  c (i) 12 (ii) 18 (iii) 11
4 **a** Geoff **b** Saleem **c** 37

5 BBC 1

  BBC 2

  ITV

  Ch4

  Ch5

6 Tom

  Jerry

  Fernandez

  Philip

  David

  Remi

7 Year 7

  Year 8

  Year 9

  Year 10

  Year 11

8 Mon

  Tues

  Wed

  Thur

  Fri

  Sat

  Sun

EXERCISE 14:7

1. **a** 3 **b** 2 **c** 1 and 6 **d** 16 **e** 33
2. **a** (i) 18 °C (ii) 17 °C (iii) 11 °C
   b 1h, $2\frac{1}{2}$h
   c (i) $1\frac{1}{2}$ h, 18 °C (ii) 3h, 8 °C.
3. **a** March **b** January & April
   c 7 **d** 20
4. **a** 39.6 °C **b** 37 °C
   c 38.6 °C **d** 2.2 °C
5. **a** 7T **b** £45 **c** £20 **d** £180
6. **a** (i) 50 (ii) 45 **b** Jan, Apr, Jun, Jul
   c 165 **d** 15
7. **a** Jamaica **b** Paris **c** (i) 3h (ii) 7h
8. **a** 4 **b** 7 **c** 1 and 6 **d** 24 **e** 63
9. **a** Week 1,2,3 in August **b** £580, £780
   c (i) 1st week in July (ii) 2nd week in June
10. **a** 18 **b** 32 **c** 32

EXERCISE 14:8

1. **a** Black **b** Blue **c** (i) 10 (ii) 30
2. **a** UK **b** Europe **c** (i) 15 (ii) 5
3. **a** £10 **b** £5 **c** £5
4. **a** Rugby **b** Golf **c** Rugby
5. **a** Pass **b** Fail **c** 25
6. **a** Lessons **b** Registration
   c 13 times as long
7. **a** Brown sugar **b** $\frac{1}{4}$ **c** 7 times
8. **a** Europe **b** $\frac{1}{6}$
   c Africa & Asia

ACTIVITIES

1. **The Dock** A practical investigation into probability. With 1, 2, 3 to move left and 4, 5, 6 to move right, the probabilities of reaching HOME and reaching DOCK are the same. If the scoring is changed to 1, 2, 3, 4 to move left, then the probability of reaching HOME is increased.

2. **To fifteen** A game of strategy, similar in nature to noughts and crosses.

3 Distance charts

Aber

3	Bisley				
8	5	Chorley			
14	11	6	Dingle		
18	15	10	4	Evesham	
23	20	15	9	5	Frimley

Gravesend

6	Heaton				
14	8	Ilkley			
21	15	7	Jamstead		
33	27	19	12	Krawley	
41	35	27	20	8	Langley

Mumps

15	Nantwich				
24	9	Oakstown			
37	22	13	Pringle		
45	30	21	8	Quigley	
57	42	33	20	12	Ringley